What Other Champions Are Saying About the Business of Being an Athlete

'Thanks for the inspiration...'

"The ability to sustain a career and lifestyle in a low profile sport such as beach volleyball takes passion, hard work, preparation, belief and determination. Kerri not only has shown these traits for more than 20 years, but is willing to share the secrets with you. As an athlete she was relentless, willing to do whatever it took to win.

Her extensive knowledge, from 1st hand experience is priceless. This book will touch on everything you need to be aware of to reach your goals, regardless of your current sporting level. It is a must have. It will be your handbook for success.

One of the reasons for our success on and off the court was our thirst for learning and understanding. We were always asking ourselves, "How do we make it better?" Kerri's book will touch on everything you need to know about how to build a winning career in sport. It is the most comprehensive account of a sportspersons journey. Whether you are a weekend warrior or a professional athlete this book will set you up on the road to your success.

An amazing athlete, teammate, mentor and now author. Kerri has made an incredible contribution to the sport of beach volleyball and the Australian Sporting Culture. Thanks for the inspiration."

Natalie Cook OAM - 4 time Beach Volleyball Olympian, 2000 Olympic Gold and 1996 Olympic Bronze

'...once you have the passion the rest starts to fall into place.'

"The Business of Being an Athlete is a very useful tool for all aspiring elite athletes, performers and their support groups. It provides fantastic practical and useful advice on many levels. I believe everybody who reads this book will find information to enhance their chances of achieving success.

I know my parents would've drawn on these when I was a 10 yr old, aspiring to be 'The World's Greatest Athlete.' With my parents in mind, chapter 9 which is all about sponsorship is the one chapter I would like to have known more about. When I was growing up my family didn't have a lot of money, so my parents worked extraordinarily hard to get me into teams that eventually took me to the top.

I also particularly like Section 1 – Passion, because I believe that once you have the passion the rest starts to fall into place."

Catherine Freeman OAM – 2 time Olympian 400m, 2000 Olympic Gold, 2 time World Champion and multiple Commonwealth Games Gold and Silver medallist

'...powerful and exciting tools...'

"There are a variety of books out there that provide athletes with the different skills and tools for creating a successful career in sport. The Business of Being an Athlete is a fantastic resource for all athletes. You'll find some unique and insightful ideas on how to build your game plan in sport and life.

You'll learn skills that will point you in the right direction to gaining an edge on your competitors....Kerri most definitely nails it when it comes to providing you with a recipe for success. An inspirational read for today's up and coming athletes, this book is filled with powerful and exciting tools and insights that will help you through the trials and tribulations of your career."

Andrew Gaze - 5 time Olympian, Basketball

'...invaluable experience..'

"Being an athlete is more than just an elite level performance every four years. It's a multidimensional landscape that presents many challenges and opportunities. This book defines the fundamental behaviours of successful athletes and articulates how to transfer your passion into commercial success off the field. The easiest way to get ahead in any field is to tap into the invaluable experiences of others and that's what Kerri provides the readers with in this book."

Grant Hackett OAM - Multiple Gold, Silver and Bronze medallist in Swimming at the Olympics, World Championships and Commonwealth Games

'The Business of Being an Athlete is an invaluable tool...'

One of the best things I heard when I was competing was "If you want to stay in front, act like you're behind." This meant that I always had to be on my toes, learning and striving to be better.

The Business of Being an Athlete is an invaluable tool full of tips on everything from setting powerful goals to securing sponsorship. I would recommend it to any athlete striving to build a successful career from the sport they love.

Duncan Armstrong OAM - Freestyle Swimming Olympic Gold Medallist 1988, Television presenter and Motivational Speaker.

'...inspiring and an impressive read...'

Over the years I have had the pleasure of meeting and observing many elite athletes. Olympic gold medallist in Beach Volleyball, Kerri Pottharst, is without a doubt one of the best.

Elite athletes possess more than just courage and determination. They have a steely resolve that ensures they get the job done. Nothing prevents them from reaching their ultimate goal. They do not waiver and they are blessed with a rich passion for competition and a general love of sport.

At the Sydney 2000 Olympics Kerri displayed all those attributes. She and her partner Natalie Cook revelled in playing in front of their home crowd at Bondi Beach. For many Sydney Olympians competing in front of their fellow Australians brought added pressure but Kerri and Nat turned the hometown advantage into a positive and came away with the ultimate prize in sport, an Olympic gold medal.

In this book Kerri shows aspiring athletes how, through sheer determination and focus, they can achieve outstanding success on and off the field of play.

I would recommend *The Business of Being an Athlete* to any young person wanting to build a successful career. It is invaluable and inspiring and an impressive read from a much-loved and admired Australian Olympian.

The Business of Being an Athlete is Kerri's blueprint to success. So many great ideas and techniques for getting the most out of life and achieving spectacular success in sport and in business.

John Coates AC – President, Australian Olympic Committee

'Kerri's book is like the inside scoop...'

Excelling in your sport is not just about swimming faster, or jumping higher – it's also about believing in yourself, behaving as a role model, and giving the sponsors value. Kerri's book is like the inside scoop on how to reap the rewards of a fabulous sporting career.

When I was an up and coming athlete I got a lot of advice and support about how to swim faster, but not many people had input into all the other 'bits' that went with it. I just stumbled along and learned as I went. A book like this would have been invaluable to me in preparing me for everything else that went with swimming fast.

If you want to learn how to maximize the rewards that can be gained from doing well in your sport, then this book is for you.

Susie O'Neill OAM – Swimming legend. Multiple Olympic, World Championship and Commonwealth Games medallist.

'The tips laid out in this book are excellent!'

The contents of this book would have been invaluable at the beginning of my career – rather than spending so much time and energy re-inventing the wheel it would have been great to have had a manual for the entire car to begin with.

The hardest thing I've had to learn over the years has been the most effective ways of networking. The tips laid out in this book are excellent! It would have also been a bonus to learn the different dress codes early on!

It's taken me years to learn much of the information that Kerri has put together in this book. Even if you think you already have a good handle on some of the topics it's great to get a different perspective to see if you can fine tune your approach.

Liz Ellis AM – Australian Netball legend

'A must read!'

"As an athlete I made the most of my career on and off the track. Building a business while being an athlete contributed to me winning Gold and provided me with a great income. Now that I'm retired I have a successful career to continue with.

In this cleverly written book, Kerri provides you with all the information you need whether you are at the beginning, middle or end of your career. A must read!"

Katrina Webb-Denis OAM - Triple Paralympic Gold Medallist and successful business woman

'I would have loved to have read this book earlier in my career...'

As an athlete, my focus in the past has mostly been on training, performing and the day-to-day processes I need to go through to get the best out of myself. It's difficult to spend time on the other aspects that are also important - PR, Marketing etc. I now realize how important the business side of being an athlete is, especially after success. I would have loved to have read this book earlier in my career to know what to expect and how to get the most out of my career off the snow.

I'm still learning every day, about *the business of being an athlete* and this book has provided me with a great tool to do that.

Lydia Lassila – Aerial Skiing Gold Medallist 2010 Winter Olympics

'...fascinating book...'

The Business of Being an Athlete is a fascinating book, filled with insights, inspiration and motivation.

Peter FitzSimons – former Wallabies Rugby Union player, Journalist, Author, Radio presenter

'...a must read book...'

Turning a childhood dream into a sporting reality takes a lot more than years of training and talent, it also takes a lot of determination, planning and guidance. All too often, athletes forget that being a successful sports person is not just about performing well in their sports, but also about successfully managing every aspect of their lives, both in and out of the sporting arena. *The Business of Being an Athlete* is a must read book to guide our sporting heroes of tomorrow, drawing from the amazing experiences and insights of a great Australian athlete.

Zali Steggall - 4 x Winter Olympian. Australia's first ever Winter Olympic medallist, Bronze in Alpine Skiing Nagano 1998

'I've never been this inspired, motivated and excited...'

"What an awesome book! I've always set goals throughout my sporting career but not like this, not this specifically. There isn't much help around to guide you in the right direction towards the business side in your sport but this is all the help you'll need. I've never been this inspired, motivated and excited!"

Jenny Owens – 2 time Winter Olympian in Freestyle Skiing 2002 & 2010

'This book is a must for any athlete.'

You couldn't ask for a better person to give you advice on this topic. Kerri's experience in this field is invaluable. She is a master at building relationships, formulating appropriate strategy and thinking outside the square. I have known Kerri since well before the Sydney Olympics and the tips and advice she gave me transformed my way of thinking about sponsorship and a career after sport.

This book is a must for any athlete.

Lauren Burns OAM - Olympic Gold Medallist Taekwondo Sydney 2000, Naturopath, Nutritionist, Herbalist (BHSc)

'...achieve success in sport and in life...'

The Business of Being an Athlete is a book that will help athletes achieve success in sport and in life. This book will give athletes and parents tools to manage their sport and their careers; it will give them the best opportunity to maximise their ability and performances, so they can turn a passion into a career. A book all aspiring athletes need to read!

Jacqui Cooper – Aerial Skiing 5 time Winter Olympian

'A fabulous read...'

A fabulous read – you won't be able to put it down. *The Business of Being an Athlete* is Kerri's blueprint to success. So many great ideas and techniques for getting the most out of life and achieving spectacular success on and off the field.

Guy Leech - World Ironman Champion & Fitness Expert

'So much great information..'

Success as an athlete is not just achieving in the pool, or on the field there is so much more. The Business of Being an Athlete shares proven methodology that every athlete can utilise to maximise their career and their bottom line.

So much great information jammed into a precise and easy to read format. From how to write your bio and set up your Facebook page, to planning and executing a goal to achieve your athletic dream.

I needed this book about 15 years ago. Future generations of sporting stars will thank you for it. You continue to be the best at what you choose to do. Well done Kerri!

Adam Pine – 3 time Olympian, Swimming, Gold Sydney 2000 4 x 100m Freestyle

THE **BUSINESS** OF BEING AN **ATHLETE**

HOW TO BUILD A **WINNING CAREER** IN SPORT

KERRI POTTHARST

The Business of Being an Athlete
www.thebusinessofbeinganathlete.com
This edition first printed 2010
© 2010 Kerri Pottharst

Copyright
All rights for the body of this text reserved. No part of this book may be reproduced, resold or used in any manner (electronic, mechanical, photocopying, recording or otherwise) without the express permission of the copyright owner. The author reserves the right to vary, amend and update this book at any time without notice.
© Kerri Pottharst 2010

Disclaimer
The author has used her best knowledge in writing this book. The author accepts no responsibility or liability of any kind for any actions or consequences as a result of using the information within this book whether or not this is in any way due to any negligent act. No guarantees of success are made. The author acknowledges that everyone's circumstances are different and the reader assumes responsibility if they choose to use any of the information contained herein. This book is general in nature and is provided for information purposes only and is not warranted for content, accuracy or any other implied or explicit purpose. This book does not provide professional advice and is not in any way recommended as individual advice. The reader should obtain their own independent advice. References to internet sites in this book shall not be construed to be an endorsement of the internet sites, the companies or organisations represented by the internet sites or of the information contained thereon, by the author, publisher or associated parties.

National Library of Australia Cataloguing-in-Publication entry

Author:	Pottharst, Kerri
Title:	The Business of Being an Athlete
ISBN:	978-0-9808533-0-8 (pbk.)
Subjects:	sport/business motivation
Dewey Number:	796.023
ISBN:	978-0-9808533-0-8 (pbk.)

Published by Kez Press
Edited by Jacki Krahmalov
Cover design by Sasha White Design
Illustrations by Megan Wisheart
Typesetting by BookPOD
Printed and bound in Australia by Griffin Press

ABOUT THE AUTHOR

Kerri Pottharst is one of Australia's most respected athletes. Together with Natalie Cook, she won a Gold medal in Beach Volleyball at the Sydney 2000 Olympic Games, which they added to their Bronze medal from Atlanta in 1996. Kerri was awarded International Beach Volleyball Player of the Decade for 1990-2000 and was Australian Champion for nine consecutive years.

In 2001, she received the prestigious Order of Australia Medal, and in 2007, was inducted into the International Volleyball Hall of Fame (Massachusetts, USA).

Kerri's determination and resourcefulness kept her dream of Olympic glory alive for over 20 years, and enabled her to travel the world making a living from professional Beach Volleyball.

Away from the court, she lives on the Northern Beaches in Sydney, Australia with her husband, Max, and their son Tyson.

Since retiring from all competition in 2005, Kerri now divides her time between her three passions – her family, coaching elite-level Beach Volleyball, and inspiring people from all walks of life to achieve excellence through her writing, motivational speaking and mentoring.

For more information, visit www.kerripottharst.com

For all athletes wanting to realise their true potential

TABLE OF CONTENTS

About the Author iii
Table of Contents vii
Acknowledgements xi
Introduction 1
How to Use This Book 7

Section I - PASSION 11

CHAPTER 1
THE COURAGE TO DREAM BIG 13

CHAPTER 2
LIVING LIFE TRUE TO YOU 19

CHAPTER 3
THE DIFFERENCE IS A (BACKWARDS) PLAN 23

CHAPTER 4
THE SECRET TO OUR SUCCESS, SYDNEY 2000 39

Section II - PREPARATION 45

CHAPTER 5
TIME MANAGEMENT 49

CHAPTER 6
BUILDING AN A-TEAM 65

CHAPTER 7
DETERMINING THE COST OF YOUR DREAMS 77

CHAPTER 8
GENERATING INCOME 83

CHAPTER 9
THE 'S' WORD - SPONSORSHIP 93

CHAPTER 10
MANAGING YOUR MONEY 111

CHAPTER 11
KEEPING RECORDS 117

CHAPTER 12
DEVELOPING YOUR MARKETING TOOLS 123

CHAPTER 13
COMMUNICATION 141

CHAPTER 14
IMAGE, WARDROBE & FIRST IMPRESSIONS 145

CHAPTER 15
NETWORKING, MEETINGS & FUNCTIONS 151

CHAPTER 16
PUBLIC SPEAKING 163

CHAPTER 17
MEDIA 179

CHAPTER 18
DEALING WITH FANS 195

CHAPTER 19
ON THE ROAD 201

CHAPTER 20
NUTRITION 213

CHAPTER 21
HYDRATION 225

CHAPTER 22
SPORTS RECOVERY 233

Section III - BELIEF 243

CHAPTER 23
THOUGHTS BECOME THINGS 247

CHAPTER 24
BELIEVE TO ACHIEVE 253

CHAPTER 25
FEARS AND DOUBTS 267

CHAPTER 26
DEALING WITH CHALLENGES 275

CHAPTER 27
SELF-CONFIDENCE 287

CHAPTER 28
NEGATIVE SELF-TALK 305

CHAPTER 29
ATTITUDE IS EVERYTHING 313

CHAPTER 30
EXCUSES - TAKING RESPONSIBILITY 331

CHAPTER 31
HANDLING COMPETITIVE NERVES 339

CHAPTER 32
AFFIRMATIONS – BE LOUD AND PROUD! 347

CHAPTER 33
SEEING IS BELIEVING - VISUALISATION 353

CHAPTER 34
HABITS AND CONSISTENCY 357

CHAPTER 35
CONSTANT DAILY IMPROVEMENT 365

CHAPTER 36
BALANCE 369

CHAPTER 37
HAVING AN ATTITUDE OF GRATITUDE 375
CHAPTER 38
WHAT I'VE LEARNED – FINAL WORDS 381
CHAPTER 39
AFTERWORD – WHAT IT'S LIKE TO BECOME
AN OLYMPIAN 385

KERRI'S ACHIEVEMENTS 389
ADDITIONAL REFERENCES 391
SHARE YOUR OWN STORIES 393
BOOK KERRI FOR YOUR NEXT FUNCTION 395
FREE BONUS GIFTS 397

ACKNOWLEDGEMENTS

My deepest appreciation goes to the following people who have contributed, directly or indirectly, to this book:

Firstly, my most heartfelt thanks goes to my wonderful teammate during the most successful period of my Beach Volleyball career, Natalie Cook. Not only did she put together the chapter on Sponsorship in this book, without her I most certainly wouldn't have found Gold at the end of the rainbow. Together we learned so many aspects that I've written about in this book. We were two individuals with one goal in mind. She will always be like a sister to me and she continues to be an inspiration in all things sport and business.

A big thank you goes to another wonderful friend, Sarah Bunting, who helped me research and write much of the Preparation section. She also proofread what I wrote and gave fantastic feedback and advice throughout the process of writing this book. Sarah's supreme work ethic, superb organisational skills and amazing dedication to this project was exactly what I needed to make it happen. Without her it may never have come to fruition, or if it did, it would've taken many more years!

To my darling husband Max, thanks for putting up with the many hours I've spent crouched over my keyboard. Your support in whatever I decide to do is unparalleled and I love you dearly for that. You are in the true sense of the word – my other half. You're my sounding board, my dearest friend and the most amazing father to our beautiful son Tyson. Thanks, also, for doing all my IT and computer stuff, for constantly reminding me to do backups and for developing an amazing website to go with this book. I love you!

To my cheeky little 4 year old son, Tyson. I hope that everything in this book can one day provide you with a career in sport, if that is the path you choose. Thanks for putting up with Mummy while I sat for so many hours in my office while you played around me or on my lap. I hope you are proud of your Mummy and that you will always believe in your own dreams and work hard to make them happen.

My deepest gratitude goes to the two most influential and amazing volleyball coaches in my world – Sue Dansie and Steve Anderson. Sue guided me with love, laughter and a 'whip' during my early volleyball years. She took a gangly, self conscious, sensitive teenager and built me into a controlled, skilful and confident Indoor Volleyball athlete. After my switch to Beach Volleyball, Steve Anderson came on board and quickly built that confident Indoor Volleyball player into a Gold Medal winning Olympic athlete. In my mind, Steve is the most gifted, intense and knowledgeable Beach Volleyball coach in the world.

To Kurek Ashley, our Success Coach in the lead up to the Sydney 2000 Olympic Games, who was the final piece of the puzzle in our search for Gold. Thanks for all your guidance, your belief and the successful mindset strategies that enabled us to believe when it most counted. Thank you for teaching me not only to believe in myself, but to help others believe in themselves as well. I continue to live by many of those strategies and I am proud to be able to write about them in this book.

My thanks also go to Phil Moreland, our supreme Fitness and Conditioning Coach. I was 33 when I started working with Phil. I'd played volleyball for the past 18 years, I'd had 4 major knee surgeries and still needed to jump up to 200 times a day for the next 2 years at least. Thanks Phil for acknowledging my history, working with my injuries and making it happen!

To Lindy Olsen, Manuela Rocker, Jessica Berg, Megan Wisheart (who also did the wonderful illustrations!), Karin Boyd-Goerzer, Una Davis, Kirstine Lumb, Julia Heuer, Angie Akers, Craig Seuseu, Kira Sutherland, Margo Malowney, Chris Lewis, Mark Thompson and Judy Goldman who gave their time to help proofread, give feedback and advice on the first draft.

Thanks to all the athletes mentioned in this book for your stories, insights and feedback that have added so much extra to the content.

A huge thanks to Jacki Krahmalov whose superior editing skills have produced a superior product, Sasha White who designed the cover and Sylvie Blair from Bookpod for the typesetting design. All three of these amazing ladies put up with my many changes and additions throughout the production process.

Thanks to my friends and colleagues who have contributed to the amazing set of bonuses that are available with this book. (The bonuses can be found at www.thebusinessofbeinganathlete.com/bonus. Register, or log-in if you have registered before, to download your bonuses.)

And finally, thank you to Dale Beaumont, Andy McCombe and Karen McCreadie who all generously gave up their personal time to help me in the very beginning with advice from their own personal experiences.

INTRODUCTION

Stepping up onto the Olympic dais on Bondi Beach, Sydney was one of the most incredible moments of my life.

Together with Natalie Cook, I had just won Gold in the Women's Beach Volleyball. To win Gold at the Olympic Games is the pinnacle of any sporting career but to do it at your home games; in the Green and Gold of Australia in front of a home crowd with friends and family, was everything I had ever dreamed of.

I was so proud and so excited and yet it felt so right! It was as if all the moments of my life up to that point had brought me to that place and I couldn't believe the explosion of emotions within me as they put that medal around my neck.

We had planned for that day for years. We had visualised it a thousand times in our minds and we had worked so hard to achieve that exact result. As we stood there on the beautiful sands of Bondi Beach, every injury, every setback and every early start was worth it. I just remember letting it all sink in and feeling on top of the world.

You couldn't wipe the smile off my face for days, and I think I slept with my Gold Medal under the pillow for about a week! Natalie and I had already won Bronze in Atlanta 1996 but it was the Gold in Sydney that changed everything. And none of it would have been possible had it not been for what I'm about to share with you in this book.

It dawned on me a few years ago how lucky I was to still be deriving an income from doing things I love and also doing things that are related to the success that I've had in my sport. I realised that so much of it has to do with having had a very 'business' type approach to my sporting career and creatively finding ways to earn income to fund my journey.

All too often I've seen really promising athletes leave a sport they love because the daily realities of having to make money and pay the bills forces them to compromise their dreams. It's really hard to train full tilt, manage your diet and get your mind in the right place when your rent is due or your credit card is at its limit.

Not many athletes want to talk about the business side of sport, and yet it is crucial to reaching your goals. It doesn't matter whether you are an enthusiastic amateur, a seasoned professional, or on your way to your first Olympic Games.

Having the right mindset is every bit as important as having the right physical training program. And seeing yourself as a business and seeking out financial opportunities is every bit as important as your diet or finding the right coaching team. In this book you will learn both the mindset and the business side to give you a winning edge.

When I first started playing Beach Volleyball in 1993, I realised that to be the best, I needed to do it full time. I couldn't expect to beat teams from around the world if I continued to work in a full-time job and only practise before and after work or on weekends.

From that moment I set about devising ways of earning income through speaking engagements, sponsorships and coaching that allowed me to become a full time athlete. I was committed to learning, experimenting, making mistakes and taking risks. I also lobbied my Sporting Federation continually to help with funding towards our training and travelling.

There are so many talented athletes. The idea of being a professional sports person is attractive to millions of people around the world. Being paid to focus on winning Gold or setting World Records in a chosen passion is a dream for so many. So what is it that separates two seemingly equally talented athletes, both with huge potential, where one 'makes it' and the other doesn't? Is it drive? Is it motivation? Is it simply talent?

I believe it's not any one of these things. I believe that those who succeed are those who have learned how to treat themselves as a business.

You need to learn from mentors and set goals, you need to market yourself, you need to develop your brand and you need to be your own PR team. You need to know how to face challenges, have the right attitude and focus. You need to stand out from the crowd and be better than your competitors. In short – you need the same skills and mindset to be a successful athlete as you do to run a successful business.

Through various channels I started to make enough money to live and invest in my own growth and development as an athlete. I would pay for additional coaching and invest in things that other players were not doing, thus giving me an early advantage.

By the beginning of 1994 I was able to reduce my hours from full-time to part-time, and I finally quit by the end of that year. I have never had a 'job' in any other area or company since.

I consider myself an entrepreneur. I have earned my income from a combination of prize money, sponsorship, speaking presentations, endorsements, media appearances, corporate team building days, commentating, TV reality show appearances, coaching and running workshops. I think I am even now considered a 'millionaire' as I own my own home on the Northern Beaches in Sydney. Who would have thought that I could have made that much money from such a low profile sport as Volleyball?

You might be thinking, "well sure that's OK for Kerri, she's got an Olympic Gold under her belt". But consider this – in Australia, Volleyball isn't even mentioned in the statistics on sporting participation. The highest participant sports include Netball, Tennis, Cricket and the various codes of football such as Soccer and Rugby. You'll rarely read, see or hear anything about Volleyball in the media and yet I have spent 22 years competing in a sport I love. And most of those years before the Olympic Gold!

So if I can do it in Beach Volleyball then so can you in whatever sport you're passionate about!

I consider myself a sporting pioneer, one of the first athletes of my generation to travel the world making a living from professional Beach Volleyball. I have also successfully managed the emotional grind of staying on top of my sport for more than 20 years.

In 2001 I had the great honour of being awarded International Beach Volleyball Player of the Decade for 1990-2000 (along with Natalie Cook and Brazilians Sandra Pires and Jackie Silva) and before I retired, I had been the Australian Champion for nine years. And yet none of it would have been possible if I had not found a way to survive financially without caving into the demands of modern life.

Being a successful athlete is not just about the sport, it's about being able to make a living from your passion so you can give it everything you've got. Only then will you ever stand a chance of being the best in the world. I only wish there had been a book to guide me when I started my sporting career. It's what every athlete should know as soon as they recognise they have some talent. If you are serious about excellence then you also have to be serious about developing your career as an athlete.

As a fellow athlete or sports person you will know the hours and dedication it takes to even be good at your sport. Add to that the stress and strain of making a living and sometimes it can be overwhelming. As athletes, most of our focus is on the physical side of our sport rather than the financial or psychological aspects. Yet we all have to pay bills and take care of our responsibilities – finding that balance and achieving the ultimate sporting dream is what this book is all about.

This book is the culmination of everything I have learned, from how to be a successful athlete by setting specific goals, having the right mindset, to effectively managing my own brand and generating income. Winning is the most fantastic feeling, and fulfilling a lifelong dream is beyond words, but building a life around your sport is just as important. Today I'm happily married with a beautiful son whose arrival into this world was every bit as emotional and significant as winning Olympic Gold.

And for the record, this book will not cover sport-specific technical training. My guess is that if you're reading this book then you already have talent and potential and are supported by appropriate experts in your chosen discipline who will guide and teach you on the technical and physical aspects of your sport.

INTRODUCTION 5

What this book will do is teach you how to take your sporting talent and turn it into a lucrative career on and off the field.

I will share a very powerful 'toolbox' full of ideas and strategies that will guide you to being the best you can be. The rest is up to you...

Good luck!

Kerri Pottharst

On the podium with Natalie at the Sydney 2000 Olympic Games

HOW TO USE THIS BOOK

We all want to be winners. It's tougher than ever to succeed on *and* off the field, and unless you have the focus, the determination and the game plan to make it, you'll live with regret: "I wish I'd listened to...." or "I wish I'd tried that...."

The Business of Being an Athlete will help you achieve the successful career you want from sport – whether you're just starting out, or you've already won accolades and you don't quite know how to take it to the next level. Remember, it's never too late to begin.

This book isn't a set of rules and regimes. We are all unique and we all travel life's roads carrying different baggage. What works for some, will not work for others.

What you *will* find in this book are tried and tested ideas, techniques and tools used by myself and other world-class athletes that helped *us all* achieve success. And it's up to you to look at the range of options, try them, and then follow through with the techniques that work for you.

In the early days of my motivational speaking career, I remember being asked quite often what I thought were the 'keys to success' in sport. I used to flounder around and mention things like dedication, commitment, teamwork, focus, and so on.

One day I sat down and thought long and hard about it. I realised that:

- You need to *really* love what you do; it's motivating, absorbing, uplifting. It makes you feel alive. That's PASSION.
- You need to put in an enormous amount of hard work and learn everything you can about what you're trying to achieve. That's PREPARATION.
- You need to truly believe that you *can* achieve the success you're aiming for. Without that belief, you haven't got a chance. That's BELIEF.

Passion, Preparation and Belief – the 'keys to success' that I suddenly realised were my 'keys' and those of so many athletes I'd met.

I've divided *The Business of Being an Athlete* into these 'key' sections:

- **Passion**

    Setting goals to achieve the success you desire, defining your purpose and planning each step of the way.

- **Preparation**

    Practical tools and strategies to develop your career, on and off the field.

- **Belief**

    Developing the mindset of a champion, creating your winning attitude and troubleshooting the obstacles.

No section is more valuable than the other. Without one, the dream cannot be achieved.

Work on them all, and you have the best possible chance of achieving everything you hope for.

I encourage you to step out of your comfort zone. If contacting potential sponsors or the media makes you anxious, try a few of the different approaches suggested, until one clicks. You'll find lots of practical techniques in this book that *will* help you make the most of your time and your efforts.

It won't be easy, and you'll need to commit more time and energy to 'the business' if you want to reap the rewards. But you will achieve, on and off the field, if you commit and follow through.

You'll notice an icon featured throughout this book:

This indicates a Winner's Toolbox exercise – practical steps to create your own unique and incredibly effective motivational powerhouse.

You'll also find lots of grey shaded boxes, which contain my own personal reflections: the highs and lows, the challenging and the light-hearted stories of my journey to achieving the dream.

I suggest you read *The Business of Being an Athlete* in full, then come back to the sections you need. There are many 'little gems' in this book that I wish I'd had on hand throughout my career.

Learning is doing, so give it a go. The benefits are life-changing.

Create Your Own 'Winner's Toolbox'

The first and most important thing you need to do is to go out and buy yourself a blank journal or folder that you can write or draw in, and store pictures. It will be for your eyes only and you'll be referring to it every day.

You'll need to be able to change things in it while you're on your journey, so make sure it's easy to add or take pages out. You could even use transparent plastic sleeves.

I encourage you to personalise your front cover with a picture of what you want to achieve, or by simply having a picture of yourself and/or your teammates.

On the cover of my Winner's Toolbox (that I started in 1998), I had a picture of Natalie and I with our 1996 Atlanta Olympics Bronze Medal around our necks, with the title, 'Sydney 2000 Going for Gold' at the top and 'It all starts with a dream' at the bottom.

If you're already an established athlete and you don't have some sort of Toolbox, then this could very easily be the tipping point that gets you to the top of the podium. Try it.

As you read through this book, do the exercises, and fill your Toolbox with as many images and motivational sayings that you can.

The more creative and visual you make it, the more it will be worth to you. It will become a powerful addition to your life. I did it, and I know it works.

My Winner's toolbox created in 1998

SECTION I

PASSION

FINDING MY PASSION

I was always into sport. I tried Athletics, High Jump (I'm 6' tall) – but stopped that when I fell on my head one day and nearly broke my neck! I tried Netball at school, but that never went anywhere. I tried Basketball, but didn't like running much. I liked Tennis, but there weren't any opportunities to go far with that. I tried Swimming, but found it really difficult as I tended to sink too quickly. One night my older brother asked me to fill in at a social Indoor Volleyball competition: "We need 6 players on the court when the whistle blows. Once that happens, you can step to the side and we'll play". But rather than stepping to the side, I stayed on and played. I was 15 years old and this is how my passion for Volleyball began.

How do you feel about your sport? Is it all-consuming? Do you look forward to getting out of bed each day because you feel you have so much to do to achieve your sporting dream? Do you find yourself constantly thinking about it? Is it on your mind just before you drift off to sleep?

Do you have the courage to make changes and sacrifice 'important' things in your life now – steady income, clothes, the latest gadgets and so on, to be able to live the life you love?

If the answer to all these questions is a resounding "yes" then I'd bet money on you reaching that sporting dream, and achieving greatness.

Studies of highly successful athletes reveal that at some point in their lives they gave up a career based on money or what others thought they should do, to pursue their passion, their sporting dream.

If you're willing to do that too, and truly go after it, then I'd say you're on the right track. You most definitely have the passion.

Receiving my first state tracksuit at 16yrs old

CHAPTER 1
THE COURAGE TO DREAM BIG

Let's start this journey and explore exactly what you want, and why.

Don't worry right now whether you feel the dream is possible or not. Dare to dream big, dream huge – it's an incredibly valuable first step.

Clear your mind of any limitations. Don't worry about how you're going to get there, we'll work that out later, trust me!

Start wide, expand further, and never look back.

Arnold Schwarzenegger, Bodybuilder, Actor, Politician

If there were no limits to what you could achieve, if there were no boundaries to how far you could go, if you had no fears or doubts about reaching the highest pinnacle of your career.... Exactly what would your future look like?

Let's call your ideal future 'The Big Picture'. No – let's take it a step further, and call it the 'Ultimate Big Picture'.

Take a risk, be daring, have some fun and paint a picture for yourself of a place that is beyond your wildest dreams.

This isn't just about the ultimate prize in your athletic career. It's important to think about all those parts of your life that affect your wellbeing and happiness, and actually in turn affect your career.

> *Excelling in athletics is great, but it is only one part of me...it's only the tip of the iceberg in terms of what I plan to accomplish.*
>
> **Jackie Joyner-Kersee,** winner of three gold, one silver, and two bronze Olympic medals in Long Jump and Heptathlon

Some areas to consider:

Health and Fitness

- Diet, exercise, image. Any bad habits?

Family and Friends

- This could be the family you grew up with or the family that you may have started with your life partner.

- Do you surround yourself with positive people? Who do you need in your life?

Lifestyle

- Your home, your possessions, your values and traditions. How could it all be more balanced?

Wealth Creation

- We all need money to live the life we dream. How would you like to create more wealth? Investing in shares, property or business?

Personal Development

- Instinctively, we know our strengths and weaknesses. What do you need to develop or grow as a person – as difficult as it may be? How can you nurture that inner greatness?

..and Finally, Your Athletic Career

- Setting goals to achieve your athletic dream will consume most of your time, so what is your pinnacle? If you're already a full time athlete, or you are setting out to become one, what really would be your ultimate career dream?

Everyone's picture will be different. For some, the first five areas above might each represent a different colour of a rainbow, all intrinsically linked together, leading to the 'pot of gold' – the pinnacle of your athletic career.

Others may dream of more than one pot of gold – perhaps the ultimate athletic career, and the ultimate partner and family life; and see these as two separate dreams. That's fine. It's your Ultimate Big Picture.

Most people wish big but actually expect very little, and in life you get what you expect. So raise your standards, cast a wide net and you'll catch more of the big fish.

Begin with the End in Mind

Time to get out your Winner's Toolbox and begin your new journey. You can use a separate piece of paper or write it straight into your Toolbox.

- ✓ Find a nice quiet spot (or if you're in a team – sit down with your teammates) and start brainstorming.
- ✓ On the top of the page write 'My Ultimate Big Picture'
- ✓ Now, close your eyes and imagine. There is truly no limit to what you can imagine. The moment you imagine something, it begins to come to life. Use the list above as prompts or headings. Play a bit of make-believe. Ask yourself these questions:

1. "If I had no limitations, who and where would I like to be?"
2. "What would I do if I had unlimited resources?"
3. "What would I do if I knew I couldn't fail?"

✓ Write for the next 10 minutes without stopping. This is called flow writing. Write without thinking about what you are going to write or how you're going to get it. Just get your hand moving and let it all out. This is a great way to get your subconscious mind to relax and be able to release your dreams onto paper.

✓ Don't get stuck on *how,* just dream...

SIZE MATTERS

After recently doing a presentation called "Turning Bronze into Gold" a young woman approached me to tell me her story of regret, of not having dreamed big enough.

She told me that while doing her final year at High School she decided that she wanted to get a mark of 97% across all her subjects. She started dreaming about the number 97, writing it everywhere – big, small, all around her room, her desk and on her books.

Guess what? At the end of the year, she received an average mark of 97% across all her subjects! A truly great result.

So, what was her regret? That she hadn't dreamed of achieving 100% instead!

Make sure your dreams are BIG.

Having a clear 'Ultimate Big Picture' will energise your mind and emotions, and inspire and empower you to do all that you can to reach it.

You'll have the foundation on which to build your life game plan; a unique personal vision of a compelling future.

Your vision will become clear only when you look into your heart. Who looks outside, dreams. Who looks inside, awakens.

Carl Jung, Psychologist

THE COURAGE TO DREAM BIG   17

All successful athletes are great visionaries. They never simply focus on their current situation; they focus on the future, and where they want to be.

Taking the time to do this I guarantee will prove to be a powerful advantage, one that will give you the clarity and perspective that you'll need to shape your decision making.

It will also give you the strength to persist when faced with challenges. You'll find ways to overcome the imaginary or the seemingly insurmountable obstacles because you now have a vision. A vision that's vivid, unbounded, and audacious.

> ### WHEN YOU'RE NOT THE FAVOURITE
>
> Back in 1997, my Ultimate Big Picture was to win the Gold Medal at the Sydney 2000 Olympics. I had to think huge to paint the picture of Olympic Gold. At the time, we'd never even beaten the Brazilians who were hot favourites to win. We hadn't even won an event, let alone a World Championship. Most athletes in this situation would have dreamed of just winning a medal. We didn't. Our vision was Gold, and to my amazement, we got it!

Enjoying the final for Gold, just as we'd pictured it.

One final word on dreaming the dream. Just make sure it's yours.

Make sure that your Ultimate Big Picture is something that you genuinely want to achieve, not something that your parents, family, partner or employer might want.

Some dreams stay in our minds from childhood, from partner expectations, or are simply borrowed from someone else. Hit the 'delete' key and make room for the dreams that really matter to you.

> **KEY POINTS**
>
> **Dream big!**
>
> **Own your dreams – it's your future.**

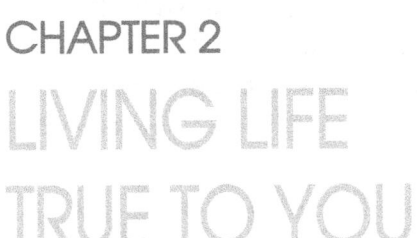

CHAPTER 2
LIVING LIFE TRUE TO YOU

You've now crafted a vision, your Ultimate Big Picture. Well done.

People often skip this step, because the picture can look so abstract, and feel so distant. But that is how it should be. The closest most people come is thinking up some New Year's resolutions.

As long as your Ultimate Big Picture is grounded in who you are, and is broad enough to encompass all the important aspects of your life, you are on the right track. If you're still not 100% clear on what you want to be, or do, or contribute in life, go back and do some more dreaming and flow writing.

If you do, keep reading. It's time to start living inside your Ultimate Big Picture.

The next step is to determine exactly *why* you want this life. What is the purpose, or reason, for wanting to achieve your dreams?

Working this out is like adding rocket fuel to your tank, to power you through the stratosphere. It is actually more powerful than the goal itself. It is your purpose that creates the burning desire and passion inside you.

Without purpose, there's no drive, no motivation.

So, to turn your Ultimate Big Picture into a down-to-earth reality, you must write out the purpose for wanting it in your life. It's about getting to the core of the dream. Put the rational, sensible part of you to one side for the moment, and ask yourself 'why'? Why do I really want it? The 'why' will tell you what's at the heart of the dream.

Finding The Core Of The Dream, The 'Purpose'

Grab your Winner's Toolbox and turn to a fresh page. Title the page: "My purpose for wanting xyz (your goal) is ...."

Spend some time flow writing again and use the questions below to stimulate your thoughts.

- ✓ In what way will your life change if you achieve your Big Picture?
- ✓ How will it make you feel?
- ✓ Will you love being there?
- ✓ Will it affect your family, friends and acquaintances?
- ✓ Will you become better known in your sport or discipline?
- ✓ Will it increase your income?
- ✓ Can you inspire others with your achievement?
- ✓ Will you be able to give more to others in some way?
- ✓ Will history be changed or rewritten?
- ✓ Will you be creating history?

An inspiring purpose is an essential catalysing force, accelerating the speed at which you will reach the Ultimate Big Picture.

Even if you don't know exactly *how* to get there or don't know what actions to take, if you have a true, clearly defined purpose you will find the way to get there.

The stronger and clearer it is, the more power you'll find within yourself to go get it.

> ### AT THE HEART OF OUR ULTIMATE BIG PICTURE
>
> Natalie and I fleshed out Our Purpose, as part of our Gold Medal Excellence plan. More about that plan later. Here are the reasons that we wanted to win a Gold Medal at the Sydney Olympics:
>
> To have a better quality of life
>
> Self discovery
>
> To become improved individuals because of our shared experience
>
> To be the best in the world
>
> To see the world and make new friends
>
> To heighten our profiles
>
> To greatly increase our income
>
> To create new and better opportunities
>
> To have the satisfaction of accomplishing our goals
>
> To leave our mark in history
>
> To represent Australia
>
> To inspire and lift others hopes and dreams
>
> To do what we love and get paid for it
>
> To make friends around the world
>
> To become better at our craft
>
> To attain our peak standard
>
> To enjoy the journey

Now you're ready to go after the dreams that no-one but you could ever dream. You'll feel a magnetic pull, newfound energy and exhilaration, and the thrill of watching your skills improve.

When you have a strong enough 'why', the 'how' will appear – it's like that sudden clarity when you de-mist your windscreen. Your vision is clear, and the way ahead is right in front of you.

Trust what feels important to you, and you will achieve greatness.

> **KEY POINTS**
>
> **Find the core of your dream, your 'purpose'.**
>
> **Your purpose will power your dream – so make it clear and strong.**

CHAPTER 3
THE DIFFERENCE IS A (BACKWARDS) PLAN

The difference between a dream and a goal is a plan.

Too many athletes treat goal setting with indifference. They dream about where they want to go, but they don't have a map to get there and they rarely write it down.

If you were driving somewhere for the first time, you'd need a map, directions or a good GPS, right? Well, why then wouldn't you use the same approach with your sporting journey?

> ## TURNING DREAMS INTO GOALS
>
> When I'm presenting, I often ask: "Who here sets goals?" On average, about three quarters of the audience put up their hands.
>
> "Keep your hand up if you've written them down." Most people take their hands down.
>
> The reality is, they haven't set goals at all. They've simply had thoughts — wishful thinking.
>
> If it's not written down and thought through, chances are, it will never happen. It will remain a 'daydream'.

Getting into the habit of setting and achieving goals will build your self-confidence and teach you where to concentrate your efforts. I now do it all the time, in all areas of my life.

> *Goals keep you focused on strategy – all the little steps towards the important outcome. Goals are a constant reminder of why you work hard – harder than someone, somewhere in the world who would like to beat you to the goal. Goals keep you motivated when you might be distracted – it really boils down to organising your plan towards winning. Once you win, you quickly realise the significance of your goal.*
>
> **Nici Andronicus,** Modern Pentathlon Australian Champion & International Triathlon World #2

Having clear goals helps you focus your energy and attention on achieving your Ultimate Big Picture. My advice is to chunk it down, and plan backwards. More on that in a moment.

In this book, we'll be focusing on how to achieve the ultimate athletic career – on and off the field. The 'pot of gold' at the end of the rainbow might be winning an Olympic Gold Medal, or becoming a World Champion, or bringing the World Cup trophy back to your country.

Goals are the steps you need to take to achieve that 'ultimate'. You think you've done goal-setting before? Have you tried doing it backwards?

Before we start, I'd like to share my seven golden rules for goal setting:

1. **Visualise before you strategise.** If you already have a picture in your mind of where you'd like to go and of what you're trying to achieve, don't be tempted to start creating your strategy or action plan just yet. Make sure you can really see it, feel it, smell it and taste it. Write how the 'ultimate' will be in as much detail as you can. You'll get to the *how* soon.

2. **Be specific.** You've got a clear Ultimate Big Picture, and you've defined your Purpose. If you aren't specific with your goals it is like going into a shooting range wearing a blindfold. You will hit something and it probably won't be what you wanted to hit. A goal like: "To have my best season ever next year" is not specific enough. To make it more specific, you could say "To win National Championships and represent Australia at a minimum of two International events in the next 12 months."

3. **Mark in the dates.** By when do you want to achieve this goal? This becomes important later as you'll need to break up that time between now and then into little pieces.

4. **Be positive.** Make sure that you are writing what you *want* in your life not what you *don't want*. If you focus on what you don't want, that's exactly what you'll get more of.

5. **Stretch yourself.** Make sure that the goal sufficiently pushes you out of your comfort zone. It must be realistic yet challenging, and beyond your present achievements. If effort and persistence are needed to reach the new level of success, it fits.

6. **Don't rely on luck.** Make sure it's in an area that you have control over and doesn't rely on fingers crossed. If it does, then you're in trouble.

7. **Write by hand.** Look, I love technology as much as the next person, but I've found that when you write something using your own hand, somehow you're more connected to it. Plus you can draw and doodle! It works for me to make my goals as creative and colourful as possible.

The kinds of goals you set may help you:

- win a specific event
- develop a new skill
- improve a current skill
- live a healthier lifestyle
- change old habits

Also, remember to make sure that your goals align with your personal values. If they don't, you'll be fighting an uphill battle to achieve your goals.

Let me explain. Values are the deep personal beliefs that guide every action you take.

For example, Greg Norman lives by this set of values and beliefs:

> *Find a better way, but don't take short cuts*
> *Always tell the truth*
> *Separate yourself from the crowd*
> *Control your emotions*
> *Get anger out of your system as soon as possible*
> *Set high standards. They will drive you to achieve*
> *DIN and DIP (Do It Now and Do It Properly.)*
> *You are judged by the company that you keep*
> *Learn the value of preparation*
>
> **Greg Norman,** Golf Champion

Take a look through this list of values for more inspiration and to clarify the values that are driving you.

Ambition, Believe In Yourself, Caring, Charity, Confidence, Courage, Courtesy, Friendship, Generosity, Giving Back, Gratitude, Hard Work, Honesty, Integrity, Laughter, Learning, Listening, Loyalty, Optimism, Patience, Respect, Responsibility, Sharing, Sportsmanship, Teaching By Example, Team Work and Trust.

What Are Your True Values?

Spend some time thinking about your core values, and write them in your Toolbox.

Values defined – now it's time to start realising your dreams. Serious dreams need serious goals, and the best way that I've found to work out my goals is to 'plan backwards'.

To create a backward plan, you need to force yourself to think from a completely new perspective. You need to work backwards from your dream – be there *right now*.

Let me show you what I mean. Imagine your ultimate dream is to reach the top of the world's highest mountain.

Now imagine you're standing at the bottom of this huge mountain, looking up. Wondering how on earth you're going to reach the top… Overwhelmed?

Now picture yourself standing at the top of the mountain, feeling exhilarated and fearless, then looking down and seeing exactly what you had to do to get there.

If you're like me, imagining that you've achieved the pinnacle of your dream seems to make the journey more possible, far less overwhelming and much more fun!

> ### LOOKING DOWN FROM THE OLYMPIC PODIUM
>
> My Ultimate Big Picture was to win the Gold Medal in Beach Volleyball at the Sydney 2000 Olympic Games with Natalie Cook.
>
> We sat down and planned out (backwards) the milestones we needed to accomplish just before winning gold in order to get that result. What specifically did we have to do, and by when?
>
> Our answer: We had to beat every team in the world, at least once, in the lead up to September 2000. We also believed that we had to win a tournament.
>
> We then worked backwards some more. What did we need to do before that 'second-to-last' goal?
>
> We looked at all the events on our calendar (18 months before the Olympics) and decided which events we should win and which events we should make the semi-finals in — as it was important to pace ourselves physically, emotionally and mentally.
>
> We aimed for no lower than the semi-finals as we knew this would put us in a good position to play all the top teams and give us a chance at winning some of those games. We also knew that overall, we couldn't match the experience that some of the other top teams had.
>
> We had to break up the journey in easy-to-achieve small, specific steps. We also looked at all the little things we had to do to win games. Physically and mentally.
>
> We worked back again and again, until we got to that day that we were writing our plan. We just kept asking ourselves, what do we need to do to make sure our previous goal is reached?

Don't just think *of* your Ultimate Big Picture, think *from* it.

Here's an example of an action plan for someone whose ideal weight is 65kg (10st 3lb):

Ideal weight goal: "I am 65kg and loving it!"

DATE	WEIGHT	EXERCISE	FOOD INTAKE
December	I am 65 kg	"Loving it!"	All of the below is a habit
November	66 kg	Walking 5 km x 3, Weights 2 x week	I love my new eating regime
October	68 kg	Walking 5 km x 3, Weights 2 x week	5 x Fruit/veg per day
September	70 kg	Walking 5 km x 3, Weights 2 x week	Healthy soups
August	72 kg	Walking 5 km x 3, Weights 2 x week	Reduce alcohol
July	74 kg	Walking 4km x 3, Weights 2 x week	Reduce coffee
June	76 kg	Walking 4km x 2, Weights 2 x week	Tomato pasta bases
May	78 kg	Walking 3km x 2, Weights 2 x week	No butter, mayo
April	80 kg	Walking 2km x 2, Weights 2 x week	Salads, no fries
March	82 kg	Walking 2km x 1, Weights 2 x week	Take out soft drink
February	83 kg	Walking 1km x 1, Weights 2 x week	Change to low fat
January 1st	84kg	Rarely	Everything

Now it's your turn. What is the Ultimate Big Picture 'pot of gold' that relates to your sporting career? Imagine having already achieved it.

What did you have to do physically, mentally, emotionally, financially and spiritually to get there?

Backward Planning Your Sporting Career

Start a new page in your Winner's Toolbox (or you can download the Backwards Planning template at www.businessofbeinganathlete.com)

1. **Write your goal as if it 'already is' at the top of the page**

    For example in 1998, we wrote 'We are Olympic Gold Medallists at the Sydney 2000 Games'.

    Tip: Write it in the present tense
    Goals stated in the future tense 'I'm going to' or 'I will' run the risk of never getting accomplished – that's why we avoided writing 'We are going to win a gold medal in Sydney 2000'. In order to achieve what you want you must first see yourself, without any doubt in your mind, achieving it. So state your goals in the present tense, as if they have already happened.

2. **Write where you are now, at the bottom of that mountain**

    For example, I wrote: 'We are ranked No. 6 in the world – 1998'

3. **Go back to the top, and apply your five senses**

    If you build the picture so fiercely in your mind, it's almost impossible not to go down the pathway that will get you there. Add some emotion to your dream by using your senses to 'colour' your Ultimate Big Picture. You've got to 'feel' it, 'see' it, 'hear' it and 'smell' it.

    For example, play the National Anthem and close your eyes. See yourself standing at the top of the podium. How does it feel? How does the crowd sound? Write it down in your Toolbox.

4. **Break the journey down into small, concise steps – working backwards**

    For example, in 1972 John Nabers watched Mark Spitz win 7 Olympic Gold medals in swimming. It was then he decided that he wanted to become an Olympic champion himself. His personal best time for 100m backstroke was 59.4 seconds. The Gold Medal in 1972 was won in 56.3 seconds. After careful extrapolation he figured that by 1976 he would have to swim 100m in 55.5 seconds to win the Gold.

That meant that he would have to improve his time by 4 seconds, which in a sprint event, is a huge chunk of time. So he figured: 4 years to train = 1 second per year. Still a significant challenge.

Swimmers train about 10 or 11 months per year, so that equated to about a tenth of a second a month. Broken down further – six days a week = 1/300th of a second per day. By training 4 hours a day, John worked out that he needed to swim 1/1200th of a second faster every hour.

(To give you an idea about how fast that is, 5/1200th of a second is comparable to the time it takes for your eyelids to touch after you start to blink!)

So for John Nabers, standing on the pool deck and saying "During the next 60 minutes I'm going to improve by 1/1200th of a second" – it became a believable dream and a great plan. And you know what – he did win Gold in the 100m Backstroke in 1976; in a time of 55.49 seconds!

Once you've broken down the steps into bite sized chunks by listing all the smaller goals that you need to achieve along the way, you're well on the way to turning your dream into reality. Taking the time to put it in writing is a significant commitment, the first deliberate step on the path to achieving your Ultimate Big Picture.

DON'T SWEAT THE SMALL STUFF

Although one of our smaller goals was to win a World Tour event before the Sydney Olympics, we never actually achieved it.

Another of our smaller goals was to beat every team at least once. We did achieve that, so the fact that we didn't win an event was OK with us.

Sometimes you may not make one of the smaller steps, but it doesn't mean you give up. Try whatever you can to keep moving forward. You can always come back to it later.

Tip: Sometimes 'stuff' happens
Try not to get too obsessed with achieving each minor goal on your way to the major goal. You might find that some steps can be skipped, some might become unnecessary and new steps might appear. Make sure you review these minor goals regularly as they will change often. You can always change it along the way if you're achieving things quicker than you planned.

5. **Detail it, date it and make it measurable**

    Your Ultimate Big Picture dream may be anything from six months to many years away. While it is important for you to have a clear picture of it in your mind, it is the smaller performance and day-to-day goals that will ultimately provide the pathway to achieving that dream.

    These are the goals that you must focus on from day to day, week to week, month by month. You can gauge your performance weekly or even monthly and you'll find that once you achieve each smaller goal, you'll naturally progress towards your Ultimate Big Picture.

I remember at school setting goals like making state and national teams for different sports and setting goals in school work. I started writing them down in about 5th grade, from memory. Nowadays, I still always write down my goals. Every year, every time I decide to do something new, even every week and then a daily list of things I want to achieve. I have a list I plan to do before I die, so I haven't achieved all of those yet and I keep adding to the list so I never feel like I've done it all!

Shelley Oates-Wilding, World Champion in Surf Ski and Outrigger Canoeing, dual Olympian in Kayaking

Tip: The more specific, the more likely
The more specific you are in breaking down your goal, the more likely you will achieve it.

- *Each step can be daily, weekly, monthly or quarterly.*
- *Use lots of detail – what, where, when, how and who.*
- *Make sure it's not cluttered at certain times. Spread the actions out so you're not overwhelmed.*

6. **Write it on something special that symbolises your goal**

    Make it colourful, use pictures, use objects – be unique!

    For example, if your dream is to win a particular trophy, find out what that trophy looks like and use an image of it as the background for writing your goals. If your goal is to lose weight, incorporate the specific number of your ideal weight into your design. Be as creative as you can, and have fun with it!

    ### BOUNCING BACK

    When I seriously injured my knee playing Indoor Volleyball for Australia in 1992, my journey to get back on the court was broken into little baby steps that I wrote all over the panel of a brand new white volleyball.

    If I ever felt defeated by pain or doubted that I'd be able to make it back, I just looked at my ball and it gave me the strength and motivation I needed.

    It started with simple things like running in water, then jumping in water, then riding a stationary bicycle. Bit by bit I moved to simple volleyball skills and added to them each month until I eventually tried to play a full game again.

    The goals didn't need to be big things, just small steps that I could focus on and think – "Yes, I can do that!" I had the ball in my bedroom where I could see it every single day. That way I was constantly reminded of my dream, and the steps I needed to take.

7. **Put your goals up where you can read them or see them every single day**

    This may sound a bit ho-hum, but I guarantee you that by reading them every day you will be so focused on your dream that you will automatically take the steps needed to reach each goal. We've all heard about hunches, intuition and co-incidence. That's your subconscious mind talking to your conscious mind. It's telling you the actions you need to take to get you to your target.

Reviewing your goals daily is a crucial part of your success and must become part of your routine. They say that the difference between billionaires and millionaires is that a billionaire checks and reviews his goals twice daily, whereas a millionaire only does it once a day!

For example, some places you could put your Ultimate Big Picture and goals:

- The wall in your bedroom
- Your bathroom mirror
- On the refrigerator
- On the microwave
- The horn on the steering wheel of your car
- Around your desk in your work place
- A little card, laminated, in your wallet
- Written on your drink bottle
- Back of the toilet door
- Outside of the glass shower screen
- Basically anywhere that you'll see if a few times a day!

8. **Tell the people close to you (or you can shout it to the world)**

    Tell the people you trust and value what your goals are. They'll support you, and maybe even help you get there. Don't let the fear of what your closest circle will think or say hold you back from telling them about your Ultimate Big Picture.

    Tip: Avoid the dream killers
    You know who they are. They're the ones who'll tell you that "you're crazy" or "you can't do that!" Steer clear. Often they're only jealous that they're not doing it themselves.

    If you're really brave, tell the media! That's what we did. Crazy, I know, but once it's out there, there's no turning back. You simply have to take action and do everything possible to make it.

THE DIFFERENCE IS A BACKWARDS PLAN

ATTENTION! ATTENTION!

Natalie and I told everyone our plans. We figured that even if we didn't get there, we'd have given it our absolute best and learnt so much along the way.

We soon found out that there were many people in our lives that could offer us help. People that we didn't even know could help and people that we hadn't dared ask.

We also started collecting everything made of gold or coloured gold – soon we were being bombarded with 'gold' from well-wishers. Gold was our theme; there was no doubt about that!

Fosters knew about our "Gold theme" and organised for us to be a part of their Gold, Silver and Bronze beer can promotion just before the 2000 Games started. Of course, we only took home the Gold cans!

9. **Take action, and do it now**

    The best laid plans are useless, unless you take action. Regrets for not doing or taking action will stay with you for the rest of your life. Don't be one of those athletes that "could have made it" or "had all the potential, but never realised it".

    You may have to alter your pathway from time to time as you discover new actions to take along the way. One action will reveal additional actions that you will need to take and the little 'wins' along the way will give you the energy to keep going.

    Make sure that you are urgent about taking action and patient about getting results.

    The fact is that the action you take today will bring you results in the future. They don't happen simultaneously.

    ### URGENT, BUT PATIENT

    I was always a little impatient about wanting it all to happen straight away and I had to learn that the work I did at training that day would reap benefits in matches in the future.

    We also knew that losing games and tournaments were all part of the learning process needed to eventually win Gold in Sydney. Sometimes that was hard to swallow, but if we went back to our Ultimate Big Picture, our Purpose and our Plan, we got back on track much quicker.

    We also realised that we couldn't do it all at once. We had to break it down into small achievable steps. That gave us the patience we needed to stay on task.

    If you're really serious about the planning that you've just done, ask yourself what you can do today that will take you one step closer to your dream. The most successful athletes are those who are willing to do more than most.

Every time you make a decision today, ask yourself this question, "Does this take me closer to, or further away from my Ultimate Big Picture?"

10. **Finally, get closer to the prize**

    What would you take home – a trophy, a medal, a shield? Try to get a little closer to your dream by bringing yourself a little closer to the ultimate prize.

    For example, find out the size of the World Cup trophy. How heavy is it? Where is it currently? Can you visit it? Can you buy a replica to put on display as a constant reminder?

> ## BRINGING IT HOME
>
> Before the 2000 Olympics I decided to research the Gold Medal itself. I found out what it was made from, where the silver and gold came from, and who made the ribbon that was going to hang around my neck.
>
> I discovered that the gold that was used to make the Gold medals came from three country NSW towns and it took them three years to mine it. The silver was donated by BHP and the Bronze medals were being made of old Australian 1 and 2 cent pieces! I immediately vowed to myself that I wasn't going to win another Bronze, I was definitely going for Gold – as the Bronze medals were probably only going to be worth $1.50!!
>
> Natalie decided that she would need a glass cabinet to display her Gold medal. Eighteen months before the Olympic Games she found what she was looking for – an upside down fish tank that she converted into a Gold Medal cabinet!
>
> She immediately started filling it with 'gold' items – in preparation for the ultimate Gold.

38 THE BUSINESS OF BEING AN ATHLETE

> **KEY POINTS**
>
> Follow the Seven Golden Rules for goal setting.
>
> To create a backward plan, force yourself to think from a completely new perspective. (You've made it, now look back to see how.)
>
> Ask yourself what you can do today, that will bring you closer to your dream.

The Gold Medals from Sydney

CHAPTER 4
THE SECRET TO OUR SUCCESS, SYDNEY 2000

Now I'll let you in on how we built our team and reveal the exact plan that Natalie Cook and I developed along with our Beach Volleyball Coach, Steve Anderson; our Physical Trainer, Phil Moreland; and our Success Coach, Kurek Ashley.

BUILDING THE TEAM AND MAKING THE PLAN

So how did we build our team? First on the team was our Beach Volleyball Coach, Steve Anderson. Back in 1995, our sport was relatively new in Australia, and the Coaches here were all still learning themselves. To become one of the best teams in the world, I felt that we had to look outside our country for the best Coach.

At that time, the Americans and Brazilians were dominating beach volleyball and had been for many years. We set off to California to try to find someone who was willing to work with us and who had the experience and passion to win.

With a coaching budget of about $500 a week and the promise that our new Coach could live with us back in Australia, we began the search. We literally "interviewed" five different Coaches who were recommended to us by some of the American players.

We asked each potential Coach to train us for two hours, on the sand, and explain to us how they would improve our game. Steve Anderson stood out immediately. We loved his philosophies and we loved his calm, confident and charismatic coaching style.

But, best of all, he had been looking for a team of tall athletic players with potential, who were open to new and innovative attacking strategies that hadn't been used before on the beach. It was exactly what we needed to match it with the American and Brazilian players of that era.

We needed a different approach, and it didn't take us long to convince Steve to give up his life in the States and join us in Australia for the next 18 months in the lead up to the 1996 Atlanta Olympic Games.

With our new Coach on board, we then added a full time Physical Trainer, Phil Moreland, to the team.

Now we'd covered volleyball skills and tactics, our bodies and training program, but what was left? Our minds!

We needed somebody to help us develop the belief we needed, so we decided to find a Success Coach. And, Nat found Kurek Ashley.

Let me tell you a little about Kurek, as having him join our team was definitely 'frowned upon' by our Sporting Body.

Kurek is an ex-Hollywood actor. He has a world record in firewalking; he's been a stand up comedian and is now a Peak Performance and Success Coach. Not someone you'd have thought could become the 'missing link' in our team. But that's exactly how it turned out. We needed that belief in ourselves, and he helped us build it.

We had worked with some sports psychologists in the past, but they never really resonated. We wanted something different, something more. We didn't want to be average; we wanted to be extraordinary!

Natalie first met the Kurek at a seminar. She was sitting in the front row and he said something that she will never forget: "No one remembers who comes second or third".

Afterwards, she introduced herself, and told him that we had won a Bronze Medal at the last Olympics. She then went on to say "I want you to help me turn the Bronze into Gold. Will you come on board?"

At just 22 years old she had the courage to ask. He said "yes," and the rest is history.

We now had our team of five, which we had decided to name 'The Dreamachine' because it was our dream to turn our Bronze into Gold and we figured we were as powerful as a machine. Without any one of us the machine wouldn't work. We were all as important as each other.

We didn't include any of the Australian Volleyball Federation's coaches as we were based in Queensland and they were based in South Australia. And for us, that wasn't an issue as we felt we had to get outside of the square, and try a different approach to that of the other teams. We often thought like this. We were always looking beyond for the best training and the best coaching – for the key to the next level.

Our team was complete: Natalie and I, Steve, Phil and Kurek. A team of five with one dream. To turn that Bronze into Gold.

Now, at this point, let me just go back to 1996, before the Atlanta games, when it was just Natalie, Steve and I. We also wanted to win Gold in Atlanta, but I know now that we didn't actually believe it as we rarely said exactly that. We used the phrase "we're going for a medal" more often than not. We also rarely wrote it down and we only had a very loose plan as to how we were going to achieve it.

At least we got what we had been talking about – a medal. But it wasn't the Gold; it was the Bronze Medal. Not a bad achievement, but clearly we got what we really only believed we could get.

So, once our team for Sydney 2000 was assembled (adding Kurek and Phil to the mix) we went away on our first team building adventure and embarked on the exact goal setting process that you've just done.

I remember my first doubt: "Look guys, if we go for Gold again, what happens if we get another Bronze or even Silver? We really do want the Gold this time, isn't there something higher we can aim for? Perhaps then we'll pick up the Gold on the way?"

Natalie then jokingly suggested going for a 'Platinum' Medal as platinum was more expensive than Gold!

We had a bit of a laugh, but realised that goals had to be tangible, and there really was no such thing as a Platinum Medal.

This is how our Gold Medal Excellence plan was born; out of a need to aim for something higher than ever before. It became more of a state of being, rather than simply a training plan to win a medal.

We went away for a weekend and we developed our plan. We called it: Gold Medal Excellence:

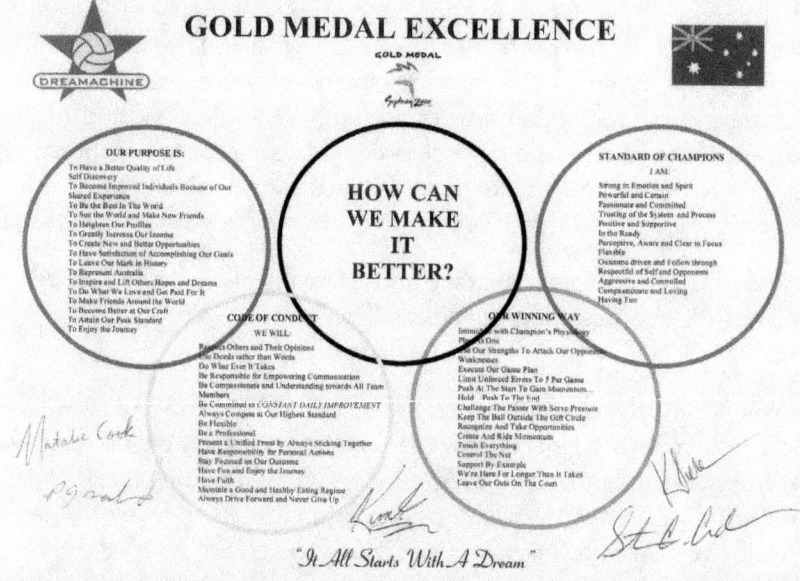

Our secret to success – Gold Medal Excellence - Go to www.thebusinessofbeinganathlete.com to see full readable version of this plan.

Each Olympic ring represented an important part of our journey.

Our Purpose

We brainstormed this list together. Steve then put it into words that were symbolic to us all. We thought of absolutely every reason why we wanted this in our lives and that purpose became our most powerful motivation.

Code Of Conduct
Every great team – sporting or business, lives by a set of rules. Why shouldn't we?

Being part of a beach volleyball team sometimes feels like being married! You're together all the time. You train together, you have meals together, you stay in the same hotel room, you travel six months or more of the year together, you're on planes sitting next to each other. You cannot get away from each other.

So we needed some pretty tidy rules to help us live together in such close proximity. We had to 'Be flexible', 'Be professional' and 'Present a unified front by always sticking together'.

Natalie and I were like sisters. I was the big sister, she was the little sister. And, we often fought like sisters! So, we had to be aware of what we showed our opponents. If they saw a chink in our armour, they would stick the wedge in and they would try and beat us with it.

We completed the rules with 'Enjoy the journey'. Of course we wanted to achieve our Ultimate Big Picture, a Gold Medal, but we also wanted to enjoy each and every moment along the way and we knew that by doing this it would be much easier to reach our dream.

Our Winning Way
This section was all about Beach Volleyball and what we needed to do to beat the best teams in the world.

I particularly liked 'Touch everything' – that meant never letting a single ball drop on the sand without an all out effort. This wasn't easy, especially playing in the height of summer in Brazil, when the sweat drips off you like a tap. You really don't want to hit the sand to pick up that ball that's a good two steps away from you. Getting up off the sand after that is like lifting a wet, eggy-covered schnitzel out of the bowl of breadcrumbs! And I can tell you, sand gets everywhere!

Standard Of Champions
I am convinced that this final ring was the most important. If we wanted a Gold Medal, we believed that we had to live our lives with the character of a Gold Medallist. We had to become Gold Medallists before the Olympics and live a type of gold medal standard. That's how we came up with the name of our plan – Gold Medal Excellence.

We had to take a look at the qualities, attributes and traits needed to win Gold. What were other successful people around us like? How did other champions in sport and in business live their lives?

We came up with a series of standards. Trust was an important one for me: 'Be strong in emotion and spirit, be powerful and certain, passionate, committed, trusting of the system and the process'. I'd played volleyball longer than Natalie and Steve. I was older than Steve our coach, so I had to put all my dreams in Steve's hands, and trust him to direct our team.

We wanted our family and our friends to still love us. We wanted to have great relationships. That led us to aim to be 'Aggressive yet controlled and compassionate and loving'. It might seem strange to put compassionate and loving on the list, but we didn't want to end up being single minded, hard-nosed, boring individuals who'd won a Gold Medal.

We really wanted to make sure that this was going to be an enjoyable journey, so 'Having fun' was also included. The successful people we knew were all having fun! And if our journey wasn't, we'd want to find a way to make it fun!

How Can We Make It Better?

This was our team motto. We asked ourselves this question whenever things weren't going to plan. This ensured that we would continue to focus on the future, rather than the past.

'The Dreamachine' started with a dream – our dream to turn Bronze into Gold.

We told everybody that we were aiming for Gold. I'm sure very few believed that we could get there, but we believed it and that was all that mattered.

KEY POINTS

It all starts with a dream.

Be the champion you want to become.

SECTION II

PREPARATION

Learning from Others

You must constantly improve and prepare yourself—improve your skills, knowledge, expertise, relationships and resources—so that when luck strikes, you have the wherewithal to take advantage of it.

Darren Hardy, publisher of Success Magazine, on Preparation

In this section I want to share with you what I have learnt over the past 25 years, which will give you a great head start on your competitors. If you take on board the tips and the advice, you'll stand out amongst fellow athletes, make enough money to be able to play sport full-time and realise your potential. And, once you've retired from sport, these skills will ensure a much easier transition into the business world.

Just remember though, it's not enough to simply read these chapters. You must take action.

Also, you should seek out mentors – people who have achieved the kind of things you want to achieve; and ask if they would be prepared to join you on your journey. Watch how others do things, emulate them and go one step further, do it even better!

Even the great Roger Federer needed inspiration from role models. He lists his role models as **Boris Becker, Stephan Edberg and Michael Jordan.**

My point is, you will get much further if you actively try to learn from others.

You may choose to learn from famous individuals, but there might be someone closer to home that has something to offer.

- If you want to learn how to become a millionaire, would you learn more from speaking to a millionaire or from speaking to someone who's been telling you for years that they are going to be a millionaire someday? Talk to the person who's been there, done that and find out how they did it.

- If you know someone who seems to be infinitely more productive than you and gets more done every day than you seem to in a week, talk to them about it. Ask them how they do it.

- If you have seen a charismatic public speaker, take notes on what impressed you about their presentation.

- If one of your teammates handles the media well, go along to a media conference and watch them in action. Or observe high profile sports stars being interviewed. Take note of how they handle themselves after a win and a loss. If it's someone in your sport, ask them how they prepare, and the kind of work do they do behind the scenes before they even face the media.

- If someone in your team or even in another sport has an amazing technique or an ability to achieve something that you currently only dream of, then ask them to show you how they do it. How have they trained and prepared to get to this point?

Yes, some people are naturally better at certain things than others. Some people are inherently persuasive public speakers and others will be natural planners and budgeters.

Of course, you won't suddenly become brilliant at everything just by talking to others. But try to get into the habit of stepping out of your comfort zone to learn from others. For every person you see doing something well, compliment them on it. They will almost always be flattered that you even noticed, let alone commented on it. Talking to them may open doors, or give you the key to a skill you've been trying to master.

> *A single conversation across a table with a wise man is worth a month's study of books.*
>
> Chinese proverb

I urge you to take this 'learning from others' mentality with you on your journey, and as you are reading through this section. Make notes about those you already know who could help you.

Don't underestimate the difference it could make to your success.

KEY POINTS

Seek out others who could help you improve.

Step outside your comfort zone.

CHAPTER 5
TIME MANAGEMENT

Until we can manage time, we can manage nothing else.

Peter Drucker, renowned Management Author and Consultant

So by now, you know your goals. You have a clear picture of what you want to achieve. Hopefully you also have a clear picture of when and how you plan to achieve it.

Feeling a little anxious about how you are going to fit all this into your already jam-packed life?

How do some people manage to fit twenty-five things into their day and accomplish so much, while others can barely fit in four or five? These people who achieve more have just learned to manage their time more effectively. We all have exactly the same amount of time in the day and once that day is gone, there is no getting it back.

You have 1,440 valuable minutes to spend each day and the secret is just working out the best way for you to spend them.

The most successful time managers follow these three steps:

- Plan
- Prioritise
- Schedule

Doing all three is critical to achieving your goals. But here's the key – making the best plan, prioritising, and working out your agenda is not going to help if you don't actually follow it!

Time On Your Side

When it feels like you don't have any time to plan, that's exactly when you need to do it. Read any successful business person's memoir, and you'll find that they spend a significant amount of time thinking and planning, before taking any action.

This exercise will help you work out where that precious time is going.

List everything that you do during a normal week. For example this could include:

- ✓ Training (all types)
- ✓ Competition
- ✓ Meals and snacks
- ✓ PR/Media
- ✓ Administration/paperwork
- ✓ Meetings/Business Functions (for example for sponsorship, media liaison, team matters). Include travel time to and from the meeting along with any preparation time for documents or presentations you are giving.
- ✓ Socialising
- ✓ Family commitments
- ✓ Goal setting/reviews
- ✓ Travel (to/from training/competition)
- ✓ Work/school/study

TIME MANAGEMENT

- ✓ Rest/recovery, including treatments such as physiotherapy, massage.
- ✓ Sleeping

Visit www.thebusinessofbeinganathlete.com and you'll find a worksheet like the one below that you can print off and fill in yourself.

Next to each activity, note how many hours per day x number of days per week that you need for that activity. Overestimate the time (most of us think we are much more efficient than we actually are). For example:

Activity	Daily Hours	Days per Week	Total Hours	Notes
Sleeping	8	7	56	
Training – skills and strength	2 x twice/day	6	24	Rest day Monday
Meals & snacks	0.5 x 5/day	7	17.5	
PR/Media	1	3	3	Updating website, Facebook fan pages, chasing media etc.
Admin/paperwork/shopping	1	2	2	Travel plans, bills, budgets, grocery shopping
Socialising	3	1	3	
Goal setting/reviews	0.5	7	3.5	Daily review/planning
Travel (to/from training/competition)	1.5	6	9	15 mins each way x 2 sessions per day
Work/study	7	5	35	
Rest/recovery	1	7	7	Physiotherapy, massage, chiropractor, ice baths etc.
Total			160	

This is how you can start to work out how you spend your 24 hours each day (or 168 hours per week) in making your goals a reality. If your total is above 168 hours, you are in trouble!

Make sure you allow time for some unscheduled interruptions such as a friend calling. Interruptions will happen and you just need to adapt your plan. Move something to later in the day or later in the week. The idea is not necessarily to plan every minute of your day, but just have a basic structure to determine how (and if!) everything fits in. That way, the week doesn't just pass by without you doing some of the key activities that are always on your list.

Recovery is just as critical on the path to peak performance as training and competition. Your body needs the time to re-build and grow stronger. Allocating sufficient time to rest and recover is critical in your planning. But resting is not an excuse to sit around and do nothing! Use this time to do your PR, media, sponsorship, paperwork and budget proposals.

> *Waste your money and you're only out of money, but waste your time and you've lost part of your life.*
>
> **Michael LeBoeuf**, Business Author and Professor Emeritus, University of New Orleans

If you are already in the fortunate position of playing your sport on a full-time basis, you will have a significant advantage of 30-40 additional hours per week over those who may be working or studying.

Use this time wisely. Be productive. Improve your website, update your Facebook fan page or chase some media stories.

> **Tip: Be honest**
>
> Be honest with yourself – if you plan to spend two hours each Tuesday on PR and goal setting reviews, don't try to do it in front of TV, or while you're chatting to friends over the internet. If you really enjoy TV or chatting, allow time for them in your schedule and when you get to that time – really enjoy it, rather than feeling guilty that you should be doing something else.

No Time Like The Present

Allocating sufficient time for everything we discuss in this book may prove challenging. Start a new page in your Winner's Toolbox and write down the answers to the questions below. It will help you figure out how you can 'gain' more time.

But you need to be just as disciplined in the planning of your life as you are on the sports field. You may decide to give up watching TV in order to plan your training or prepare sponsorship proposals. Or you may decide to start listening to audio books or self-improvement CDs while travelling, rather than just wishing there was less traffic.

Ask yourself these questions:

- ✓ What can I give up in order to fit everything in?
- ✓ Is everything I have listed really necessary?
- ✓ What are my highest priorities?
- ✓ Are there times during my week where I can combine two activities? For example, on long journeys to/from training and competition, could this time be spent returning phone calls?

Urgent Versus Important

In his book 'The 7 Habits of Highly Effective People', Stephen Covey suggests a time management technique that involves dividing your 'To Do' list into four quadrants based on importance and urgency.

Covey suggests that it can be easy to get caught up doing all the 'urgent' things and not allowing time for the things that are important to you but are not urgent. Examples of 'urgent, not important' activities might be certain phone calls, interruptions, or meetings you really didn't need to attend. Be careful – these activities may appear urgent, but ask yourself whether spending time on them will help you achieve your goals.

Addressing tasks that are ***important*** but not urgent is the real key to achieving your goals faster.

Activities in this category are things like planning, goal setting, enhancing your skills and true recreation.

Allowing time in your schedule for these types of activities ensures you are not always focused on short-term goals or immediate issues. You'll find yourself making headway with some of the 'bigger picture' items too.

> *The key is not to prioritize what's on your schedule, but to schedule your priorities.*
>
> **Stephen Covey,** Management Expert and Author

Visit www.stevencovey.com for more resources to help you with time management.

To Do or Not To Do

The next step is actually putting your activities into a weekly planner. This could be in Word, Excel, your phone, your diary, Outlook or any other diary or calendar-planning tool including good old-fashioned pen and paper. Find what works for you.

You can download an example of a weekly planner on our website, www.thebusinessofbeinganathlete.com.

Next, to get the most out of your week, you need to write up a 'To Do' list each day.

Here's how:

- ✓ Write down everything from your schedule that you planned to get done that day.
- ✓ Review the list and number your top 5 tasks, 1 to 5 in order of priority – '1' is something you need to do first (not one you'd like to do first), and so on.
- ✓ Switch your phone to voicemail. Close down your emails, Facebook and website. Focus!
- ✓ Work through your list from 1 to 5.
- ✓ Do not cheat and jump a task to get to one you'd prefer to do first.

- ✓ At the end of the day, spend 5 minutes preparing your To Do list for tomorrow. If you don't, you'll waste time in the morning trying to recall where you left off the day before. Look at your weekly planner for the next day, list the activities (and the 'leftovers' to follow up from today). Re-assign tasks 1-5.
- ✓ Clear your working space ready for a clean start the next day.

Reward yourself when you have completed all 5 tasks on today's To Do list. Rewards could be as simple as watching that TV show you recorded last night, reading a book or magazine, chatting with friends online, taking a walk on the beach, downloading music, or enjoying a nice hot bath!

Whatever it is, choose something that makes you feel good.

When Your To Do List Starts Weighing You Down

Do some activities seem to stay on your To Do list forever? Do you find yourself avoiding activities that seem monumental or incredibly tedious? Do you skim through the list to find the easiest or quickest things that you can tick off straight away?

No Time to Lose

Is your schedule impossibly tight? Try this simple activity:

- ✓ Keep a diary of your week in 15-minute intervals. Be precise, don't guess. It's surprising how quickly 15 minutes can pass if you aren't keeping track. Look closely at where you are spending quality time and where you are wasting time. Do you really need to check your emails so often during the day?
- ✓ Re-prioritise. Are there activities you could delegate? Can you do some activities less often? The simple test of priority is asking yourself: Will doing this activity really get me closer to achieving my goals?

I realised early on that working haphazardly through a list of items is neither effective nor efficient in the long run. You may get through some of the more urgent items on your list, but you never get around to the ones that are *important, but not so urgent*.

> **Tip: Learn to Touch Type**
>
> If you can't already touch type to a decent speed – and I mean using all your fingers across all the keys – then you definitely need to learn! It is probably the best skill I was ever taught as it makes me so much more efficient.
>
> So much of your day-to-day life is spent on the computer; touch typing makes everything so much faster – whether you're sending emails or typing up a business proposal. There are many free online tutorials to help you, or programs you can buy. Although it might be slow progress at first, persevere and you will be amazed at how much more you can get done.

Procrastination

Procrastination is simply a habit. A habit you can change. It is a real time-killer, and can stand in the way of achieving your goals.

There's an element of procrastination in nearly all of us but some of us are worse than others. I admit to being guilty of it from time to time, but procrastination can really be damaging if you let it get out of hand.

>
> ***Discover Your Procrastination Triggers***
>
> Pull out all your To Do lists from last week.
>
> ✓ On each day's list, circle the tasks that didn't get done.
>
> ✓ Now, go through each day's list, and looking at the circled tasks, cross out all those tasks that didn't get done because of a third party (for example, the doctor cancelled your appointment). These weren't your fault.
>
> ✓ Look at the circled tasks that remain. Does this tell you where you are procrastinating?

I want to share some helpful techniques from Motivational Speaker, Jason Gracia, that may help you win the battle against procrastination. Visit www.motivation123.com for more.

Choose a few techniques that appeal to you and start using them right away. Yes – today! I guarantee you will get more done in less time. They've worked for me and I know they'll work for you.

Just do it. Be accountable. Follow through. You will be amazed how far it gets you in life and in your sporting career. It is such a simple thing and it makes such a difference.

Technique 1 – Give It 5

- Find a task on your list that you just can't seem to get to, even though you know it needs to be done. For example your tax return, calling the doctor or taking a step towards your Ultimate Big Picture. It can be anything at all, just something that you have been putting off.

- Next, think of one small step that you could do right now to make a start. Give that task 5 minutes. That's all. **Just do something**. A mere 300 seconds is nothing.

- Once you've given it 300 seconds, it's so much easier to just give it a few more seconds. If you can't do more than 5 minutes initially, make a note of when you will spend another 5 minutes on it. That next 5 minutes will definitely be easier than the first. I guarantee it.

- Raise the bar and extend it to 10 minutes.
- Do it. Right now. Don't come back to this page until you've done it!

Not so daunting, was it?

If it is a task that you need to do again in future, try writing up some notes on how to make it more manageable next time. For example, if you procrastinate with your tax return, perhaps allowing a certain amount of time each month throughout the year would be more effective than leaving it to the last minute and struggling with the burden. Can someone help you - your accountant or partner, or a trusted friend who enjoys budgets and finances?

Technique 2 – Switch It Off

If you find yourself irresistibly drawn to checking emails or Facebook or watching TV instead of working through your To Do list, then make a commitment to 'not switch them on' until you have completed a certain number of activities on your list.

Better still, actually go to the wall and unplug the TV or computer. Don't cheat and check Facebook through your mobile! Remove the temptation. Switch them all off.

If you know you will struggle with this, tell those you live with about what you are doing and ask them to help you implement it.

If there are TV shows that you really want to watch, record them and watch them later without the ads – you will save time, achieve more, and really enjoy the program.

Technique 3 – The Competition

Use your competitive nature to your advantage – both on and off the field:

- How quickly can you get through your To Do list?
- How much can you get done in 5 minutes?
- How many productive phone calls can you make in 10 minutes? Plan your calls and know what you want to say. Don't waste time.
- Use your stopwatch.
- Find a way to make it a game or a challenge (anything!) to make it fun and easy for you to get things done.

Technique 4 – Break It Down

Got some monumental, overwhelming, sigh-inducing tasks on the list? Break them down.

One at a time, make a list of all the smaller tasks needed to complete that big task. Go into as much detail as you can. Once you have your list of 'mini tasks', decide on three things that you can do right away. This might be to:

- Make a phone call
- Research online
- Send an email

Whatever it is, just do something to start the ball rolling. You will feel elated at having made a start and the momentum will see you through the completion of this task.

Technique 5 – On Your Marks, Get Set

Distractions, distractions. It's the "I'll just do this first…" syndrome. If you find it really hard to get started, try to make the repercussions more vivid in your mind.

Imagine a distraction causes you to miss a World Championship event…. I might just check Facebook one more time before I go on the court… oops… whistle blows… you're disqualified.

OK, unrealistic perhaps, but taking it to the extreme in your imagination might bring to life the potential effect that these distractions are having on you achieving your goals. So:

- Get to your desk
- Make a start
- Wasting a second can quickly turn into wasted hours

Technique 6 – Time Of Day

Sometimes, scheduling tasks at the wrong time of the day can be a huge factor in why they just don't get done.

Some people are more productive in the morning, some in the evening. Some love exercising at the crack of dawn, some find they perform better later at night. Think about what works best for you (and your team) and adapt your schedule around it.

If you leave all your tasks for the evening but you know you're really a morning person, then set your alarm 30 minutes early every day, and start doing tasks first thing. You will be amazed at how much you get done in those 30 minutes! For me, if I have cleared my desk, cleaned up from breakfast and am organised by 9am, I know I am going to be productive for the rest of the day.

Technique 7 – Trade Me

Chat to your family, flatmates or teammates about sharing or trading chores and tasks. Sometimes, just by talking about it, you can find a better solution. Someone else might quite like doing some of the things you hate and vice-versa.

Technique 8 – HELP ME!

Actively seeking help can be liberating! Jason Gracia says you ask for help "Not because you don't know how to do it but just because it will make you move!"

Consider paying someone to do some of the things that are taking up your time. Can you pay a bookkeeper, administrative assistant or handyman to help out? The outlay might seem like an extravagance initially but it will take these tasks off your hands and ensure they get done well, and on time. It nearly always turns out to be money well spent in the long run.

> ### THE WRITE FRIEND
>
> I had been thinking about writing this book for over two years. I had been actively collecting material, doing research and recording stories over many more years.
>
> But I was so busy with all the other things in my life, even though I really wanted to write it, I just couldn't make a start on the actual book.
>
> Then by chance, I was chatting to my friend Sarah, who was between projects, and I asked her if she'd be interested in helping me. She said yes and within two weeks, we had started writing!
>
> Having Sarah on board also meant that I had to commit to the project. We started to tell people about it. I mentioned it in every interview or media opportunity I could. By talking about it, everyone expected to see something soon and that drove me to ensure it really happened.
>
> I'm still busy with all the other areas of my life but I've made the commitment to find time to do this too. If I hadn't had that conversation with Sarah, it might have been years before I found time to make a start!

Technique 9 – Delete It

Sometimes (just sometimes) there is a task on your list that really doesn't need doing. If nothing much in your life will change if you don't do it, then here's a tip – delete it!

This is especially true for any little job that has been on your list for weeks or months. Why do you keep avoiding it? Maybe it's because it's just not that important after all.

Feel the joy when that pressure's gone, and the task is off the list.

Technique 10 – I Can Do It

Sometimes we convince ourselves that a task is going to be harder than it really is.

In this case, some positive self-talk can go a long way here. Gracia suggests before you start the task, consciously tell yourself "It's not hard. It won't take long. I'm sure I can do it, or at least learn as I go."

Remember 'The Little Engine That Could'? ...I think I can... I think I can...

Technique 11 – The Glory

As with most of our journeys as elite athletes, the hours, months and years of training are gruelling for a few minutes of glory at the end. But it's the glory that keeps us motivated and the adrenaline of winning – the payback for all those years of commitment – is unlike anything else you will experience. We finally reach that pot of gold at the end of our rainbow.

Whatever you are putting off, the more you focus on the drudgery of the route to the goal, the more negatives you associate with it and the less likely you are to act. Instead, flip this over and focus on the pot of gold. Imagine a completed To Do list as a minor win; a win that gets you closer to that major win, that pot of gold.

Technique 12 – Inward Outward

Do you sometimes feel that you have been super-busy all day, but you don't have much to show for it? Or that you've had so many interruptions, it's hard to concentrate on any one thing at a time?

Grouping activities into two 'types' can result in huge increases in productivity:

1. **Inward Activities**

   Things you do by yourself without interacting with anyone else. This could be replying to emails, planning a budget, scheduling your training program, writing or reviewing a sponsorship proposal and so on. Anything where it's just you, working alone.

2. **Outward Activities**

    Activities where you need to interact with other people, such as phone calls, meetings, answering questions, listening to others.

I get so much more done when I tackle the same type of activities in a big chunk. This means that you allocate say, two hours of your morning solely to 'inward' activities. You switch off your phone. Close your email. Don't answer the door. You focus solely on your inward activities with no distractions. After your two hours is up, you might change it up and do a whole chunk of 'outward' activities – returning phone calls or holding meeting with teammates.

Give it a try. I have been surprised how much more I get done and how much more satisfied (and more sane) I feel at the end of the day.

Technique 13 – Handle It Once

I've found this one works in my home life just as well as in my business life. As far as humanly possible, you touch each item once and only once.

Let's take the example of a bill coming in through the mail. Typically, you might:

- Collect the bill from the mail, put it on the kitchen bench until you get chance to open it later.

- Some time later you open it and put it in your pile of things to do/bills to pay.

- A few days later, you look at it, maybe pay it or maybe put it back in the pile to deal with closer to the due date.

- At some point later, finally you pay it.

- Once you've paid it, you move it to a pile of 'Things To Be Filed' (because actually bothering to file it right now would involve getting off your chair...!)

- At some point in the future (which could be weeks or even months later) when you get round to doing your filing, you file that piece of paper in the correct place and don't have to look at it again.

How incredibly inefficient it is to handle each item five or six times?

Now, 'handle it once':

- Open it, pay it, file it. Done!

Around the house, this principle works just the same when you are clearing up or putting things away. Don't just move an item to another place before you get around to dealing with it properly.

You'll be surprised at how much more efficient you will be when you make this a principle throughout your life.

Technique 14 – Keep it Simple

Say you're going to do something.

Do it.

Once you have mastered time, you will understand how true it is that most people overestimate what they can accomplish in a year – and underestimate what they can achieve in a decade!

Anthony Robbins, Self-Help Author and Success Coach

KEY POINTS

Take action towards your goals every day.

Set your priorities and allow time for them in your schedule.

Persevere when you really feel like giving up.

Think of the goal, not the process.

CHAPTER 6
BUILDING AN A-TEAM

The bottom line is, you simply can't do it all by yourself. It took me a long time to figure this out. When everything rests on your shoulders alone, facing the unexpected can overwhelm you to the point where you may start to second-guess yourself. To question whether it's all just a pipe dream.

Ultimately, your level of success depends on the quality of the team you build around you. When you're ready to take on the world it is of utmost importance to hire the right people in order to win. You need a team, even just a few players, who will inspire you, energise you - a team that's brimming with integrity, optimism and drive. That's the team that will help you win Olympic Gold.

FROM THE LAUNCH PAD TO THE STARS

I was part of a Beach Volleyball team with Natalie, and together we were part of a much bigger team (See Chapter 4, The Secret to Our Success.). In addition, there were also those close to us and those within our environment - some we paid and some who were on board with us just for the anticipation of an amazing journey.

Natalie and I had a brief split in our Beach Volleyball partnership in 1997/98, so when we came back together, we sat down with Kurek, our Success Coach, and he had us draw a model of the team we now wanted to rebuild. He wanted to point out to us that we relied on many of these people who were holding us up and pushing us to the top.

With this in mind, we drew what started out as a pyramid, but quickly turned into a rocket ship as we loved what it represented – communication, observation, navigation, exploration, power and speed whilst propelling you towards the stars, higher and higher than you've ever been before!

We also liked the fact that we could see ourselves in front, steering the ship, with our support crew, the engine, pushing us toward the top.

On a team building weekend with our new team – From left; Steve Anderson (our Beach Volleyball coach), me, Kurek Ashley (our Success Coach), Natalie and Phil Moreland (our Fitness and Conditioning coach).

Have a look at the best athletes in your sport – who do they have on board their rocket ships?

Who do they associate with and who mentors them? If you're not able to see it immediately, ask them! Top level athletes and successful people love to talk about how they reached the top.

You may even find that by asking, they then come on board as one of your mentors. You'll never know unless you ask. Or, they may recommend someone who can help.

If my Beach Volleyball partner Natalie hadn't had the courage to approach Kurek Ashley at a Success Seminar back in 1997, who knows if our rocket would have reached the heights it did.

Is there a missing link on your team, someone you need to join you on your journey, right now?

> *I have always had a coach and mentor and I try to find the right person for me in each of the areas I need support at the time. It changes all the time but I always feel that I couldn't have achieved nearly as much without the great team around me.*
>
> **Shelley Oates-Wilding,** World Champion in Surf Ski and Outrigger Canoeing, dual Olympian in Kayaking.

Who Do You Need On Your Dreamachine?

This will vary depending on your sport and whether you compete in a team or as an individual. Your age, sporting status and financial circumstances may also affect who you can enrol to join your team.

> *It's a big step in your development when you come to realise that other people can help you do a better job than you can do alone.*
>
> **Andrew Carnegie,** Entrepreneur and Philanthropist

I believe:

- If you have a dream, but no team – then your dream is unachievable.
- If you have a dream, but a bad team – then your dream is a major challenge.
- If you have a dream and you're currently putting your team together – then your dream has potential.
- If you have a dream and an awesome team behind you – then your dream will become reality.

Food for thought: the bigger your dream, the more attractive it will be for people to join your team.

The process of determining who is on your team will be a never-ending one. Why? Because as you work towards your Ultimate Big Picture, things will change. You will change. Your needs and their needs will change.

Take a look at the list below. Multiple roles may be taken by the same person or some may not be required at all. What is most important though, whether your team is large or small, is that they all work together as a coherent group, focused on the same goals.

Title	Role
Manager	Guides and mentors you throughout your career. Negotiates your playing contract. Often looks after all off-field issues such as flights, accommodation and travel, allowing you to focus on training and competition. Liaises with media to set up opportunities and interviews for you. Liaises with sponsors after a deal has been procured by an Agent or can sometimes secure sponsorship and endorsement contracts themselves.
Agent	Procures and negotiates endorsement deals and sponsorships to get the best deal for you including salary and contract terms. Markets you as a brand. Earns a % of the athlete's salary and of all endorsement deals.
Coach	Provides technical coaching and direction.
Strength/ Conditioning Trainer	Works with you on improving your physical conditioning through gym sessions, weights, cross training, sprints, jump work/plyometrics and any other physical aspects relating to your specific sport.
Training Partner(s)	Depending on your sport, a regular reliable training partner allows you to practice your skills at an appropriate level outside of competition.
Dietician/ Nutritionist	Determines the best nutritional program to keep your body in peak physical condition, based on your age, level of competition and circumstances specific to your sport.

Sports Psychologist	Focuses on the mental side of your game to help achieve peak performance. They specialise in psychology and/or kinesiology, which can affect your performance in sport.
Success Coach	Not an 'official' title, but for us our Success Coach helped us with our belief system. They teach you the relationship between successful patterns of behaviour and the patterns of thought, and can help overcome any limiting beliefs.
Mentor	Guides you, shares their skills and their own experience with you. This is typically a person who has already done what you want to do.
Doctors, Physiotherapists, Therapists, Chiropractors, Osteopaths and any other medical experts	These specialists understand your body and your sport, and ensure that you are fit, healthy, recovered and ready for competition. They can also help you prevent injuries. Note – Make sure they are familiar with drug laws relating to your sport so that they are aware of the medications you are and are not allowed to take.
Masseur	Aids recovery and can help prevent further injury. It's best to employ a trained masseur, familiar with your sport and your personal circumstances, such as previous injuries.
Accountant	Gets your finances in order for your annual tax return, and provides guidance in sound money management and ways of minimising tax. Note – Earning money overseas is different from earning money in your own country. Make sure your Accountant is aware of the implications.
Web Designer	Creates and builds your website. Every athlete needs a website to communicate – with fans, sponsors, potential clients. Ask around - you may find that you can negotiate a website as a sponsorship.
Financial Planner	Helps you manage your money and achieve your financial goals, which may include various forms of investment and tax planning. Only use a trained professional, and check their credentials beforehand.
Lawyer	Checks all contracts before you sign. Choose an independent lawyer who is employed by you (not by your Club) so that you can be sure they are looking after your best interests.

Ask yourself – Who is on my team right now and have I included all of the people I need to help me realise my goals?

Teaming Up

This next exercise will help you build your very own A-Team, unique to your circumstances.

Sit down with your current team, teammates or family and make a list of the support you need in order to achieve your sporting goals.

Then, make a list of the people who might fill these roles or who could suggest others to fill these roles.

Speak to athletes who have worked with these people and ask them for feedback.

If you're going to have a meeting with them, write a list of questions before you go, such as:

- ✓ How long have you been in this role?
- ✓ Who else do you look after?
- ✓ How often will we meet/speak and how do you manage if more than one of your athletes needs your urgent attention at the same time?
- ✓ What are your fees/how are you paid?
- ✓ How flexible are you with your time?
- ✓ How many of our practises and competitions can you attend?
- ✓ What is the length of the contract and under what circumstances can I break the contract?
- ✓ How would our relationship be affected if I have to move interstate or overseas?
- ✓ Are you prepared to travel with me internationally?

Build your DREAMACHINE – no one succeeds alone.

BUILDING AN A-TEAM 71

Just after the Olympic final, our team was allowed on the sand and we embraced as one

Fans cheering for the "Dreamachine"

Tip: Trust your instinct

This is your team, and there should be a great spirit within the group. Make sure everyone you hire is dedicated, committed, fun to be around and always has your best interests at heart.

Trust your inner voice. Even if many athletes are using a particular person on their team, if that person doesn't feel right for you, they have no place on your team.

Managers/Agents Versus Doing It Yourself

Hiring a Manager or Agent is a big decision. Don't rush into it, especially if you've just won a big event and your name has been splashed across the media.

Seek advice from coaches, other players, even family. Above all, make sure you feel that the potential Manager or Agent is someone you could trust. Be wary of those who promise all sorts of deals and opportunities.

Know the fees and commissions they will be charging. Ask them how much time they will commit to you and your business dealings. Ask how often you will meet or talk on the phone and what will happen while you're overseas or if you need to move interstate. Finally, have a lawyer advise you on the contract before you sign.

BANKING ON SUCCESS

Over the years, before and after my Gold Medal win, I tried working with a handful of Agents and Sports Management companies. Initially I thought that they would be very useful in helping me find sponsorship and then managing that sponsorship.

When I signed up with one of these companies prior to the Sydney 2000 Olympics, I was quite excited that they actually took me on board. They had much higher profile athletes on their books, so I felt quite proud. I felt like I'd made it!

I quickly realised, after time passed and nothing much happened, that it was just as hard for them to find deals as it was for me.

> I also realised that they were spending 99% of their time with the high profile athletes and the remaining time on me. It made sense, as their big athletes were bringing in the big dollars.
>
> Eventually I went back to looking after and managing myself and found that I was successful in arranging a few deals leading up to the Sydney Olympics.
>
> In fact, Natalie and I signed our biggest ever sponsorship deal with the Brisbane based bank, Suncorp Metway, a year out from the Olympics. They seemed to believe in us as much as we believed in them and wanted to be on board when we won.
>
> I don't think that an Agent would have been as successful in signing that deal as we were because it was 'us' that Suncorp believed in. Perhaps they wouldn't have felt that as keenly if they were dealing only with the Agent.
>
> However, in saying that, I've also got to mention that as 'amateur' Agents we made a mistake in determining the final amount as we'd left out the soon-to-be-introduced Goods and Services Tax. This meant that we duped our bottom line by 10%. An Agent wouldn't have done that.

There are positives and negatives to managing yourself. Try it and then try working with a Manager or Agent. Contracts have end dates, so just make sure that you can get out of it easily if you need to.

In his book Jonah – My Story, Rugby great Jonah Lomu talks about how his Manager, Phil Kingsley Jones, sometimes got a hard time for being over-protective of him. Certain sections of the media felt that Phil was only looking for ways to line his own pockets. But Jonah had total confidence in him and knew that he was only ever looking after his interests – especially once his career took off, and he became a highly marketable athlete.

You have to trust your Manager 100%, and believe that they have your best interests at heart.

Natalie displaying our biggest sponsor to date, Suncorp Metway, just before the 2000 Olympic Games.

All In The Family

When you first start out on your chosen sporting path, it's usually your parents who sacrifice many hours of their time and often large amounts of money to enable you to follow your dream.

They may initially take on multiple roles – from Manager and Agent, through to Coach, Nutritionist and even Training Partner. For many families this works well and helps keep costs down. For some athletes, this arrangement (or parts of it) continues through into adulthood and there are many instances of elite athletes competing on the world stage whose parents still take a very active role in their careers.

However, for some families, it can also lead to conflict and stress. There may also come a time when you simply outgrow your parent's ability to coach or manage you. It's time to look at engaging a professional who can take you to the next level. If you feel this decision could cause tension within your family, then discuss it with a trusted friend or someone within your sport first, who understands your circumstances and has your best interests at heart.

But be honest with your family. Having the support and love of your family is so important while you pursue your dream, no matter what their role.

My biggest fans, Mum and Dad.

Keep The Dream-Killers At Arm's Length

Finally, but most importantly, think about who else are you are associating with that might have a powerful influence on you.

If you're surrounded by turkeys and ducks, go swim in another pond!

Anonymous

Dr. David McClelland of Harvard University concluded after 25 years of research that the choice of a negative 'reference group' was in itself enough to condemn a person to failure and underachievement in life. Stay away from selfish, negative, egotistical people.

The people that you interact with day in and day out are the most powerful influences on your life and will determine whether you stick to your goals or whether you simply give up.

They don't push you hard in any specific direction, they just 'nudge' you bit by bit, over time, until eventually you realise the impact they've had.

Jim Rohn, famous Entrepreneur, Author and Motivational Speaker says: "You will become the combined average of the five people you hang around the most."

It pays to stop and ask yourself, every so often, whether the company that you're keeping is helping you move towards your goals or pulling you away from your goals.

Keep away from people who try to belittle your ambitions. Small people always do that, but the really great ones make you feel that you, too, can become great.

Mark Twain, Author

KEY POINTS

Build your own quality A-Team.

Surround yourself with a circle of successful, positive, encouraging people.

CHAPTER 7
DETERMINING THE COST OF YOUR DREAMS

Your goals are clear, and you've worked out who you want on your A-Team. So how much money do you need to make it happen?

Budgeting can seem tedious, even a little daunting, especially if you've never created a budget before. Here's my little tip – don't think of it as a torturous chore, instead, focus on the outcome. You'll know exactly what you'll need to generate in sponsorship and other income, to get you closer to that Ultimate Big Picture. Budgeting is not rocket science and you'll feel great once you've done it.

Presenting a budget to a sponsor also shows your commitment and planning skills and gives them a very clear idea as to where their money will be going. Sometimes just the very fact that you have prepared one will give you a professional edge over your competitors.

In The Money

This next exercise will help you gain a clearer picture of all the incoming and outgoing cash, so that you know where you're falling short.

Start by listing your annual income. Go to our website, www.thebusinessofbeinganathlete.com and download the Income and Expenses template. Write down all your current income sources and how often each is paid (weekly, monthly or annually). Only include money that is guaranteed to come in such as wages, funding, approved grants, study allowance and so on. Don't include income such as overtime, unless it is regular and reliable.

This is a very simple example. Yours may be more complex.

Income	Amount $	How often	Convert to Annual	Amount $ per year
Wages	$250	Weekly	x 52	$13,000
Study allowance	$200	Fortnight	x 26	$5,200
Training grant	$3,000	Year		$3,000
Sponsorship	$500	Monthly	x 12	$6,000
Total annual income				$27,200

Now, in a separate table, write down all the costs you incur every month. Be as accurate as you can with your estimates. You'll probably include things like:

- ✓ Training
- ✓ Equipment
- ✓ Coaches
- ✓ Medical appointments
- ✓ Massage
- ✓ Supplements, protein powders, energy drinks, recovery drinks

DETERMINING THE COST OF YOUR DREAM

- ✓ Travel (air, train, bus, car rental, taxi, fuel, parking)
- ✓ Accommodation
- ✓ General living expenses (rent, food, entertainment, clothing, bills, etc)
- ✓ PR
- ✓ Management
- ✓ Tax
- ✓ Accountant
- ✓ Other advisors
- ✓ Office equipment
- ✓ Stationery
- ✓ Phone
- ✓ Internet
- ✓ Computer
- ✓ Printing
- ✓ Postage
- ✓ Sponsor expenses
- ✓ Promotional expenses
- ✓ Any other related expenses

Tip: Minimise the guesstimates

If you don't know how much you spend each week or month on certain items, then keep track for a couple of weeks in a notepad or on your phone every time you spend something. It's surprising how quickly small items add up.

Tip: Include the 'freebies'

If you currently receive any of these items or services for free through a sponsorship deal, don't forget to include them in your expenses as they are still real costs. Estimate their value. If that sponsorship was to end, you'd still have to have enough money to pay for those items or services later.

Tip: Be optimistic, but realistic with travel costs

Travel costs can add up, especially if your sport involves interstate or international competition. List every event you would like to compete in this year. It's better to include every potential event cost even if you're not sure yet if you'll qualify for them all. This could be your best year ever! If some events run together in close geographical proximity, think about how you will travel between them. Consider how many nights you might be in each place. Many people find it easier to consider an 'average spend per day' when on the road to cover general expenses, for example $65 per day (but decide what is appropriate for you).

So for an example 'Event A' costs might be:

Event A

Accommodation	5 nights @ $100 =	$500
Food, general expenses	$65/day x 5 days =	$325
Travel (return airfare)		$1,200
Total Event A		**$2,025**

Now total up the costs from all your events to form the potential travel costs for the entire year.

Remember, your budget is not set in stone, it is just your best estimate at the time you put it together. It will change and evolve as your season progresses. If you aren't sure of some costs, use your best estimate to work it out and add 10%. It's better to over-estimate slightly than underestimate.

This is a very simple example. Again, yours may be much more detailed.

Regular costs	Amount $	How often	Convert to Annual	Amount $ per month
Training venue	$50	Weekly	x 52	$2,600
All travel	$16,700	Year		$16,700
Accommodation on tour	$12,500	Year		$12,500
PR, Promotion	$1,200	Year		$1,200

DETERMINING THE COST OF YOUR DREAM

Phone/Internet	$150	Month	x 12	$1,800
General living	$200	Weekly	x 52	$10,400
Total expenses				$45,200

Now you'll have a picture of the real income you'll need to cover all your expenses.

Total income	$27,200
Total expenses	$45,200
Net profit/loss	= Income minus expense
	= $27,200 - $45,200
	= *(-$18,000)*

In this example there is a shortfall of $18,000. This means that you will need to find $18,000 additional income in order to break even at the end of the year. This figure can be given to your Manager/Agent, sporting body and even directly to your sponsor to help substantiate your request for funding.

> *Tip: Track it now*
>
> It's a good idea to keep track of your actual costs on a weekly basis ongoing – partly for tax purposes as we discuss in the chapter: Keeping Records, but also so you can see where your money is really being spent. It will help you create a much more accurate budget next year.

KEY POINTS

It's not rocket science. Create a budget.

Overestimate on expenses, rather than underestimate.

BORAL OLYMPIC TIMES

ISSUE 3   JULY 1996

BEACH VOLLEYBALL'S DYNAMIC DUO SMELL GOLD AT THE END OF THE OLYMPIC RAINBOW

When the 26th Olympiad kicks off in Atlanta in July, there'll be a few extra athletes joining the Australian quest for sporting supremacy. Beach volleyball will make its debut as an Olympic sport for the first time in history, and right up there in medal contention will be two young women determined to be the first to bring home gold.

Dynamic duo Kerri Pottharst and Natalie Cook teamed up only twelve months ago but in that time have become major players on the international circuit, currently ranked third place in women's beach volleyball. They come second only to the USA and Brazil, countries where this sport has been a huge part of their lifestyle for many years.

South Australian Pottharst, 30, and her Queensland partner Natalie Cook, 21, have had a sensational year that culminated in a silver medal at the world titles in Rio in February.

Pottharst and Cook fulfilled two big ambitions in Rio – to finish in the top three and to beat one of only two world-series teams they had not overcome; the number one US and Brazilian teams. They achieved both, beating the Americans in the semi-finals and finishing runner-up to the Brazilians.

Beach volleyball is a relatively young sport in Australia, as the national beach volleyball competition, the Pro Tour, was established in 1988, but the general public has taken to it in droves

Natalie Cook (left) and Kerri Pottharst (right), have enjoyed sponsorship support from Boral at a number of beach volleyball tournaments around Australia.

and tournaments are now played every weekend in all states throughout the summer months.

"In the States they've been playing beach volleyball for 15-20 years. They started playing for T-shirts and records, now they're playing in million dollar tournaments," says Kerri. In California, beach volleyball draws such enormous crowds that huge grandstands have been erected and 137 permanent courts are marked with the two kilometre stretch from Manhattan Beach to Hermosa Beach, where the game originated.

Kerri and Natalie realise that while they have already proved they have what it takes to be champions, they still need to continue their learning curve if they want to make it to the top.

"Brazil and the US have the tactics, the strategies and an instinct for the game that we are now trying to develop and perfect. We have to cram all those years of experience into a much shorter period but we know that we have the skills to match them and there's every chance we will be in medal contention at Atlanta," adds Natalie.

Standing at 185cm and 181cm respectively, Kerri and Natalie are effectively the tallest women's team on the world circuit and their height superiority means that both can play the dual role of attack and defence. Until recently, the prevailing wisdom meant these roles were split between a tall (attacker) and a short (defender) player. By teaming up, these ladies have taken Australian women's beach volleyball to a new level.

Australia will also field two other beach volleyball teams in Atlanta. The second women's team of Anita Palm and Liane Fenwick is ranked ninth while Julien Prosser and Lee Zahner will be 15th seed in the men's competition.

The Australian Olympic Beach Volleyball Team will compete on Atlanta Beach from July 23 through to July 28.

Boral were one of our first big sponsors that helped us manage the costs of training and travelling in the lead up to the 1996 Olympic Games.

CHAPTER 8
GENERATING INCOME

> *The secret to getting rich is to find out what you absolutely love doing and then to work out how to make money out of it.*
>
> **Richard Branson,** Entrepreneur

Before we get onto the holy grail of Sponsorship, it's worth taking a moment to consider other ways that you can be proactive about bringing in additional income.

While it's great to land a big Sponsorship deal, it is a hugely competitive field and you need to really excel in many unique ways to achieve it. I really hope that you will, but in the meantime you can be doing lots of other things to generate cash.

Bring Your Employer On Board

Many athletes will need to work full or part-time in the early stages of their sporting career, in order to fund their training and attend events.

Try to get the support of your employer. This could take on a variety of forms such as:

- Allowing you more flexible working hours around training
- Allowing you additional time off for competition
- Supporting you financially
- Purchasing equipment or sportswear that may carry their logo
- Becoming your sponsor

You never know until you ask!

However, just be cautious about how you present this plan. It may shock them to hear that you eventually want to quit your day job and become a full-time professional athlete, especially if you've never discussed your sport before. Don't go in cold. Try pinning some photos of your sport around your desk, and casually mention an event or a competition in conversation every so often.

Many employers admire the qualities of drive and motivation needed to realise the goals you have set yourself, but treat this just as you would any other business negotiation.

Plan your strategy and determine exactly what you want to ask them. Be ready to describe your short and long term goals for your sporting career and prepare a budget to present to them (like the example in the last chapter).

If your boss turned to you and said "Sure, we'd love to support you, what do you need?" you must be ready to give a clear answer.

Be specific. If you want more flexible working hours, what exactly does that mean? Are you asking to come in at 10am every day, or just two days a week? If you know specific competition dates, tell them the exact dates you need, allowing for travel and recovery/acclimatisation if necessary. This will allow your employer to look at their plans for the year and see if it's possible to accommodate you.

It's also a good idea to prepare a proposal. This document could contain a brief history of your sporting career to date, some photos of you winning, and the detail of what you would like from them for the next year – for example, specific dates to attend events, flexible work hours on certain days, financial support, and so on. Also include a description of what you would hope to achieve in your sport, for that year.

This gives the decision makers something professional and tangible to take away and discuss. It also shows you have thought it through, and shows you are a committed professional, at work and on the field.

Whether or not you are successful, always try to stay on positive terms, even if they are not willing or able to support you now. They may become a supporter (even a sponsor) at a later stage.

Hold A Corporate Event

Another way to earn some extra money is by running a corporate event. The beauty of these events is that you can make them fit around your training and competition schedule, and they are also another way to make valuable contacts.

They could take the form of:

- A tennis tournament
- A beach volleyball corporate day
- A rugby games day (skills, drills and mini comps)
- A soccer skills day or 5-a-side tournament
- An Olympic 'themed' day with lots of different fun events

Brainstorm an event that you could run. You might run it with a couple of teammates or include athletes from another sport.

Once you have an idea for an event, work out the costs and what you can charge. Of course, your sport and your profile will also play a part. You want to get something for your time and you want people to use you again, but don't want to price yourself out of the market.

Make a plan of how many hours it will take you to complete the event to help you work out what to charge. Include:

- Hours in preparation (be realistic, things often take longer than you think. Allow time for getting extra equipment together if you need to source some and pick it up).

- Hours on the day itself, including set up and pack up. Usually you would allow more hours for more participants as you may need to set up more fields/courts and source more equipment.

- Hours for any staff or assistants you need on the day or before/after.

- Hours after the event – to assess how it went, speak to the client and send a thank you note, perhaps with some photos.

Then total up your hours and see how many hours the event will take overall. Multiply this by the rate you'd like to charge per hour and see if this gives a realistic overall fee to charge. That gives you a good basic starting point.

Don't forget the extras. You may need to include equipment hire costs. Check whether you'll need Council approval or any other type of license to run your event if you plan to use a public space.

You may decide to charge more or less, depending on the circumstances, your profile, experience and anything else you may also be doing in conjunction with this particular client.

Another option is to charge a set amount per person participating. Check out what other people or companies are charging for running similar days (if such an event exists) so you know how you fit into the market place.

Now you're ready to promote your special event, and I suggest you follow a few simple steps.

Think about why a potential client would want to hire you, and how the event could benefit their organisation. The 'reasons' for hiring you might be to:

- Build strong relationships
- Build moral
- Improve communication
- Create team power
- Encourage creativity
- Develop new skills
- Harness positive attitudes
- Share leadership
- Create lasting memories
- Return to office more motivated, as a stronger team!

You can include these 'reasons' in your promotional material.

Next, add an 'Events' page to your website, and blog that you offer corporate events. Let your friends and colleagues know and get them to spread the word. Think about which companies could benefit from your event and approach them. Personal contacts through friends are a great way to get started, as word of mouth is very powerful.

Have an e-brochure ready to email to anyone interested with some great photos. If it's your first event, include photos of yourself (and any other athletes involved). If you've run events before, include photos taken at those events as well as some testimonials. Make sure that the e-brochure is professionally produced.

Follow up emails with a phone call, and try to find out more about your potential client's needs.

Some may have team building goals, or are trying to boost morale after a merger. Some may have no specific objectives and just want to have a great time after a particularly stressful or busy period at work.

Listen carefully, and try to express how your event would satisfy these needs. Once you are booked, make sure your event delivers. You are more likely to be hired again or for your name to be referred to another company if you tailor your day to meet their needs or requirements.

I have run many corporate Beach Volleyball days with a range of clients from small companies through to big name corporates, for 10 people through to 200 people. Let me share some gems that will help yours run a little smoother:

- It's preferable to have one point of contact at the client's company – it's more efficient to have one clear line of communication. Ask them to pass on any relevant information to the participants, such as when to arrive and what to wear.

- (Warning: Don't overlook this point about what to wear, include footwear. It sounds obvious, but some companies don't pass on this information as they like these activities to be a surprise. If you're not careful, you could have people turning up in suits or high heels to play your sport!)

- You will often get a wide variety of abilities and ages at a corporate day. Ensure there are activities suitable for all. Be sure to ask your client what the male/female and age demographic of the participants are. This just allows you to plan more effectively if you know your group will be mainly active males aged 20-something, or mostly a mixed group of office-based staff aged 45+.

- Have a plan in place for warm up, icebreakers, fun drills, an opportunity to play with (or against) you, and perhaps a small competition at the end. Keep it focussed on their desired outcomes.

- Be well prepared and ensure everything runs on time. Often corporates have a very limited amount of time for an event – perhaps it is part of a conference or they are taking time out of the office to be with you. Work out how long you will need to set up so you are completely ready before they arrive on site. Get friends or maybe some of the juniors from your club or sport to assist – it's great experience for them. Keep to your schedule and make sure you finish on time. They have come to learn but also to have fun.

- Wear your competition gear, if possible. It's exciting for others to feel like they're playing with professionals!

- Have a basic medical kit on site including some ice packs or ice. You must have your basic First Aid certificate or ensure that one of your staff or someone on site has one and knows what to do if there is an injury.

- Get insurance. Depending on the rules within your country, make sure that you have the required insurance that will cover you fully if someone is injured. You may also get participants to sign a waiver, which releases you of all liability in case of injury.

Finally, a day or so after the event, call your client. Try to get constructive feedback so you can improve for the next event. Was the event what they expected? Did they feel it helped in building morale/team bonding etc? What did they like most about the day? What could have been done better? Would they use you again? If yes – ask straight away – do you have a date in mind?

If their experience was positive, ask if they'd be willing to give you a testimonial for your website.

More Sources Of Financial Support

Once you start looking, you might be surprised to find a number of Government grants or scholarships that fit your situation. Consider:

Federal Government or State grants

- Search online to find out what is available at the State and National level.

- Keep an open mind and consider all possible options for funding that might be applicable to you. Grants come under many different headings. This could be male/female, elite/international level competition, indigenous, country/city, by age group, regional etc. There will usually be an application process where you need to meet certain criteria, and submit by a particular date.

- Before spending time on the application, find out as much as you can about what they are looking for, and whether you are eligible to apply.

- Speak to the staff in charge and tailor your application to meet their needs – just as you would for a job interview.

Training grants through your sport's governing body.
- Similar to the Government or State grants above. Do your research both online and by speaking in person to your sport's governing body. You never know what's out there until you ask.

Scholarships
- Look for elite level scholarships to schools or universities both in your own country and overseas.

- Investigate which colleges specialise in your particular sport and what they can offer in terms of facilities and elite level coaches.

Other sources of funding
- Philanthropic organisations seek to do good by helping others in the community. There are philanthropic organisations in every country so search online to see what is local to you and whether any of their grants or assistance could be relevant to your own situation. For more information go to www.philanthropy.org.au.

- Search the internet for Foundations and Trusts that seek to help inspire young people achieve their dreams. A great one for women in Australia is World Surfing Champion, Layne Beachley's 'Aim For The Stars Foundation' – www.aimforthestars.com.au. Perhaps your country has a National Sports Commission or National Sports Foundation you could apply to?

- Find out if there is one government department that coordinates grant opportunities nationally. In Australia, visit www.grantslink.gov.au for more information. Search under sport to see if any of the options are applicable to you. Don't be afraid to think outside the square to see if any of the grants are relevant to your situation but always phone them to clarify the opportunity before you spend time on the application.

Organise your own fundraiser

- Be open and upfront about your need to raise money and where the money is going. You could organise anything from a movie fundraiser at the local cinema through to a dinner or a major function where you and several other athletes feature as guest speakers. Include a raffle or silent auctions and ask local businesses or other elite athletes and local celebrities to offer prizes.

  (Warning: Be careful to check all your potential expenses versus the potential income to determine if you are really going to make enough money from the event to make it worth the hours and effort. It will take more time than you anticipate and costs can quickly escalate without very careful planning.)

Our Athen's fundraising dinner MC'd by Larry Emdur. I'm sitting on the couch with Summer Lochowicz, Mark Williams and Julien Prosser (Australian Men's team.)

Finally...Thank You!

Thank everyone who helps you along your journey – large and small!!

Depending on what you are thanking them for, you might send

- An email (at the absolute very least)
- A thank you card in the post
- A photo of you competing, preferably featuring their equipment or their logo
- A report of the event, or your progress to date
- A special delivery of flowers, chocolates or wine

You never know when you may need assistance again in the future and a small thank you gesture can go a long way.

KEY POINTS

Think outside the square, how you can generate extra cash.
Remember to say 'thank you'.

CHAPTER 9
THE 'S' WORD - SPONSORSHIP

In the early days I tried to wear as many of my sponsor's logos as I could. This is an extreme example, but it worked! Later I learned that it was more about relationships than just logo branding.

Sponsorship is a two-way street. Like most relationships, there needs to be effort on both sides to make it work. I've met some athletes who regard sponsorship as a golden egg, a gift almost. But I find those sponsorships simply don't last – there's too much taking, and not enough giving back, and the sponsor moves on to the next relationship.

In the early days of our Beach Volleyball career, Natalie and I would send out proposals cold. Our target sponsors had probably never heard of us, let alone met us, and the end result would inevitably be a resounding silence – no response whatsoever.

We soon realised that we needed to get out there and meet potential sponsors, and network. Our early sponsorships were obtained through people we knew. We attended all sorts of functions, and were always on 'sponsor alert', ready with a verbal proposal, just in case the person standing next to us represented a company that we could team up with.

Once they were on board as a sponsor, we treated them as if they were part of our team. We communicated with them often. In the early days we mostly used mail. I'd put together a monthly newsletter with copies of all the media coverage we'd received, and post it to them. Nowadays it's all about using Facebook and other social media.

We also visited the sponsor, and talked to their staff about our journey. We tried to think up different ways to help them. We held team-building events on the beach, and spoke at their functions. In return, our sponsors were very loyal and supportive.

Always remember that there might be someone watching that wants to sign you up or sponsor you. It might be only at a local competition but you never know when the next door will open for you.

Shannon Eckstein, World Ironman Champion

In my opinion, there are few athletes better at securing sponsorships than my Olympic Beach Volleyball partner, Natalie Cook. When we started out, few athletes in Beach Volleyball were sponsored, particularly in Australia. Our sport simply didn't have a high enough profile. Not to be deterred, we knew it had the potential to attract sponsors, so we started from scratch and learnt along the way.

I've asked Nat to write this chapter, as not only did she play a key role in acquiring sponsors when we played together, but she has been able to secure significant support to continue her Olympic career and also support her business goals.

Enjoy her unique take on sponsorship.

I was never afraid of trying something new. Bolle suggested branding on my body, so I tried it. It looked great at first, but add sand and sweat to the equation and it made for a bit of a mess at the end of the day!

The Sponsorship Game

Sport is a game, and because I have played sport for so long, I now consider my life to be one big game. Games are supposed to be fun. Your objective is to find a way to win the game.

Speaking from experience, it doesn't always go to plan. Sometimes you win, sometimes you lose. The next time you play the game you have a better idea of what to do or not to do. The Sponsorship Game is the same. To play the game you need to know the rules; to win the game you need to understand how to use the rules to your advantage.

Let's roll the dice, and I'll show you how to play.

Be Clear On Your Objective

Your sponsorship objective: To gather as much money/products/services as you can to cover your expenses so that you can participate fully (or at your best) in your sport and subsequently all the other games in your life.

Learn The Rules

These are set by all parties involved and sometimes not divulged in time frames that suit you. You have to find out whilst you are in the game.

For example when you play Monopoly for the first time, there are so many rules to learn. So instead of reading the manual cover to cover, most people jump in with the attitude: "I'll learn as I go". The first time you land on a square and someone says, "no you can't do that… you have to do this", you don't give up. You learn the rule, and you know next time. That is how you learn in the Sponsorship Game too.

Some rules seem to be enforced more than others. Sometimes the referee doesn't notice something and you can get away with it, sometimes they make a wrong call and you have to deal with that. It's just the same in the Sponsorship Game.

Ok so it's now GAME ON. You can't score points from the sideline; you need to be on the court.

What Do You Need To Get Started?

Begin by filling your sponsorship toolkit. You need to gather items or produce items that will ensure you are prepared for all situations, ready for when you meet a potential sponsor. It should include the following (note – Kerri describes how to create them all in Chapter 12, Developing Your Marketing Tools):

- **Business Cards** – you need to leave your mark wherever you go. Find a creative designer to produce one for you, so that when the potential sponsor reads your card, it leaves an impression.

- **Biography** (Bio) – a colourful, one-page account of yourself. This should include your history, results to date and your future aspirations.

- **Pictures** of yourself – both portrait style, and of you in action.

- **Facebook Page** – keep it professional and clean, fun and engaging. Register your full name (the name fans and sponsors know), not a nickname.

- **Twitter** – same as Facebook

- **Website** – These days, having your own website is crucial! It serves as an initial contact point and it displays all your information and achievements. Try to register a URL in your full name (the name fans and sponsors know), for example, www.fredsmith.com.

- **Email** – once you have a website address, you can create a more a professional email address like fred@fredsmith.com rather than fredsmith@hotmail.com

- **A creative sponsorship offer** – more on this later.

Some of these items will cost you money. Some you may be able to put together yourself, but it's very hard to do everything alone. Try to get support in some of the areas where you are weaker such as preparing your offer using Word or PowerPoint. Ask friends and family to help you. Do you know someone who might open some doors for you or get on the telephone to find out the right person to speak to? This is another time where it's often not *what* you know but *who* you know and having family and friends supporting you can be really beneficial.

Now you have your toolkit, where do you go from here?

Sponsors considering supporting an athlete will see them fitting into one of four main tiers. Here's where you need to be honest. For years I wanted to be in Tier 1, but it was clear to others around me, and the sponsors, that my sport simply wasn't - regardless of how much I talked it up.

Tier 1 – Professional, High Profile Sport

Global sports such as football, rugby, tennis, golf.

Tier 2 – Professional, Lower Profile Sport

Less visible sports, such as Beach Volleyball. Once every four years it is the greatest event to watch but otherwise it gets little media attention.

Tier 3 – Semi Professional/Amateur

Yours may or may not be a visible sport, but your commitment or achievements to date could see you falling into this tier.

Tier 4 – Playing for the love of the game

Community sports – any kind, at any level.

Once you know where you fit in the picture, you can better prepare yourself to play the Sponsorship game.

Tier 1 athletes often have Managers who can attract highly recognisable brands for sponsorship (for example, Toyota, Coca-Cola, American Express).

Tier 2 athletes need to work hard to sell themselves. You will be successful if you attend lots of functions and learn to network. Often a sponsor is drawn to you because of your energy and the way you engage them and others. Consider local or national brands with which you have a good fit. Consider those that have a strong local presence and may be interested in you and your passion, dreams and commitment.

Tier 3 athletes need to take the same approach as Tier 2 athletes, however personal relationships are even more important in this category. Success may be more at a local community level, for example, local businesses that are interested in supporting a local athlete.

Tier 4 athletes will also need to network, but will usually have greater success in attracting those businesses who are interested in grass roots level community development, particularly junior teams.

There are obviously exceptions to the rule, so even if you fall into the Tier 2 category, you can try and play in the Tier 1 market. Just be realistic about what you are up against. It depends on who you know and being in the right place at the right time. So keep an eye out, but my advice is not to spend much time in the tier above yours, as you may get disheartened.

Cash Vs. Contra

You might be surprised to know that contra (receiving donated products or services from sponsors) is as good as cash. Many items that you need in order to compete can be covered by contra sponsorship. That means companies sponsor you by donating 'items' as opposed to cash. It can still save you considerable amounts of money, as you no longer have to buy these items. The benefit to the sponsor is that it is often much easier for them to organise. They are often much more likely to enter into this kind of arrangement especially when you are starting out, than one that involves them giving you money.

I've had many great contra deals over the years that have included swimwear, eyewear, sunscreens, supplements and nutritional products, electrical products and even a car. This all adds up and has saved me a lot of money.

I have been with Oakley Sunglasses since 1993. It has been a long lasting partnership that I have loved being a part of. Once you are in the Oakley team you are there for life. Loyalty is very important to most sponsors.

And, even though we were on the same team, Kerri was sponsored by Bolle sunglasses and her relationship with Bolle began in 1989. She wrote to them asking for a pair of sunglasses to use during her first ever tournament of Beach Volleyball. She has been sponsored by them ever since and still to this day receives eyewear and clothing, even though she retired 6 years ago! And, it's all due to the great relationship we've built with them over the years.

What Do You Need, and What Can You Offer?

In your Winner's Toolbox, make a list of everything you spend money on each year to train (you can copy these items from your budget). For example:

Protein powder	$500
Gym	$1000
Running shoes	$500
Clothes – training/competition	$1000

Now, your first challenge is to get the items on your list for free. If you're successful in getting all the above for free, you will have saved $3,000 cash! Remember though, in return for these products you have to be able to provide that value back to the company supplying the product.

So that you can be clear in exactly what you want (in terms of sponsorship), before you start preparing your sponsorship proposal consider the following:

- WHY do I want sponsors? ("To enable me to quit my job and train full time, to win a Gold Medal, to inspire others, etc.")
- WHAT do I want from and in a sponsor? ("Free flights to attend competitions")
- HOW do I get it? ("Try to meet potential sponsors at the next Travel Expo")
- WHO do I want as an ideal sponsor? ("GoFar Travel Agency, FlightsRUs Agency")
- WHO am I? What do I, as a person, bring to the table? ("Energy, speed, strength, commitment")
- WHO do I know that can help me? ("Cousin John, Neighbour Fred Jones")
- WHAT do I have to offer a sponsor? ("Competition clothing featuring their logo, their banner ad on my website")
- WHAT do I need (resources) to get what I want? ("Complete sponsorship toolkit, finished website")

Why Sponsor?

Put yourself in the Sponsor's shoes. Consider why they might want to take on a sponsorship in the first place, and in particular, what you (or your team) could bring to that partnership.

They could be looking to sponsor for any number of reasons, including:

1. Raising brand awareness – your profile gains their brand more exposure
2. Improving credibility of their brand – for example the Meat Corporation may want to promote the health benefits of beef, and featuring a healthy athlete in their campaign makes their claims more believable.
3. Generating positive PR by showing their support of a local athlete
4. Promoting a new consolidated brand after a merger
5. Motivating staff – the company may involve you in team-building exercises
6. Assisting or increasing sales – they may take you to meet key clients, to win sales
7. Opening up new markets, particularly if they are new in the community
8. Launching a new company – they may be looking to raise their profile
9. Countering negative publicity, by aligning themselves with the positive attributes of a successful athlete
10. Building a brand's personality, by using your face in their campaign. This could be particularly attractive to a commodity brand such as energy, water, washing powder, soap and so on.

Who Is Not Your Perfect Match?

In the early days, I used to think that any company that was willing to give us money was a great sponsorship match. We were ecstatic if anyone gave us anything! But I soon realised that not only is our image continually associated with their product, but they need to be a good fit for us too.

What would you personally feel comfortable endorsing? Try making up a list of products or activities that you would *not* feel comfortable endorsing, for example, cigarettes, alcohol, fast food, gambling and so on.

Be careful of any potential sponsorship conflict. If you compete in a State, National or International league or competition, be aware of the event's sponsors as you could create conflict if their sponsors and your sponsors are from the same industry. For example, when Kerri and I were competing on the National Beach Volleyball Tour in Australia in 2004, the major event sponsor was Vodafone, a mobile telecommunications company. When we signed on to play that season it was made clear that we could not seek sponsorship from any other telecommunications company, such as Telstra or Optus.

Kerri spiking on the Vodafone National Tour.

Check your player agreement documents or contracts with the league or competition as to which industries or companies you need to avoid.

If the sponsor is suggesting a level of commitment that you are not able to give, make it clear from the outset. You know how much time you need to train and compete, so consider how you would be able to fit sponsorship activities into your schedule.

Preparing Your Offer

Research the companies you are considering approaching for sponsorship, both online (their website, Facebook/Twitter pages, Google) and by looking at their current advertising campaigns. Understand who their target market is. Understand the key messages they are trying to communicate in their campaigns – Strength and Reliability? (a Bank); Power and Agility? (a Small Car); Attitude and Energy? (a Fashion Label).

Approaching a potential sponsor is exactly like preparing for a job interview. It will stand you in very good stead if you can show you have done your homework and that you know their company and their brand.

Remember I mentioned earlier that you should have a 'creative sponsorship offer' in your sponsorship toolkit? Well now it's time to create that offer. You need to sit down in a quiet place, think about the potential sponsor's needs, their brand values, how you would relate to their target market, and anything else you've learned about them. Your task is to come up with an offer that shows your UPOD – unique point of difference. Something that only you can bring to the table.

Imagine a desk with 1000 proposals on it. How will yours stand out?

Your 'offer' to the potential sponsor needs to paint a vivid picture, to entice them, and to help you get your foot in the door. Be clear on what you can do for the sponsor, what you are good at, what you like to do, and what you need. An offer idea could be along the lines of:

1. Win a beach volleyball party with Kerri Pottharst and Natalie Cook
2. Laps to London - Swim laps with an Olympic swimmer

3. $1 per Kilo – Weightlifter selling to the meat industry

4. SAIL on now! – sailing team with a twist on the word SALE

Your offer needs to be able to be presented in three ways:

- **Verbally** – This is the most powerful way, preferably in face-to-face meetings where you can articulate your story. If you aren't such a good talker or seller then take someone who is, or chose a different method. In the meantime, work on your 'elevator pitch'. This is the ten second pitch you have ready to fire off when the opportunity arises (why 'elevator'? Imagine you are in a lift, the door opens at the 10th floor and Richard Branson walks in... you have ten floors to pitch your offer, what would you say?). Practise pitching at events – if you found yourself at a table with business owners, or even the General Manager, could you talk your offer up? Be ready, because once you start playing the game these opportunities will come your way.

For example, a friend of mine had always dreamed of singing the National Anthem to open a big Football game. He didn't know how or when that could possibly happen. One day he walked past the coach of a team playing the game. He stopped immediately and told him of his dream and asked how to go about it. He took the opportunity and got to sing!

A variation on the 'elevator pitch' is the 'BBQ bite' – similar, but dropped a little more casually into conversation. Work on this too.

- **Electronically** – PowerPoint presentation, PDF, email or on a website.
- **In hard copy** – Brochures, flyers, postcards etc

Once you have a foot in the door, it's worth considering whether you could *present* your offer in a creative way; in a way that will really capture their attention.

Imagine a potential sponsor's reaction, if you:

- Sent a tray of sand to potential sponsors asking them to take off their shoes and socks, and wriggle their toes in the sand whilst reading your offer, which by the way, is written on a volleyball. (Beach Volleyball athlete)

- Hand-delivered bottles of water that feature a sticker on them outlining your dream. (Swimmer)
- Delivered model race cars with an invitation to do some hot laps with you. Better still take them out in the car for a spin at 200kms an hour, and then hit them up for a sponsorship deal! (Racing Car Driver)

However... A Word Of Caution

Just make sure your idea is going to engage them and not put them off. It usually works better if you already have a contact in a company and have perhaps previously discussed how you might work together.

Knowing them also gives you an insight into the personality type you are dealing with and the kinds of ideas that are more likely to work. If someone receives some bizarre delivery from a person they've never met – they might just think you are a little weird and throw it in the rubbish!

Now, Spread The Word

Next, go out and meet as many people you can and tell them about your dream, and your 'offer' (see Chapter 15, Networking, Meetings & Functions, for tips on doing this effectively).

Align with a community project or charity. This will allow you to meet lots of people. Major companies and their executives often attend charity events. It is a good place to meet them and help out a good cause too.

Introduce yourself, and tell them what you do. Find a common interest – sport, music, travel, and so on. Ask what they do and ask how you can help them (be ready with some suggestions here if they aren't so forthcoming, such as 'team-building', 'speaking', 'advertising').

Don't forget to ask for their card so you can send them your offer or even better drop it off in person. Give them your card as well. It is important to be clear and upfront with what you want and what you can offer, so you don't waste their time and they don't waste yours.

Sometimes you may also need to get on the telephone and cold call. Depending on the size of the company you will need to talk to the CEO, or the Marketing or Sponsorship Manager. Get the details from reception and then call back. Don't leave a message unless you have met them previously. They will probably not call back unless you are already well-known. You really need to talk to them in person, and once you leave a message you are reliant on them to respond.

Selling your offer can be the most difficult part, but it's like public speaking – you just need to have a go. Each time you do it you will get better and you can make minor adjustments after every pitch. It is OK to say the wrong thing; you just need to learn from it. Practise, practise and practise some more.

Take some professional courses in presentation skills and influencing people. It can also be a good idea to start at the bottom of your wish list of sponsors so that by the time you get to the one that you really want, you have perfected the pitch.

And, don't be discouraged by the "no's." There are many possible reasons why a sponsor will say no. In some cases they may genuinely like your team and your goals but may have just been told the week before that they are to cut back on all spending outside of television advertising and in-store sampling. The more "no's" you get the closer you often are to a "yes"!

There are also some companies that don't actually want to say no. They may be indecisive or they don't want to hurt your feelings. They have little intention of going through with the deal and it may seem to drag on and on. After a period of time if you get the feeling that discussions are not progressing, it's useful to ask the hard question straight out, in a nice way. Often by asking for them to make a decision either way, you may even get a "yes" or in the case of a "no", will save you time on an unlikely sponsorship.

In saying that, don't count the cash until you've got the contract and the ink is dry. It may still take time or circumstances may change, even after the verbal "yes" or a response via email.

Negotiations And Contracts

Once you have sold the offer, what follows next is a negotiation period. Sometimes it's easy and simple. Sometimes it's time consuming and complicated.

Suffice to say, if it is too hard for you to negotiate your own deal then I suggest you find someone to help at this stage – perhaps a family member, a Manager, or even a teammate.

After both parties agree upon the deal you should enter into a written contract. This can be as simple as a one page Memorandum of Understanding or as complex as a 50 page document, depending on the company and size and scope of the deal.

There are a few things you'll need to consider in a contract:

- Term – how long the contract runs, for example 12 months or 3-5 years. For Olympic sports 4 years is a good term. I would recommend at least 12 months with an option to renew. If you are happy with the deal, then the longer the better.

- Payment terms – amounts, method and frequency.

- Other areas where they might be able to help – in terms of provision of services such as travel expenses, food, clothing and kit, accommodation and so on.

- Obligations – to the sponsor and vice versa.

- Termination clause – if either party isn't happy, what can you do?

Go to www.thebusinessofbeinganathlete.com to view a contract example.

Once you have signed the deal, you can celebrate! Congratulations are needed here on a job well done. Enjoy the moment.

However don't rest on your laurels. You now have a sponsor that you need to take care of and manage. Servicing and delivering are important parts of this last phase.

Taking Care Of Your Sponsors

Once you've got them, *look after them*. It is much easier to keep them than get new ones.

- Be a great ambassador.
- Send them regular updates.
- Blog about them on your social media sites. Whether it's text, audio or video, be sure to send them copies or links.
- Keep in regular personal contact.
- Offer to do speaking appearances when it fits into your schedule.
- Send photos especially where their logo is included – the bigger the better!
- Give them memorabilia.
- Ensure you mention them on radio, TV, newspaper and in any other mainstream media appearance that you do. Send them copies.
- Most importantly – *under* promise and *over* deliver! This will make it much easier to enter into long-term relationships of 3 years or more, as well as make it easy to re-sign a sponsor when the term of the contract expires.

Delivering (On And Off The Field)

Following through is very important for long-term relationships and ongoing sponsorships. Keep training, because sponsors like winners and your commitment to be the best.

Personal development is also a great way to enhance yourself and what you have to offer. Through personal development activities such as attending courses, reading books, listening to CD's, watching DVDs, attending functions with high profile industry speakers, you will continually refine and enhance your unique point of difference, your UPOD.

THE 'S' WORD - SPONSORSHIP 109

It didn't take us long to realise that most photos were taken from behind!

Summary – The Keys To Winning The Sponsorship Game

- Understanding Yourself
- Developing Your Offer (Creativity)
- Networking
- Selling
- Servicing
- Delivering
- Maintaining the Relationship!

You don't even have to be the best athlete. We have seen over the years that there are lower ranked players in many sports making more money in sponsorship than some top ranked players. You just have to be good at the above list (or find someone that is good in the areas you need help with and enrol them in your dream).

The most important part of the whole process is understanding and packaging your offer. Preparation is absolutely key to success. You need to know your UPOD, what you can do for a sponsor and the value you can provide. Then you can match this with the people you meet and it is all practice selling the dream. It is a numbers game. Don't take it personally, develop a *thick skin* and persevere!

For further information on Natalie Cook please visit www.nataliecook.com

KEY POINTS

Know your Unique Point of Difference.

Persevere. For every 99 that say "no", I will say "yes".

Treat your sponsors like gold.

One of our most lucrative sponsorships was with Grand United Health Fund. They had us on billboards in Sydney and Brisbane!

CHAPTER 10
MANAGING YOUR MONEY

When I left my full-time job and regular income, I must admit, not only was it a struggle financially, it was a little scary. A little voice inside kept questioning: was I really good enough to derive a living through sport?

But gradually over the years, as my training started to pay off and we became more successful on the court, we won more prize money. Sponsorship dollars increased and I was able to derive a reasonable income solely through sport, and long before I won a Gold medal.

Now my Gold medal and my profile have opened doors that I would never have dreamed of and I have developed many avenues that allow me to make a good income through my own ventures, even though I have been retired (as a full-time volleyball player) since 2005.

What Should I Do With All This Cash?!

What a fabulous problem to have! If your sponsorship, endorsement and/or prize money dreams have been realised, you may suddenly have more money that you ever imagined.

It's worth taking a moment to consider the best way to handle this new situation. Getting that flash car might be another dream and it may feel amazing to achieve it, but you should consider the bigger picture too. Statistics show that 70% of lottery winners have used up all their money within 3 years. I'm not suggesting that coming into all this money after years of dedication in your sport is an act of chance, but it may feel like you've won the lottery if you suddenly come into a large amount of cash after barely scraping by for so long.

Wouldn't you feel pretty lousy if in five or ten years' time you have absolutely nothing to show for all your hard work and success?

As with any business, the more successful you become, the more your costs will increase. There will be more people on your A-Team to pay, and as your profile rises, more people will want to join you. Always seek advice from people around you that you trust, not people who are making money from you. Only bring on people that you truly need and are adding value and helping you achieve your goals. Make sure they have your best interests at heart. Some people see you earning lots of money, and try to jump on board for the ride.

Here are some things you could consider if you do end up earning the big bucks:

- **Talk to other successful people.** Talk to those you trust, both from within your sport but also from other sports and businesses. Ask questions and truly listen to their answers. What have they learned and what would they do the same or differently if they were starting out on their careers again or were in your position right now?

- **Get professional help.** Find the names of Financial Planners that your valued friends and colleagues recommend and trust but ensure they are totally financially independent, not earning a commission from your decisions. Get a list of qualified Certified or Chartered Accountants.

- **Check your accountant 'knows' sport.** Make sure the Accountant you engage is aware of the following areas that are particular to athletes:

    i. Hobby or Business – if you earn income from sport you should seek advice as to whether you are merely earning income via a hobby or you are in fact in the business of sport.

    ii. Income Averaging – athletes who are assessed on their sporting income can benefit significantly by achieving average tax rates much better than a typical tax payer in the early stages of their career provided their tax return is lodged and 'Income Averaging' is applied.

    iii. Setting up a Structure for Image & Likeness – there are many advantages to a sports person transferring their 'Image & Likeness' earning ability to say a company or trust. Entity structure advice should be sought if endorsement income is possible in the future.

    iv. Salary Packaging – in many cases athletes are employed by 'Non-Profit Organisations'. They can elect to package their salary into fringe benefits such as home loan repayments and possibly achieve better tax rates.

- **Set aside enough money for taxes.** Ensure they can be paid as soon as they are due. Do not touch this money!

- **Take your time before you spend.** Wait a month or even a few months before you make any big decisions. Do your full research and if you don't have time, find other people you trust to do the due diligence for you. Is this really the right financial decision for you now and in the future?

- **Find a safe place to hold your money.** Look for short to medium term options where your money is earning some interest while you make your decision. These days, online banking often offers better interest rates than high street banks, usually with unlimited access and no fees. But shop around and see what is best for you.

- **Work out how to derive a secondary income from your cash.** There are plenty of ways to do this, such as earning dividends from shares, investing in property and so on. Diversify your portfolio if possible so that you don't have all your money in one place. If you decide to solely invest in the share market and there is a share market crash or global financial crisis, your entire wealth could be lost.

- **Educate yourself.** Knowledge is power, and puts you in a better position to make sound decisions. Research online, attend free seminars, read books, visit your local library and chat to others. There is so much information out there that is readily available and often free. Fix a date in your schedule and commit to doing some self-development!

- **Pay off any bad debts.** Bad debts are items you've purchased using high-interest credit cards, where you haven't paid the balance in full. The item you purchased continues to lose value and the amount you paid for it continues to increase. Examples of bad debt include expensive cars, top brand clothing, and so on. Bad debts will burn big holes in your pockets, so pay these off first.

  (Note: Good debts are often tax-deductible debts that produce more wealth in the long run. For example an investment debt that creates value like a student loan, real-estate loan, home mortgage, and business loan.)

- **Make a wish list.** Research how much the things you want actually cost – you might be surprised. Shop around. You may have plenty of money suddenly, but that's no reason to be taken for a ride. Be aware of people trying to persuade you into deals because they see you have money available.

- **Take a holiday.** When your schedule allows it, truly enjoy your time off from sport. Relax and enjoy the fact that you are able to live your dream.

- **Make a budget.** If you are earning more money than ever before, but also seem to be spending more than ever before, then try doing a revised budget – just as we talked about in the chapter: Determining the Cost of Your Dreams. It's worth tracking your spending (every cent!) for a week or two or even a month if you can. This will really allow you to see where your money is going and the changes you need to make to reign things in.

- **Get insurance.** Your car, your house, your life. How are you covered if you are injured through your sport? Make sure that your valuables can be replaced if they are damaged or stolen.

- **Make sure your will is in order.** This may seem like a strange thing to say when you are at the peak of your physical fitness, but setting up a will just allows you to choose where your money goes.

- **Give back.** This could be to your family who have supported you to reach this level of success or it could be to a charity or other organisation.

KEY POINTS

It's OK to reward yourself now, but think long-term.

Research investment opportunities.

Please note that the above is for information purposes only and does not constitute financial advice, merely my own suggestions of things to consider. You may wish to consult a licensed financial professional for financial advice based on your own circumstances.

CHAPTER 11
KEEPING RECORDS

If your life is worth living, it's worth recording!

Anthony Robbins, Self-Help Author and Success Coach

Keeping a record of your sporting career will not only make a great keepsake, but it can be a really valuable tool, to help *build* your career now. It will help you with media, writing your bio, putting together sponsorship proposals, making speeches, completing your tax return, and perhaps even if you write your own book in the future.

There are many ways you can keep records, so choose the methods that work best for you, and stick to them, at home or on the road.

You may choose:

- **A diary, journal or notebook.** When you write about what you're thinking, feeling or even wondering about, you tend to gain clarity and understanding. It's a good way to release pent up feelings and frustrations, and you can list the pros and cons of taking different courses of action. It's also a great place to record wins, funny stories and exciting events.

- **Keep your journal in a safe place.** Write in it as frequently as you like and don't beat yourself up if you haven't picked it up for a week or a month or so. Just write where you left off.

- **A collection of scrapbooks.** Use these for all your newspaper, magazine or other media clippings. I currently have over 20 big scrapbooks. They include my very first local newspaper clipping from when I was just 16 years old, right up until a recent print-out of a story on my entire career from an American Volleyball website. I've kept everything and it's a fantastic keepsake and memory. I also used some of them when I went to sponsor meetings to show them how much media I was generating and I will use them when I write my autobiography in the future.

- **Computer folders, Portable Hard Drives, DVD and USB Drives.** There is so much information out there on the Internet. I love to collect articles or photos to use for different projects. I collect folders on different subjects, such as Nutrition, Plymetrics, Coaching, Motivation and Goal Setting. You never know when you'll need this information, so it's great to collect it as you go. You can read it at your leisure and have it handy when you need it.

  Remember – Always, always have a back up and back it up regularly.

- **Your mobile phone.** Great to record interviews, take photos and collect links and interesting facts.

Whatever you choose, make sure it's something you can keep safe, find easily and won't lose. For each entry, record the date and location.

What Should I Record?

Here is my list of the bare minimum you should be recording:

Your results

If you're in a low profile sport, there may not be an official record of your results as you journey through your career. When I was playing Indoor Volleyball, there wasn't one. I kept a list myself and I have used it many times on my website and for interviews.

Even if you are in a high profile sport, you may need to keep a record in the beginning, until you reach National competitions, where your results are more likely to be recorded.

In any case, it's great to have a record of your progress throughout your journey.

Competitor information

Collecting information on competitors is something that simply must be done by all athletes – it made an enormous difference to my sporting success.

I made notes after almost every match that we played, especially the games at the highest level and the games we lost. Because we played up to 100 matches per year, I found that by the end of the season I relied on this information to remind me of how we played against different teams, what worked and what didn't work. I recorded things like:

- Name and country of the opponent
- Date, Event, Score
- Weather conditions
- How the match progressed
- Critical turning points
- Our game plan
- What worked and what didn't work against them in our offence and defence
- Tendencies of our opponents
- Which opponent was the weaker, that we could win more points on
- How I/we felt during the match

Your achievements

- School awards

- Recognition by your club/sporting body – Most Valuable Player awards, Most Inspirational, Rookie of the Year, etc.

- Community awards

- Record of national or international ranking

- Any other significant achievements or goals you have reached

Media

- Newspaper and magazine clippings and articles

- Transcripts from websites or online articles

- TV and radio interviews

Income and expenses

- Keeping track of your income and expenses is required by law. You must do this in order to submit your tax return at the end of the year. Keep *all your receipts*.

A Final Word On Expenses

Many of the costs associated with being a professional athlete can be claimed for tax purposes (including this book!), whether you are working from home or on the road. Check what is allowed in your own country with your Tax Office or Accountant, but in my opinion, it's better to keep a record of *everything* as you go along. It would be a shame to find out later that you could have claimed something if you'd only kept the receipt.

Before you start, ask your Accountant how they would prefer your expenses to be recorded. They may offer to do it for you (at a high hourly rate!), but it's really something you can easily do yourself, with a bit of planning.

Splitting costs into expenses at home and overseas is usually a good idea as you may be able to claim for different items when you are travelling.

Here are some simple steps to help you keep track of expenses:

1. For each event or trip away, write the details of the trip on the outside of a clean envelope. Depending on how many receipts you accumulate, this could be one envelope per event or at least one per country so you keep currencies together.
2. When you arrive in a new country and you exchange money, keep the exchange receipt so you can convert it into your own currency on your spreadsheet later. If you haven't kept that receipt, there is a website that can give you the exchange rate of that country on that particular day - www.xe.com/ict
3. Ask for a receipt for *everything* you spend! Whether it's a take-away coffee, groceries, an airline ticket or a new camera.
4. Have a quick look at the receipt as soon as it's handed to you. If it's not obvious what the receipt is for (or it's in a foreign language), write a note on the top, along with the date and location. It's a good idea to always carry a small pen with you for this.
5. Put the receipt in your wallet.
6. Every day transfer all the receipts into the relevant clearly marked envelope.
7. Once a week or at the end of your trip, transfer all the receipts into a spreadsheet that you will give to your Accountant for tax purposes. (The Australian Taxation Office publishes 'Record Keeping' guidelines and it is as easy as logging onto their website and downloading publications that will inform you of exactly what is expected.)

Here's how my Accountant likes me to record my expenses:

Airfares (including departure taxes etc)	Date	Amount Paid (excluding Australian GST)	GST Paid (Australia Only)	Invoice Total	Currency	Conversion Rate	Total ($AUD)
Sydney – LA return	21/5/10	1363.64	136.36	1500	AUD	1.0000	1500
LA – Miami – LA	30/5/10	555.00		555	USD	1.11	616.05

Accom-modation & Meals	Date	Amount Paid (excluding Australian GST)	GST Paid (Australia Only)	Invoice Total	Currency	Conversion Rate	Total ($AUD)
LA – Hilton Hotel	21/5/10	230		230	USD	1.11	255.30
Miami, Backpacker	30/5/10	85		85	USD	1.11	94.35
Total		-	-	-			349.65

Go to www.thebusinessofbeinganathlete.com to download a sample template for recording Tax Expenses.

RECORDING, WRITING FOR THE FUTURE

If I hadn't kept such good records throughout my journey, the process of writing this book would have been a lot more difficult, even impossible!

The great value of writing a book, whether it's a biography or some sort of self-development book, is that it can generate income for many years to come.

It's a great marketing tool, and you'll be able to sell it online, at events, while you're speaking at the back of the room and even in large quantities to groups with the same interests.

It will also be a great resource and learning tool for others that may follow in your footsteps.

While it is a very lengthy and time consuming project, the better your records – clearly detailed, and kept from the very early days, the easier it will be to write your book, when the time comes.

KEY POINTS

Your life is worth recording, so do it regularly.

Receipts are valuable.

CHAPTER 12
DEVELOPING YOUR MARKETING TOOLS

For a business to succeed, there are three unavoidable 'must-haves'. A business must have:

- A quality product offer
- Strong financial management
- Great marketing

Likewise, for an athlete to succeed, they also need the three 'must-haves'. If any one of these factors is missing, the success you dream of is unlikely.

You are the **'quality product offer'.** You're now pretty savvy on the importance of **managing your finances.** It's time to move on to the third 'must-have' – **marketing**, so you can effectively build your brand – YOU! Earlier, Natalie described the ideal components of a sponsorship toolkit: a bio, business cards, e-brochure, photos, your own website and social media pages. These marketing tools can be used for many purposes, and in this chapter we'll look at how you can make yours really stand out.

1. **A Well-Written Biography**

    Spend the time and effort to get your bio right. It's an important introduction (of you) to the world.

A biography is simply a brief overview of who you are, along with your relevant experience and achievements. It could be used:

- By journalists, writing articles about you
- By commentators, talking about you
- By TV hosts, interviewing you
- For Awards ceremonies
- In press conferences
- On your personal website
- On your own social media pages such as Facebook and Twitter
- By potential sponsors or employers
- By your fan club
- By motivational speaking clients

It's a good idea to read other people's bios, before you write your own. Look at bios from within and outside your own sport – online, in books, and in magazine articles. Get ideas about content, layout and formatting. Decide on a style that works best for you.

Here are some tips to creating a professional bio:

- **Start with a concise statement.** It should include your name, and introduce you to the reader. It should also give the reader a sense of how long you have been playing, or even your crowning glory to date.

- **Continue with a less formal statement, which builds from your expertise.** This could be a special approach you have, or unique skills or a conviction.

- **Include something unique about your journey.** Perhaps an injury you overcame, or the young age you started playing or the inspiration behind your career so far. Make it warm and friendly. This style is generally much more engaging than reading a straight list of facts. People want to learn about you as a person and your journey.

- **Make the reader hungry for more.** End the bio with a statement that will make them keen to know more. This part of the bio can be changed, depending on where you plan to use the bio. It could state your next goal on your journey, your next book release and so on.

Remember to write in the third person. Use 'He' or 'She' rather than 'I'. Even if you are writing your own bio, it's much more professional to write in the third person so it reads as if it's been written by someone else. It allows you to be more objective and the reader will also have more trust in the information.

Make two or three different versions that can be used for different purposes. If you're asked to supply your bio, don't be afraid to ask how much information is required. Your versions could be:

- Short – around 5 or 6 sentences

- Medium – around 1 page

- Long – up to 2 pages, including all your achievements, your journey, educational background and key results and awards

Your bio should evolve as you achieve new things – it should be constantly changing. Make sure your bio is always up-to-date with the latest information.

However, before you give it to a new audience, it might be worth tweaking it, to make it more relevant. For example, if a school requests your bio, you might include more information about managing your training program along with your schoolwork or any particular school-age achievements. If a function is requesting you to make a speech, you might include reference to your other notable public speaking engagements.

Make Your Bio Better Than The Rest

Two elements of a bio that athletes often forget to include are photos, and contact details.

People love to see photos. They get a much better feel for you as an athlete and also as a person. Use one of your best photos of you in action, but make sure it's flattering – we don't all look great in every sports photo! If you can, have some professional photos taken and add these in as well so they get to see how you 'scrub up' off the sports field.

Don't forget to include your contact details along with your website, blog and other social media pages so they know how to reach you, or where to look for further information.

Finally, I would recommend getting a professional copywriter to look at your bio and improve it. It will cost a little extra money but it will make such a difference to the final piece. Get other people you trust to read it and give you feedback.

Save it in PDF format, so that you can email it as a smaller file size.

Go to http://www.kerripottharst.com/Biography.htm to see an example of my own bio that has evolved over the years and is always being updated and improved.

2. **Sharp Business Cards**

It's important to get your business cards professionally designed. Add a photo, and list your best achievements or some of your goals and dreams on the back.

Tip: Business Cards
Keep them in a card holder so they don't become worn and dog-eared.

3. **Memorable Autograph Cards**

Being ready to sign something shows you have planned ahead and are committed to your fans. Use one or a few of your best photos on the card. Choose a glossy finish and don't skimp on the quality. If you already have sponsors or someone who may be willing to start sponsoring you, ask them to cover the cost of production (they may even be able to do it in-house which won't cost them much at all) and in return print their logos on the cards.

On the back you can again list some achievements, or your favourite quote, or your goals for the year. Make sure you leave room for an autograph and dedication.

Again, be creative and be different.

Here are some examples of my autograph cards, which have always been paid for or produced by sponsors:

Autograph card sponsored by Bolle and Crocs

Autograph card sponsored by Vodafone

4. E-brochure

Many requests for information on you, or your team, will come through your website, blog or email address. Having an E-brochure (saved as a PDF) ready to send straight back ensures that you appear professional, efficient and organised.

Here's an example of an E-brochure that I send to my prospective speaking clients:

5. **Professional Photos**

   Now, if you're going to go to the trouble, time and possibly expense of doing all or some of the above, you're going to need some impressive photos that can only be done by a professional photographer.

   Part of presenting yourself as a professional athlete is also having great photos for your bio, autograph card, website, blog and many other places. It is really worth spending some money in this area. The reader's eye is immediately drawn to images, whether in printed media or online, so poor photos can ruin even the best-written bio or article.

   Perhaps you know someone who is a professional photographer that may want to do this for you to help you on your journey? Remember, if you don't ask, you'll never know! Even if they give you a great discount, that's a start.

   Important Tips For Photo Shoots:
   - Take some time to really think about your image, wardrobe and overall appearance as it can make such a difference to the final outcome. Take some photos in your normal sporting attire as well as casual or more formal clothes. See the chapter: Image, Wardrobe & First Impressions.
   - Relax and enjoy it. Using someone you know to take the photos will help you relax.
   - Make sure you've had a good sleep the night before so you look lively.
   - Ensure that you will own the copyright afterwards. That means you can use the photos whenever you need to, without having to pay an additional fee every time. You may pay more for this initially, but it will save time and money in the long run.

   You may only have one crack at it, especially if you're paying the photographer, so be prepared to look your best.

130 THE BUSINESS OF BEING AN ATHLETE

One of my favourite professional photos taken not long after the 2000 Games. I use it often when asked for a photo to go with an article, blog or in a corporate newsletter.

This photo was taken more recently. It's good to keep your photos updated.

DEVELOPING YOUR MARKETING TOOLS 131

Have fun with your photos. They don't all have to be serious. It's good to have a variety of shots.

Don't be afraid to show off your assets!

6. Your Own Website

Almost every professional athlete (or aspiring professional athlete) has their own website. If you haven't done so already, register your name as your URL – such as www.kerripottharst.com, as soon as you can. Even if you are not ready to start your own website, this will ensure that you own that URL (so no one else buys it and tries to sell it to you for a high price when you become a big star). Registering a URL will involve a small annual fee, and it is often more cost effective to register for more than one year at a time.

Your website will be your communication, PR and marketing 'hub'. It will tell your story and be the place that people will go to find out more. You can add to it as often as you like and remember that anyone can see this information – from friends and fans through to media, sponsors and competitors.

Before A Designer Creates Your Site

- Consider other websites that you really like (both for sportspeople and other businesses) to help you decide on a style and layout that would work for you. If you like a style or a particular site, find out if local web developers could do something similar or contact the designer who made that site and chat to them about it. Their contact details are usually at the very bottom of each web page.

- Write down what you want your website to do. Is it really just an online brochure or would you like it to be more interactive so that you can chat with your fans? Is it more of an online diary? Some blogging sites are now so sophisticated, that if they are used effectively, you hardly need a separate website. Take a look at Basketball legend Kobe Bryant's Wordpress site at www.kb23.com. See more examples at www.wordpress.org.

- Using Wordpress or something similar saves you the cost of a web designer and developer but you will need to put more of your own hours in to the initial set-up. There are options suited to every level of technical expertise (or lack of!) so consider your options and research which one would be best for you.

DEVELOPING YOUR MARKETING TOOLS

- Note: If you choose this option, just be aware of any potential limitations in case you want to make your website more sophisticated in the future. For example, will you be able to send an e-newsletter to individual names in your database? Can you add a shopping cart? Can you manage promotions or special offers? These things may not be applicable to you but it's worth thinking ahead.

- Your website should *definitely* have a CMS (content management system), which allows you to change text, photos and add pages yourself both from home and while you are on the road. Constantly updating your site with interesting info and pictures, will not only give readers a reason to want to return, but it will also help your site rank higher in search engine results.

- It's important to remember that you don't have a full content management system, then you won't be able to update the website yourself. You'll have to have updates done by your developer at an extra cost each time.

Check out my website at www.kerripottharst.com and if you like it, contact Trimax Solutions at www.trimaxsolutions.com and mention you're reading my book. They give special discounts to athletes.

Tip: Choose for the long-term
I strongly recommend that if you use a web developer/designer make sure it's someone you trust, who will be there to help you grow. You don't want to be switching developers as time goes by as this will only incur extra costs.

Consider Your Target Audience

- Keep the text simple, and consider who might be visiting your site. Make sure you use the appropriate tone for the kinds of visitors you expect.

- People will scroll down if they are interested enough, but if possible, pitch each page so it fits within the screen size. That way, they can see it all without scrolling.

- Include a links page, with links to other sites that might be useful to your visitors.

What Should I Include On My Site?

Your website might include any of the following:

- Your bio
- Latest news, or an option to subscribe to your newsletter
- User registration to build your database
- Results
- Photo gallery with great photos
- Media releases
- Blog or a link to an external blog
- Coaching tips
- History of your sport
- Sponsors/partners/supporters' info and links
- Links to other relevant websites
- Fans and membership info
- Contact details
- Links/integration to Facebook, Twitter and other social media
- A forum for fans (to ask you questions and chat)

It's also worth considering the use of other online tools such as Flikr and YouTube. You might want to have them embedded into your site to save the development of photo or video display.

What Will It Cost?

- Depending on the complexity of the design (and if you choose to go with a full content management system, which I recommend), prices start at around $1000. You could choose a professional web company, or a freelancer, or maybe just a friend who will do it as a favour. Get a written quote, and ask their fees if you need changes made once the site is complete.

- Don't forget to include the monthly website hosting fee in your budget. You might be tempted by free hosting offers, but check the fine print and understand the level of support they offer, and the amount of content you can upload (especially if you want to include lots of photos and videos on your site). It's also a good idea to do a quick search online to see if there are any disgruntled comments from customers who've had difficulty with the hosting company. The last thing you want is for your site to be constantly crashing or freezing. Hosting fees start at around $20 per month.

Setting up a website way may seem like a large expense initially, but if you update it regularly and use it well, it will become an extremely important part of your Marketing toolkit.

7. Facebook, Twitter And Other Social Media

Using Facebook and Twitter to keep your fans, supporters, sponsors and the media up to date with your journey is an absolute must. With over 400 million active users (when we went to print) Facebook is one of the most popular and fastest-growing social media sites in the world. The main advantage of social media sites over traditional media is that they allow you to interact with your fans. 'Friends' can share opinions and give feedback. It's a two-way conversation.

Another great thing about having a page on Facebook is that it will usually rank higher in the search engines than your own personal website. This means that people may find your Facebook page before they find your website. This happens because Facebook is searched for so regularly by millions of people, that it comes up near the top of the search lists.

You can get your own website to rank higher by optimising your site for search engines such as Google, but this will take SEO (Search Engine Optimisation) technical knowledge as well as time and effort. Your own page on Facebook will usually rank much higher on Google soon after you have set it up. You can then link from your Facebook page to your own website.

Search engines will also find you more easily if you set up a personal URL using your name in your Facebook page such as www.facebook.com/federer. You do this through Facebook Account Settings under *username*. You may need to try a few options to find a suitable name that is still available. Do the same on Twitter.

Link all your social media together so that you only need to upload once, and that post will show on all your social media pages. You can do this using sites such as www.hootsuite.com, or similar.

Tip: Keep it clean

Facebook, Twitter and other Social Media pages are a great way to present yourself as a professional athlete. They are not the same as your private Facebook or MySpace pages that you share with your friends. Keep them separate and be aware that anyone and everyone can see what you post – media, potential sponsors, sporting bodies, coaches, supporters, competitors and so on. Think about how you want to show your image to the world. Refrain from swearing and being too controversial. Be a great role model and act with integrity and professionalism.

Facebook Superstars

Barack Obama, the current President of the United States, uses Facebook and his page has over 12 million fans, growing by 100,000 per week!

Roger Federer, Tennis champion, has 4.2 million fans and grows by about 17,000 per week. Click 'like' on his page and see what he posts. He's a great example.

Misty May-Treanor is another Olympic Beach Volleyball Gold Medallist who also has been on the TV show 'Dancing with the Stars' in the US. She competes in a relatively low profile sport, but now has over 550,000 followers. See her page and how she links to her blog and website.

Tip: Keep learning
Do a short workshop or course on how to get the most out of using Social Media. Subscribe to sites like www.mashable.com and read social media experts' blogs. It's well worth your time, and will make your pages more enticing to readers.

> *Communication works for those who work at it.*
>
> **John Powell**, Award winning Composer

Regular Updates To Social Media & Website

Don't write a novel – catch their attention so they want to read more, and want to check out your other pages. Tell them something they don't already know.

Whether you are training at home or competing on the road, update often. Keep it interesting. Research has shown that updating your website, blog or Facebook page every day is not necessarily more beneficial than updating it once or twice a week. The most important thing is the quality of the posts and whether they are of interest and relevance to your audience. Look at the posts of high-profile athletes, to get a feel for what's of interest to their audience.

Your updates to your website, blog or social media could include:

- Sending newsletters to your database/network/contacts

- Links to newspaper articles about you

- Articles or interesting stories about your journey

- Adding or changing photos and videos

- Giving your fans access to information or personal insights that they wouldn't get elsewhere. How you feel about the competition you've just completed, tips and insights into your lifestyle, habits, diet and training regime

- Where you are in the world right now and what it's like

- Posting answers to common questions being asked by fans or younger athletes looking to get into your sport

- Uploading videos from YouTube

- Adding links to other websites

Tools You'll Need To Step It Up

If you're going to have a great website, blog or Facebook page, you'll need these tools:

- **Digital Camera.** Good quality, vibrant photos really capture an audience. However, always make sure the photos look professional or they will detract from your site.

- **Video Camera.** Loading video clips onto your site, blog or fan page or linking to YouTube can really enhance your communication. People love to see you in action or being interviewed and often will prefer to listen to a video than read text. Media may also request footage of you and if you can supply your own good quality video, it's a real bonus. The video quality on some digital cameras is good enough to upload to the web, so you may not need an extra camera.

- **Voice Recorder.** Use the voice record option on your computer, your phone, or you might prefer using a portable digital voice recorder. You can record interviews, and upload as podcasts. (I also use voice recorders to record reminders and spur-of-the-moment ideas, and to help prepare speeches.)

- **Database Software.** A well maintained contact list or database (using your website or programs like Outlook, Excel, Access or ACT!) can be an extremely powerful resource. It enables you to keep track of your contacts, and communicate with them more effectively. Having a great contact list has been one of the most valuable tools I've had over the years. Not only does it allow me to include notes about each contact, record when I last spoke to them, and write a summary of what we discussed to jog my memory for next time, it also allows me to send out newsletters or press releases to groups of individuals quickly and efficiently.

KEY POINTS

Having great marketing 'tools' is a must-have, to help you stand out to media and sponsors.

Invest the time and the money to develop the best tools you can.

CHAPTER 13
COMMUNICATION

The way we communicate with others and with ourselves ultimately determines the quality of our lives.

Anthony Robbins, Self-Help Author and Success Coach

The way you communicate with others says a lot about you. If you're serious about creating a career from sport, it's a good idea to follow basic business protocol when it comes to communication.

Be professional with everyone you deal with in relation to your life as a professional athlete – media, sponsors, businesses, your governing body, your coach, trainer, manager and even your parents or friends if they are fulfilling any of these roles in your professional life.

Business people will get incredibly frustrated if you don't respond to their requests for a week or more when they can see you have been on Facebook every day.

Your ability (or inability) to communicate well could make or break a sponsorship deal or play a factor in your relationship with the media. You may be dealing with people you've never met so their first impression of you is through your communication skills, whether via email, on the phone, or face-to-face.

Email

Email is a fast and efficient way to get information out to people instantly, no matter where they are in the world. However, there are some drawbacks to email and it's not always appropriate for every situation.

- **Be informative but brief.** Everyone is busy so cut to the chase – get to the point, and include details only if they are relevant.

- **Create an email signature.** Include your contact information, links to your website and social media, and a quote about you.

- **Check your grammar and use spellcheck every time.** Poor spelling make you look instantly less credible. Make sure you re-read your emails before you press 'send' for poor grammar or expression – spellcheck won't pick up 'two' instead of 'too' or 'their' instead of 'there'. If you aren't sure which to use, look it up online.

- **Use correct sentence case** (capital letter at the start of each sentence) **and correct spelling.** Don't use all upper or lower case, texting shorthand such as pls, thx, u, or 2, or emoticons. It is simply not appropriate in a business context.

- **Check the tone of the email,** to make sure you're sounding friendly and approachable, not demanding, offhand or abrupt. Sometimes rearranging paragraphs can help.

- **Consider getting a separate email** address for your professional and personal correspondence. This is especially relevant if your personal email address is something like sexyblondeontour@hotmail.com

- **Don't attach too many** (if any) **attachments** unless someone has requested them. People often don't open them, either because they are too busy or for fear of viruses. You could ask the recipient first if they are happy to receive an attachment or if possible just embed the text of the attachment into the body of the email.

Telephone

Often we can get caught up in an email exchange for days, going back and forth with questions, when a quick phone call would have sorted it out in a few minutes. Don't fall into this trap, especially if you're trying to arrange a meeting or co-ordinate diaries. Your time is valuable. Pick up the phone.

- Plan what you are going to say before you call and be ready to leave a clear and concise voicemail if the person is not there, including how they should get back to you. Repeat your name and number twice if you leave a voice message. It can be frustrating for your contacts to miss your call but then receive no voice message.

- Keep conversations short and to the point. Everyone is busy and mobile calls can be expensive. Keep your own costs to a minimum when you can.

- Be considerate about the time of day you are calling and try to call within business hours unless there are special circumstances. Double check time zone differences if you are calling overseas.

- When you start the conversation, ask if they are able to talk right now. This allows the receiver to decide whether it's better for them to talk now or call back later. You don't know where they are or who they are with.

- Have you listened to your voicemail lately? If not, listen. Do you sound professional and upbeat? Change your own voicemail monthly. Clear your messages regularly and always return calls as soon as you can – at least within 24 hours. If you need to, set aside a certain time each day that you will return all calls together.

- When you answer the phone, smile and say, "Hi, this is Kerri", rather than just, "Hello?" People can hear the smile in your voice.

- Call back if you get disconnected.

- Ask permission before putting someone onto speakerphone. If you are in the car, let the caller know and introduce them to anyone else who is with you. This will avoid any potential embarrassing situations and ensure everything remains confidential.

Face-to-Face

How you conduct yourself at functions or meetings or when you're introduced to someone who could help you – can make or break your career.

Practice the tips in the following chapters. Learn how you can conduct yourself more professionally in person, and in return, be perceived as the positive, committed athlete you want to be.

KEY POINTS

Learn to use the most appropriate method of communication for each situation.

Always be professional in your business communication.

CHAPTER 14
IMAGE, WARDROBE & FIRST IMPRESSIONS

When asked, "What was the first thing that you bought when you first won some money?" Roger Federer replied – "I improved the contents of my clothes cupboard".

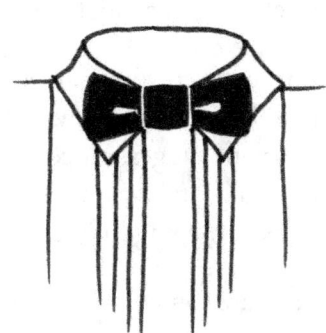

I've learned over the years that many people judge you on the way you present yourself, and the way you speak and act.

If you walk tall, smile confidently, look people in the eye and appear successful, people will immediately think that you are, even before you open your mouth to speak. Studies show that up to 90% of your communication is done without words.

Your image, as perceived by others, is conveyed through:

- The way you dress
- The way you stand
- How you speak – both in the vocabulary you use and your tone of voice

- Your facial expressions
- Making and keeping eye contact
- Your gestures
- Your behaviour

The way you conduct yourself both on and off the sports field is also an important factor in whether or not the public recognise you as a role model. This can considerably affect your chances of securing sponsorship.

First Impressions Are Important

You only have 7 seconds to make a first impression. In those 7 seconds people assess your appearance, demeanour, mannerisms, body language and clothing. They determine your age, income, marital status and education level – in 7 seconds!

Throughout your career, you'll have many opportunities to meet new people and form new business and social relationships. Like it or not, everyone judges. Once people have formed an opinion, it can be very hard to change it. The opinion they form in that first 7 seconds often forms the basis of the ongoing relationship with you. Leave them with your best.

Here are some quick tips on making a great first impression:

- **Be on time.** If you only remember one thing, remember this!
- **Try to be yourself** and relax.
- **Practice a great handshake** – firm but not too tight. Smile, look them in the eye, say your name and that you're pleased to meet them.
- **Take pride in your appearance**, and pay attention to detail
- **Practice great posture** – back straight and head held high. Face the world with a smile. You will feel and look more confident. Try keeping your hands lightly clasped in front of you if you tend to fidget.

- **Be positive.** Look like you want to be there and greet people warmly, but don't overdo it. Watch the mood of the other people for a while and take your cues from them. Use positive language when you speak and if possible avoid criticizing or complaining – try to see a positive in every situation.

- **Don't over-think what you are going to say.** The words you speak make up less than 10% of the message you are sending, so maybe have a few comments prepared but let the conversation flow naturally. Listen to what others are saying and focus on them, not yourself. This means asking questions about themselves and their opinions, such as "What do you think of…?" or "Where did you…?" rather than starting sentences with "When *I* was at…" or "Well, *I* think…"

- Some people like to **imagine they are meeting an old friend**. It can help you feel less nervous and more open to them. Your body language and demeanor will reflect this too.

- **Visualise the event** before you go there, just as you might visualise a big competition. Imagine yourself talking positively and confidently to lots of different people. This can really help you relax and appear friendlier.

Wardrobe And Style

It's also important to dress for the occasion. I learned at an early stage that the way I dressed for different functions affected people's initial perceptions.

- **Dress appropriately.** If you are not sure of the dress code for a function or meeting, call the organisers and find out.

- **Make sure you have the right kind of clothes** – that you know you will feel comfortable in, ahead of time. This will make you *feel* more confident. Also, ensure that they are clean and ironed well before you're due to step out the door.

- Take the time to **dry or style your hair** completely.

- **Pay attention to basic grooming.** Check that your fingernails are clean, your breath is fresh and your shoes are immaculate. These small details are noticed if overlooked.

- **Go easy on aftershave or perfume.** You don't want to overpower someone with your scent.

- For men in a corporate environment, **clean-shaven** is usually recommended. If you have long hair, it should be neat and generally tied back.

- For ladies, **be careful with makeup.** If you aren't sure what is appropriate, less is more. Find a local makeup or image consultant to give you some advice on style and makeup including what would work well for you and your skin colour. Or check out makeup tutorials online for quick and easy tips.

- **Get professional advice** from a stylist or hair and makeup artist if you are not sure how to present yourself off the sports field. This applies to guys as well as girls! Professional stylists can advise you about the kinds of clothes that suit your body type and the best colours for your skin type and hair/eye colouring. They can assess your current wardrobe and take you shopping to find clothes that would work for you. The right look can make a huge difference in your life and boost your confidence off the sports field.

- **For television appearances it's best to dress in simple outfits** of solid primary colours. Steer clear of black and white, as they don't work well on TV. Also avoid plaids, patterns, stripes (unless very thin) and spots. Wear minimal jewellery, and nothing that is visually or aurally distracting (ladies – avoid bangles).

What Do The Different Dress Codes Mean?

It's always a good idea to check with the organisers of a function but here's a basic guide:

- **Black tie** – Men: tuxedo and bow tie or very smart dark suit and straight tie. Plan ahead if you need to rent your tux. Ladies: long evening dress for women, not knee length.

- **Business attire or day formal** – Men: suit. Ladies: smart tailored clothes.

- **Formal** – Men: suit and (usually) tie, dress shoes. Ladies: evening dress, but this can vary from event to event. Check with the organisers to be sure.

- **Semi-formal** – Men: anything from a suit (usually without a tie), through to smart trousers and jacket. Ladies: smart tailored clothes.

- **Cocktail** – Men: dark suit. Ladies: knee length or ¾ length cocktail dress.

- **Country Club** or **Golf Club** – Men: collared shirt or polo shirt with trousers, and closed toe shoes. Ladies: collared shirt or polo shirt with tailored shorts or skirt. Check with the venue.

- **Smart casual** – Men: collared shirt or polo shirt with trousers. Ladies: slightly dressy casual or tailored clothes.

- **Casual** – can depend on the venue. Casual for a beach function can mean shorts and t-shirt, but casual in a function room in a large hotel can mean closer to smart casual attire. Whatever the venue, if it's a function that you have been invited to as a professional athlete, casual still means you should look good. Clean clothes, no rips or holes.

- It is usually acceptable to wear a small sponsor logo on a shirt to a function so long as it is in keeping with the general attire and look that is required. Check with the host or venue if you are not sure.

KEY POINTS

Dress as you want to be seen: committed, professional, upward-bound, and ready to take on the world.

Dressed to impress at our 2004 Olympic Fundraising Dinner where we framed and auctioned off autographed swimsuits!

CHAPTER 15
NETWORKING, MEETINGS & FUNCTIONS

Every best friend was once a perfect stranger.

If you are new at networking, don't panic! We're all first-timers at some point, and practice *will make it easier.* **Practice at smaller functions first, where you feel more comfortable.**

Try making the effort to meet people you don't know at your next function, rather than just staying with the crowd you came with. This is especially important if you are involved in a team sport when it's often far easier just to stick with your teammates. But this is just where you can stand out from the crowd and be noticed. Be brave and take that step across the room to introduce yourself to another person or group – they will appreciate it and admire your confidence. Once you have met one new person, they will often introduce you to others.

Networking simply means meeting new people in a business or social context, having a chat and sharing contact information. Networking is a simple, effective tool that can open many doors. It is nearly always the case that your best opportunities will come from who you know, not what you know.

It's not about trying to hand out as many business cards as possible to everyone you meet. It's about getting to know people and building relationships over the long term. It's better to have really met and gotten to know five people at a function, than to have handed out thirty cards but not be able to really remember anyone. You may not know how someone could help you today, but perhaps in a few months or even a few years time they may have the perfect opportunity or contact for you.

Make the most of every event – they are great opportunities to expand your network and make new acquaintances.

If you do get invited to an event, function or meeting, here are some tips that may help:

Before The Event

Always RSVP to an invitation. Send it as soon as you can so you don't forget. If you can't attend, reply politely, for example: "Thank you for your kind invitation to….. Unfortunately I already have something on that night, but please keep me in mind for similar events in the future." When you RSVP, mention any special dietary requirements to allow the chef time to plan ahead.

Find out the dress code before the day and make sure you have appropriate clothing.

If you are presenting or are expected to speak, plan and practice before the day.

Define your objective in going to this meeting or function. What would you like the outcome to be? Is it to widen your network in general? Are there specific people that you want to meet? If so, what do you want to say to them? Plan for this, to make sure that you are ready when you finally do meet them.

Find out about the company you are visiting or the function you are attending before you arrive so you can talk knowledgeably. Understand them and what is important to them. Who is organising it, and why? Who is likely to attend? If they have recently undergone a merger or a re-brand or have received some media coverage, ask them about it in a friendly way. You will gain an insight into their business too. Planning ahead will also help you feel more confident about talking to others at the function too.

Prepare the 'elevator pitch' (refer to Chapter 9 - Sponsorship on how to do this). Practice it and use your own words so it sounds natural and you feel confident saying it to new people. Be enthusiastic and positive about who you are and what you do or what you want to achieve.

Be prepared to answer common questions about being a sportsperson. People are often fascinated by your lifestyle and your commitment. They want to hear something more than just "I like it" or "I am good at it" so rehearse what you will say if you are asked how you got into your sport. If you have any funny stories to throw in, even better. They don't always want minute detail but they do want to get a feel for your lifestyle. Answer them honestly and with enthusiasm, even if you have to repeat the same thing to every new person in the room!

If it's appropriate and you have the time in your schedule, volunteer to help at the function. This could be to 'meet and greet' when people arrive (a good chance to say hello to everyone and then follow up with people later), assist with registration, act as MC or help to set up or pack up. People will appreciate your assistance but make your request at least a week before the event to allow them time to plan, and only offer if you can commit to seeing it through.

Don't Leave Home Without...

...your trusty networking tools! Be prepared – as the Scouts say, and arm yourself with:

- **Plenty of business cards.** Ensure they are in good condition and not dog-eared or dirty. Get a business card holder.

- **A small pad and pen** to jot down notes or anyone's contact details if they haven't brought a card. You might also use your phone for this purpose.

- **The invitation or contact details**, including the address of the function or meeting and the name of the person who invited you.

- For meetings, any information you have been asked to prepare in advance or that you think could be useful for discussion, such as a budget or your schedule for the year.

What Do I Do On The Day?

Be on time! Never keep people waiting. It can make you seem unreliable, or give the impression that your time is more important than theirs. If you know you are *always* running late, allow for this in your planning – even put the event 15 minutes earlier in your calendar. If on a very rare occasion, there has been an emergency and you are late, call ahead and let the people you are meeting know what has happened and when to expect you.

Smile as you meet people and shake their hand with a good firm grip. Practice your handshake so it's not too hard or too soft. Smiling is such a basic thing but it's easy to forget especially if you are feeling nervous yourself. Even if you aren't feeling confident, just fake it!

Listen actively – this takes practice. Hearing is a physical activity. Listening is a skill. Nod your head and use positive body language. Maintain good eye contact with the person speaking and ask relevant questions when there is a break in conversation. If you find it hard to maintain eye contact then practice with a friend. (No matter how much you might be tempted, it's rude to look over the shoulder of the person speaking to see who else is in the room or find someone more interesting to talk to!)

Find a way that works for you to help you remember names. Repeat someone's name when they introduce themselves, "It's nice to meet you, James" and repeat their name in your head three times. Use their name in conversation several times if possible while you are talking to them (people love hearing their own name). Introduce them to other people that are with you: "James, have you met Margaret?" If their name is unusual, ask them to spell it and clarify how to pronounce it. Ask them if you are saying it correctly.

NETWORKING, MEETINGS & FUNCTIONS

Be positive, enthusiastic, alert and friendly. Look like you want to be there and are interested in what people are saying. Your attitude could mean the difference between a sponsorship deal going to you or a competitor. Or it could bring the media onside, rather than offside.

> *Tip: Be your fabulous self*
>
> Have a favourite word and use it often. Mine is 'fabulous'. What is a word you use often that people remember you by? Try to show your authentic self – you are fabulous – let others see you. This is the best way to build your personal brand. Turn up as yourself 100% of the time, people want to know you, they want to help you and they enjoy your brand. Be unique and be honest.

Asking questions is often a great way to stimulate conversation without having to actually say much yourself. Typical icebreakers:

- How did you come to be at this event?
- Do you know....? (the same people you know attending). If so, how do you know them?
- Where do you work?
- What was the highlight of your day? week?
- What do you like to do in your spare time?
- What do you think about....? (current affairs).

> *Tip: Be in the know*
>
> Read the paper or online news and sport often. Be informed about what's currently happening in your own sport, other sports and what's happening in the news so you can ask intelligent and informed questions or answer questions knowledgably.

- Where are you from originally? (if you meet someone with an accent). How long have you been in this country? How often do you go back to visit? What do you miss about your own country?

If someone is genuinely interested in you and your story, they may ask at the meeting or function if they could help you in some way. Be prepared for how you might answer this question. It may be appropriate to ask them if they had something in mind, or perhaps to thank them for their interest or generosity and arrange a meeting at another time (this also gives you time to work on a proposal).

Remember to switch off your phone (or put it on silent). Don't check text messages during a function or meeting. Let it go to voicemail. If you expecting a very important call that you must take, let those around you know ahead of time. When the call comes in, excuse yourself first and then leave the room. Finish the call as quickly as possible and return to the room. Apologise.

Unless it is absolutely unavoidable, never initiate a call, answer a call or send a text during a meeting or function.

Free alcohol at a function is never an excuse to drink more. Stick to your limit and keep a clear head.

Ask to meet someone in the room if you don't know them.

Invite people straight away to join you on your journey: "Would you like me to add you to my mailing list so you can follow my journey to ….?" or similar. Take their business card or make a note of their details in your phone or on your notepad with a brief description of what you promised to send them.

Ask for referrals. If you've just given a presentation or you've acted as MC, and people are complimenting you afterwards, ask them for a referral! Ask them if they know anyone who needs a great speaker or MC. Ask them to hand on your card. Never miss an opportunity!

Don't be afraid of moving on, after you have chatted to someone for a while. Politely say: "Excuse me, it has been a pleasure talking to you".

At the end of the function, **thank the host** and the person who invited you.

Ultimately, be yourself and have fun. Successful networking will happen if you are genuinely interested in meeting new people who could help you on your journey. People are much more likely to keep in touch and do business with people that they know and like.

After The Event

Did you know less than 1% of people follow up after an event or meeting? Be part of that 1%.

Depending on the amount of time you chatted or the outcome of a conversation, send a thankyou note or even a quick email: "Thanks for your time, I enjoyed meeting you, maybe we could get together for a coffee sometime to discuss..."

Take out all the business cards you received, and add some notes, when and where you met them, what they look like or their spouse or children's names or if they are about to go on holiday.

Next time you speak to them, ask them how their kids are or how their holiday was. They will be impressed you remembered. Write a summary of their info in your contacts database (refer to the chapter: Developing your Marketing Tools) so later on you can remember who, when, what and so forth.

If you told them you would send them a follow-up note, add them to your newsletter or email them about something, then do it straight away. Make a note in your database of the date and what you've sent.

Write one thank you note every week. There are so many reasons to thank people but few people take the time to do it. That little expression of gratitude will be remembered.

Other Ways To Build Your Network

If you are currently working, find out how you can become more involved in company activities. You never know when it will come in handy down the track, whether asking for additional time off for training, sponsorship or even helping you to fundraise. If people get to know and like you, they will be much more receptive if you need their help at some point. Look for opportunities such as:

- Volunteering to be on the social committee.

- Getting to know your co-workers in other departments. Try inviting them to a social lunch or arranging an inter-departmental sport or a quiz.

- Writing for your company newsletter.

- Starting up a lunchtime sports team or running/walking group.

- Starting a social lunch once a month. It could have a different theme each time. If the company won't pay for it, get everyone to bring their own packed lunch to a meeting room. Encourage senior managers to attend as well as junior team members. It's great for overall team and staff morale.

- Offering to run a coaching workshop in your sport at lunchtime.

- Offering to give a talk about your lifestyle and training/competition program. Your co-workers will often have much more support and understanding for your situation if they know more about your determination, discipline and how you are fitting all these additional things into your life. It's also great public speaking practice.

- Starting a co-worker mentoring program if one doesn't already exist.

- Getting involved with charity work. If your company isn't already aligned with a charity, find out if you can start working with one.

Be proactive about expanding your own network of contacts. How could you improve your network in your own sport? Get to know the people who work in your sport, your club or your sport's governing body. Know them by name. Be polite, friendly and interested. Ask them how they are, how their day is going. Make a note if they are going on holiday and ask them about it when they return. Be positive at all times and constructive if you need to give them feedback. They may prove to be extremely important to you and you may need their help in future.

Try networking en masse. Consider giving a speech about yourself to schools, universities or an external group such as a Rotary club or Charity, who are often looking for speakers. It's good practice and the experience will be useful later in life when you may do more public speaking or media interviews. Be clear with your message if you want to get something out of it and tailor your talk to the group you are speaking to.

Huh? Good Table Manners?

This may seem like a strange topic to include, but just for a moment imagine that a potential sponsor has invited you to a large function.

As the up and coming Next Big Star, you are seated at the head table with all the big wigs in the sponsorship world and all eyes are on you. You look around at their faces, you look down at the multitude of plates, glasses and cutlery laid out before you and rack your brain as you try to remember what your mum said all those years ago about table manners...

You may think it's irrelevant but this company is potentially thinking of having you represent their brand. You would be wearing their logo and as such, they are seen to be endorsing you and your behaviour. If all goes well, they may invite you to client dinners as the star attraction. You need to know how to conduct yourself.

Potential sponsorship deals can be laid to rest if a sponsor feels you lack the class or sophistication required in a social setting, and off-putting table manners can fall into that basket.

You should have listened more closely to your mother, right? Here's a reminder of what mum knew best:

- Wait for other people to start sitting down before you sit down.

- Unfold your napkin onto your lap. If it's one of those really huge napkins, it's OK to leave it folded in half on your lap.

- Sit up straight and keep your elbows off the table.

- Only start eating when everyone at your table has been served, unless the host tells you to start sooner. It's a good idea to let someone else start eating first just to make sure you're not jumping the gun. Someone may be about to give a welcome speech or say grace.

- Confused about which is your bread roll? Remember: drinks to the right, solids to the left. Your water and wine glasses are to the right of your plate; your bread roll is on the plate to your left. The red wine glass is slightly larger than the white wine glass.

- If faced with an array of cutlery, start using the cutlery from the outside and work your way in towards the plate, using one set for each course. Rest your fork over your knife (on your plate) when you are eating.

- Once you have picked up a set of cutlery, it shouldn't go back on the table.

- Break your bread roll into small pieces with your fingers. Don't slice it with your knife. Butter small pieces and eat them one at a time. Don't butter the whole roll at the same time or use it to mop up sauces or gravy unless you're dining alone on your couch at home.

- Take small bites. As well as being more polite, this allows you to keep conversation going with other people at the table. Cut your food up small enough so that you don't have to open your mouth wider than the Grand Canyon to get a mouthful in. Pieces of salad and vegetables should not be hanging out of your mouth.

- This is one time in your life when you are not in a competition. Slow down. Relax. Enjoy the meal and the conversation and let your stomach digest your food.

- Swallow your mouthful and if necessary, wipe your mouth on your napkin before taking a drink.

- If you take a mouthful of something too hot, subtly take a drink of cold water. It's really not a great look to spit it out onto your plate.

- Ask someone to pass you something if you can't reach it. Don't stretch across the table. You could knock something over, get mashed potato all over your new clothes, or worse, give someone a whiff of your armpit.

- Compliment the chef or the meal or at least find something nice to say at the end of the meal. If it was really bad, compliment the company or the flowers on the table.

- Excuse yourself from the table to do anything related to personal hygiene or grooming, including applying lipstick, removing food from teeth, burping, sneezing, brushing your hair and so on. Never use your napkin to blow your nose. A definite no-no!

- If you get up during the meal, place your napkin on your chair so that the waiter knows you are coming back. After the meal, place your napkin to the left of your plate, or if the plate has been cleared, it can be placed in the centre of the place setting.

- If you spill something, apologise and help clean it up with minimal fuss.

- When you have finished, put your knife and fork together parallel on your plate.

Business Meetings And Functions Overseas

Culture and protocol in other nations can be very different from your own. If there's any chance you could have any business meetings or functions whilst overseas, take a little time to research what is expected in that country. The following sites may be useful:

www.kwintessential.co.uk - Etiquette, customs and protocol guides around the world

www.cyborlink.com - International Business Etiquette and Manners

> **KEY POINTS**
>
> **If you are new to networking, don't panic. Relax, practice, and you *will* get better.**
>
> **Be your self (but remember Mum's table manners).**

CHAPTER 16
PUBLIC SPEAKING

Everyone has a story, and as an athlete, if you can tell your story (even if you're not at the end of your career) you will inspire others and potentially earn extra income to help you achieve your dreams.

There comes a time in your sporting life when your performance on the field will lead to people wanting more. That means media appearances, and possibly requests from schools or clubs or charities to speak in front of a live audience.

Are you a fearless public speaker? Or, are you like most people, mildly terrified at the prospect of addressing a crowd?

According to most studies, people's number one fear is public speaking. Number two is death. Death is number two. Does that sound right? This means to the average person, if you go to a funeral, you're better off in the casket than doing the eulogy.

Jerry Seinfeld, Comedian

Some view public speaking as a task to be avoided at all costs. Try to see it as a challenge, and use it to help further your career, and inspire and motivate others.

> ### TURNING A FEAR INTO A LUCRATIVE CAREER
>
> While I was competing, public speaking was not something I did very often. But I knew that if I became good at it, it would really help my profile.
>
> I also knew that if I kept improving my profile and gaining more and more exposure in the media, sponsorship opportunities would present themselves more often. This in turn would enable me to keep playing the sport at a high level.
>
> Public speaking also became a great way to earn extra income and fund many expenses. Today it's my main career, providing me with my biggest income stream.
>
> It didn't come naturally and I've had to work very hard at it. Once I realised that people enjoyed hearing my story – of suffering a major knee injury, and making a comeback to compete and win at the Olympic Games, I wanted to get better at telling it.
>
> I went to see other people speak at functions or at media conferences to see how they dealt with the cameras and the audience. I was always watching and listening to other people around me to see how I could improve.
>
> The lessons that you learn as an athlete are invaluable and are applicable to all areas of life. It's these lessons, the skills and tools that you pick up along the way, that motivate and inspire others.

Keys To Becoming A Great Motivational Speaker

When a speaker is good, the audience knows it. You know they know it because they scribble down notes, clap appreciatively, laugh and maintain direct eye contact with you for almost all of the time.

When a speaker is bad, they know it too. The audience is notably uncomfortable. They don't buy what you're saying. They become restless and speak amongst themselves. They stare off into space and may even fall asleep.

PUBLIC SPEAKING 165

It started off as one of the scariest things I've ever done, but I pushed through the fear and now I absolutely love speaking and inspiring others.

As a speaker, I've been both, and experienced good and bad audience reactions. But I do make a conscious effort to learn from each speaking experience and try to improve. I'll make a note of what I was talking about at the time and either keep it in (if it got a great response) or throw it out (if it didn't work or didn't get a good response).

Sometimes, in the past, it wasn't my material. Sometimes it was me and my attitude. I know that when I'm 100% pumped and motivated to tell the story and let my passion come out naturally, I always give a great presentation.

Be your authentic self and be proud of who you are.

So what makes a great speaker? Contrary to popular belief, most great speakers are not born, they are made.

Posture

Posture is really important. Standing tall and appearing relaxed gives an impression of confidence – even if you don't feel it!

So, shoulders back, chin relaxed and level, and stand with one foot slightly forward (whichever foot feels most comfortable) to help you balance naturally. Practice a range of natural looking hand gestures.

Dealing With Nerves

Feeling nervous is totally normal. The quickening of the heart and the pumping of extra blood and adrenalin prepare your body to perform. The same happens just before a competition. And, like sport, the more prepared you are the less nervous you will be.

- **Prepare, prepare, prepare.** It will help your nerves so much if you know that you are as prepared as you possibly can be – both for your speech and for any questions you may be asked. Professional speakers spend days rehearsing.

- **Breathe.** Before you go on stage, do some breathing exercises. Breathe in slowly, hold your breath for a few seconds and then breathe out. Put your hand flat on your belly button and feel it move out as you breathe in, and in as you breathe out. Focus your attention on one point and listen to your breathing. Breathing helps slow down adrenaline.

- **Never apologise for being nervous.** That's like saying to your opponent, "Oh sorry, I probably won't win this game". Don't draw attention to it. Remember nervousness doesn't show one-tenth as much as it feels.

Trust me, the more speeches you give the easier it gets. The better you get, the more confident you will feel.

- **S..l..o..w d..o..w..n.** When we are nervous, we often tend to talk faster. People may struggle to hear or understand you, which makes it much harder to get your message across. Make a conscious effort to speak more slowly and vary your pace. Pause when you say something profound or ask a rhetorical question – leave time for your words to sink in. Don't be afraid of silence for a few seconds.

- **Laugh.** Telling a funny story early in your presentation can really help both yourself and your audience relax. But be careful with jokes. Unless you're a great joke teller and the joke is applicable, it might be better to avoid comedy.

- **Be natural and down to earth.** Especially if you already have a high profile as an athlete and many people know of you, but have never met you.

- **Drink water.** Drink *lots* of it before you go on and make sure you have a glass nearby while you're speaking if you need to moisten your mouth and lips. People don't mind at all if you pause and have a sip. It actually makes you appear calmer and more relaxed.

- **Eat – even a little.** If I'm speaking after the meal, I find that I like to eat just a little bit of the dinner or lunch being served just to satisfy my hunger. I save the dessert for my reward, when I'm done.

- **Don't drink any alcohol,** as much as you may be tempted to settle your nerves. It may backfire and you could slur your words or forget your presentation. You don't want to be memorable for the wrong reasons.

Above all, have fun! Try not to see it as a chore. Enjoy the moment. Just be you and have a great time.

THE FIRST STEP, TAKING THE PLUNGE

I vividly remember my first ever big speech.

I was talking to about 1,500 accountants from Ernst and Young. I was sitting next to Herb Elliot (Australian sporting hero and one of the World's greatest Middle Distance Runners) and was just about to go on. My speech was written down, word for word and I was nervously gripping my papers.

> As I looked down to the carpet awaiting my turn at the lectern, the swirly pattern on the carpet started to move! I was seriously hallucinating. Herb recognised my nerves; obviously he'd heard my quickened breath and probably my loudly beating heart! He put his hand on my shoulder and said "Kerri, don't worry, you'll be great..."
>
> That small vote of confidence calmed me down and by the time I got to the lectern, the room had stopped spinning! I went on to read my notes, word for word, but with as much emotion as I could and I got a huge applause.
>
> There's always a first time for everything and I so much wanted to inspire others that I got through that day and have gone on to become a confident and well respected motivational speaker. I now do about 30 speaking presentations each year – without reading my notes, and I love it!

To Use Or Not To Use Notes

If you're a beginner, you'll benefit from using a script or some notes, however once you become more comfortable speaking in public, you will start to rely more on your memory.

Just remember that it can be quite boring for the audience when a speaker reads from a script, so keep constant eye contact with your audience in between sentences or paragraphs. Using notes or cue cards, and memorising part of the speech is better, as long as you can expand on your notes.

Speaking from memory is for the more experienced speaker, and you will get there with practice.

I've changed what I do over the years and now have a very simple system where a few key points form the 'core' of all my presentations.

When I sit down to prepare for my next speech, I decide which other stories are relevant to the audience and the time I have been allocated. I then slot them in on either side of the core.

Finally, I type it out on one A4 page in a really large font, giving each point a different colour so it's easy to glance down and be reminded of the next point, if I need to.

After almost 15 years of giving motivational presentations I can now speak for anything up to an hour, about my journey and all the lessons I've learnt, without using my notes. I've become so familiar with my story that I sometimes hear myself speaking and I can think about the next section already and work out how I'm going to use the 'bridge' to get from here to there.

However, my notes are always there as a backup. Especially if I have what I like to call, a 'brain blip' and forget where I'm at! I rarely use the notes, but I know they're there, so it makes me feel more confident and secure.

What's Your Story?

The best advice I was ever given was to grab a bottle of wine, invite some friends over for dinner, set up a recording device and have them direct questions toward me about my life and my journey.

You can do the same. It doesn't matter how old you are or how long you've been involved in sport, you'll already have some interesting stories and there will no doubt be lessons in those stories that you can pass onto others.

You can then transcribe your recording (or ask someone to help you), and put together what you would think would be a great presentation.

Write it out in full to begin with, read it out aloud and time it. Work it, mould it, and re-write it. If possible, practice in front of some supportive friends who will give you valuable constructive feedback.

At www.thebusinessofbeinganathlete.com you'll find a step-by-step approach on how to professionally structure your speech.

A Word Of Caution

If you are an expert in a particular topic, and someone asks you to talk about something else that you know nothing (or very little) about, my advice would be to say no.

You may scrape by if you're lucky, but if you are being paid to give a presentation, then you should be the authority on your topic and you should be 100% across everything about it.

Let someone else take that gig and wait for one that is more suited to your own personal skills.

Connect With Your Audience

Find out as much as you can about why you have been asked to speak to a particular group so that you can make your stories relevant to them. Spend 50% of your preparation time on making your speech more relevant. Consider their age, their background, why they would be interested in you, and collect information, material, and anecdotes that would appeal to them.

Don't lose sight of your objective for speaking that day (you should be able to describe your objective in one clear sentence which could be something like "Today you're all going on a journey. A journey that ends in Gold.")

Make sure your presentation is: interesting, entertaining, inspiring, passionate, amusing and makes the audience feel comfortable.

Props

Think of some things you can bring along that back up your story and that are interesting for people to see. I use:

- A volleyball that I wrote all my goals on after seriously injuring my knee
- My Olympic Medals

- The original Gold Medal Excellence plan that we put together to help us achieve our Gold Medal, and

- A tiny swimsuit which I pull out when I talk about overcoming fears and doubts!

You can use anything. Be creative, but make sure it's relevant.

Other Visual Aids

Just because technology is available to use, doesn't mean you need to use it. I've watched some athletes give great presentations just by using photos and videos. I use an introductory video and then I use my props.

If you're going to use a PowerPoint presentation, make sure you don't just read your slides. Include photos and if you have specific points on your slides, they should be short one-liners, from which you can expand. Avoid having lots of text on your slides, otherwise the audience will read, rather than listen to you.

Good Planning

Good planning is critical for a good presentation. Like any other endeavour, to do it well, public speaking requires time spent preparing. World Leaders spend many hours preparing for their public addresses, and most have teams working on those speeches.

However, even if you don't have your own speech preparation team, you still need to devote solid time to preparation beforehand.

Success depends upon previous preparation, and without such preparation there is sure to be failure.

Confucius, Teacher & Philosopher

Develop a checklist for presentations that you can use for each event to make sure that you don't forget anything. This should include:

- Preparation required before the day

- Everything you need to think about and take on the day itself

- After the event – sending thankyous and getting testimonials. Also, time devoted to writing a description of how the presentation went, and thoughts on how you could improve next time.

Talk to the function organiser well in advance, and if you plan to use any IT equipment, find out if you need to bring your own laptop, leads and adaptors, or if you can simply plug into their system with a USB drive. Is there a particular format your photos or videos should be saved in? Think it through and ask. Never assume.

What to wear? It's a good idea to dress professionally. If you expect your audience will wear business attire, then you should too. Even if it's a more relaxed atmosphere, you should still present yourself in a professional manner.

On the day, arrive early to familiarise yourself with the room and the amenities. If you can, make sure everything is working: the lights, the DVD player, the computer with your PowerPoint presentation, the microphone, the flip charts, and so on. More importantly, make sure you know how to work with them.

You may not be a professional speaker, but struggling with audio-visual equipment just distracts and annoys your audience. You want them on your side.

Practise standing on the stage, at the lectern and walking along the stage. Imagine the audience is there and you're speaking to them. Ensure that everyone in the room can hear you.

Have your script, your notes or your cue cards, your props and any other items for your presentation ready to go. If you're being introduced from within the crowd, decide whether you'll bring them up with you or arrange them on stage prior to the beginning of the event.

Give yourself the opportunity to meet with your audience before your presentation. I often found that audience members would start asking me questions about my journey beforehand. I would start answering, then stop, and tell them that they would have to wait for more from my speech.

This would get me really 'warmed up' and by the time I hit the stage, I felt like I'd already started and was totally at ease.

Knowing Your Material Gives You The Ultimate Confidence.

Make sure you know your presentation inside-out. Rehearse your speech out loud in full, many times beforehand. Use a digital video recorder to record yourself and watch it back. It might make you cringe at first but it's a really valuable tool to improve your performance.

Do not rehearse your speech on your audience! Peter Sheahan is a successful Entrepreneur, Best Selling Author and Public Speaker who is able to command $25,000 for a 45-minute keynote speech. But before he gives a speech of that value, he takes a complete week off and rehearses that speech for 8 hours a day, 5 days straight. That's why he earns $25,000.

Visualisation can work just as effectively in your sport as it can before public speaking. Visualise yourself doing well and giving a successful presentation. Think to yourself "I know my subject well. I have prepared myself for questions. I know how I am going to answer."

The Delivery

Try not to stand behind the lectern throughout your entire talk. It puts a barrier between you and the audience, and they feel it. However, if you're just starting out, your knees are trembling and you feel more secure standing behind the lectern, do it – just don't lean on it.

An impressive opening is a great way to instantly bond with the audience. You need to grab their attention, include them, and make them hungry for more. After my introduction video, which shows the last few points of our Olympic final, I launch straight into a really funny moment that happened not long after we were awarded the medal. It warms me up, warms the audience up and everyone laughs and wants to hear more.

You could also tell a dramatic and thought provoking story, or ask a relevant question that people can relate to: "Have you ever...."

Next, tell the audience what you are going to talk about during your presentation, and then launch into it.

Make eye contact throughout your talk. Look around the room and actually engage with individuals as you are speaking. Hold their gaze until you've finished that point or sentence. They will think that what was said was just for them.

Learn how to harness the positive energy within the group by complimenting them, smiling, and making them feel good.

Try not to just flicker around the room with your eyes. They will notice it and you will lose their attention. It may be difficult in the beginning, but it will be easier with practice.

Ensure that you pronounce things properly and that you articulate well. Take the trouble to form and express words accurately and audibly.

Remove all "ums" and "ahs" from your vocabulary. A good tip I was given once, was to just replace them with "so".

Finally, wrap it up with your keys points and if appropriate, ask for any questions. For many public speakers, the question and answer session can be the most nerve-wracking time of all. Michelle Bowden, renowned Australian Public Speaker and Influencer recommends the following 4 steps to ensuring a really warm and positive question session:

- Acknowledge the question and thank the person asking

- Paraphrase the question in your own words so that everyone in the room can hear

- Answer the question

- Ask the person if that answers their question

After the question and answer session, thank the audience for their time, and finish with a strong close.

> **Tip: Learn it, burn it**
> Practise your opening and your closing until you know them word for word. These are two of the most crucial moments of your presentation: getting the audience's interest and then leaving them with something to remember you by.

Get A Great Testimonial

At every opportunity, after every public speaking event, ask for a testimonial. You won't always get one, but often you will.

You can use testimonials on your website, business proposals, marketing collateral, business cards and in many other places. Testimonials are especially valuable because they offer an independent opinion of your talent, and people reading them tend to have more faith in others' opinions. It's also great to have testimonials from high profile clients or companies as these may influence other prospective clients.

Follow up any conversations on the night with a thankyou email on the next business day. This gives you the opportunity to also ask for the testimonial again when they are at their desk and more likely to be ready to write it.

Dale Beaumont, International Bestselling Author and Entrepreneur suggests this formula for getting great testimonials. Send the person an email and very kindly ask if they would mind giving you some feedback on the following questions (don't use the word 'testimonial' as it can put some people off responding):

- Were you unsure about engaging me?
- What made you decide to use me?
- What specific benefits did you get?
- Who would you recommend me to? And, why?

Once you have their replies, you can then edit and summarise their four answers and send it back to them to approve. Ask them if they would mind if you use their feedback in your marketing material and on your website. Also ask if they would mind sending a photo of themselves to be used next to their feedback so people can see that they are a real person.

> ### YOU'RE NEVER TOO OLD
>
> I really do love motivational speaking now – sharing my story and the lessons I've learnt along the way. It's a great feeling to know that I'm motivating and inspiring others.
>
> The most rewarding comment I've ever received was from a lovely older woman at an International Women's Day breakfast. She was around 70 years old and came up to me after the presentation and told me that she was so inspired, that it gave her reason to keep on running!!!
>
> To inspire someone twice my age, with twice as many years' experience in this world makes me feel pretty good.

Spreading The Word

When you first start out, even getting a gig can seem daunting. Building your experience is the key to success. Try speaking to a wide variety of groups.

Offer to speak for free to Schools, Charities, Rotary Clubs, Men's Clubs, Women's Breakfasts and so on. No matter what your age or experience, it will really help to build your confidence and refine your presentation.

Once you have done this for a while, and have collected some great testimonials and know that you are improving, then you can list a price and get a profile with all the Speaking Bureaus in your country. I am listed with about 20 Speaking Bureaus in Australia that I update with newsletters at least every six months. This keeps them informed and helps to ensure I am in the forefront of their mind. That way, when a client calls and they need a speaker, they will hopefully think: "Kerri would be good for that."

Referrals are one of the best ways of spreading the word, especially in the business community. Be proactive about actively asking for referrals. Ask everyone!

I include 'Motivational Speaker' on my business card and I am always telling people that I am a Speaker. I am also an MC, opening up more opportunities for work.

Being punctual and organised is really important, and will be noticed by the client. You are much more likely to get booked by the Bureau again if a client finds you easy to work with and professional. Once you have the appreciative testimonials, you'll be unstoppable!

> *The goal of effective communication should be for listeners to say, "Me, too!" versus "So what?" Learn to express, not impress.*
>
> **Jim Rohn,** Business Philosopher

KEY POINTS

Volunteer to speak for free so that you can practise and build up your confidence.

Prepare, prepare, prepare.

Be yourself. Make it interesting for your audience and enjoy it.

Follow up afterwards.

CHAPTER 17
MEDIA

Press coverage and publicity are great ways to build your brand. They increase awareness, broaden your target audience and draw attention to your talent.

As a professional athlete, the media will become part of your life. The amount of media you attract could be a deal-maker (or breaker) for a potential sponsor. In this chapter, we'll explore ways you can sway the media to help you, rather than work against you.

Remember, you are a role model – on and off the field. People are watching you and your behaviour. The way you react when competing and when being interviewed says a lot about your true character.

Ask, And Ye Shall Receive

My number one strategy for increasing media exposure: ask for it!

Start with your local newspaper and radio station. These media outlets need stories. It's an area where my success rate was almost 100%. I simply picked up the phone or sent out a media release with a strong angle, making it impossible for the media to ignore.

The key is to ensure there is value for the media in your story. Why would your story make someone interested to look at their paper?

Work Out A Strong Angle

When you approach the media, you need an 'angle'. You need a reason for them to be writing the story on you – a special event, a slant or spin on a particular situation, a hook that gets them interested and one that their readers would find fascinating.

If you just emailed the media with: "Hi, I'm Joe and I'd like you to write a story on me.." chances are, they won't bother. Some journalists receive hundreds of emails a day and they don't have time to figure out who you are or what the story might be.

Make it easy for them, and come up with something interesting yourself. Read the sports section and watch the sports news in your area to see the kinds of angles that are used to write stories about other athletes and their teams. Could yours be a 'human interest' story?

A good angle might be, for example:

- If you're about to leave the country to compete in an International event

- If you've just won an event or a special award

- If you've just been selected for a team or squad

- If you've had to overcome an injury and you're now back, fit and raring to go

- If you've just been struck with an injury and you've got weeks or months ahead of you to rehabilitate and you're determined to make it back.

- If you have a family member competing in the same sport and you have to compete against them.

- Relating your story to a current relevant news topic. For example, if there is a heatwave on right now, your angle might be about what you are doing to deal with it and how you will be better than the competition on the day.

- The media love surveys. Set up your own survey on your sport using a free site like www.surveymonkey.com and report the findings to the media.

Be specific in your angle and work out your message and consider the target audience of that media.

A great journalist friend of mine, Judy Goldman, who has worked in various parts of the media for over 20 years, says it's the '-est factor' – the biggest, newest, sexiest, fastest, best, oldest, youngest, and so on. Think about your angle and find one that works for the message you want to get across.

Write A Press Release That Gets Attention

A press release (also known as a media release, news release or press statement) is a written document sent to journalists in order to obtain free publicity. Releases can also be sent to editors, or producers at newspapers, magazines, radio stations and television departments.

Want to get your press release noticed? Make sure you:

- **Focus on one great angle.** The journalist isn't interested in helping you make money or drive visitors to your site. They are looking for a story of interest to their audience. Don't clutter it with too many angles. Keep it simple.

- **Use a catchy headline.** This should be your most exciting piece of information or news. Write it like the headlines you see in the newspaper every day. You have 15 seconds to grab their attention. Your headline and first few sentences will determine whether they read further or your release ends up in the bin with the 300 others they have received that day.

    Download examples of media headlines that you can use at www.thebusinessofbeinganathlete.com

- **The lead paragraph should include the who, what, when, where and how of the story.** If the reporter were only to read this, he'd have everything he needed to get started. It must capture his attention enough for him to read further. For example this could be:

    "Joe Smith, rising star of Rugby League is one step closer to his dream of being signed by a major team, after scoring three tries in Manly's 18-12 win over rivals Balmain last night."

- Following the lead paragraph, the rest of the release **expands on the claims** you have made in your heading and introduction. Use quotes (you can quote yourself) or an expert to add credibility to, or develop your angle.

- **Stick to the facts.** No exaggeration, no selling, just facts.

- **Write in the 'third' person** as if someone else is writing the story about you, never use 'I' or 'we'.

- **Use clear, simple language.** Avoid jargon, waffle and phrases that may not mean anything to the reader. The same applies with acronyms – unless you are talking about something that's universally well known.

- **Use 12pt font, and 1.5 spaces** between the lines.

- **Try to make your point in one page or less.** The shorter, the better.

- **Include a sentence or two describing yourself and your journey** (assuming they don't know you).

- **Add all your contact details at the bottom,** along with links to your website and blog, or social media pages, in case they need further information.

Think Up A Visual

Next, think of a photo opportunity that could accompany the story. If you have a photo already, it must be good quality, and you must own the copyright (or get permission from the photographer to use it).

Every little idea helps when getting media involved. If you come up with an interesting idea for a picture, the media might turn up and give it greater prominence in the local paper or even TV!

Send, Then Follow Up – Get On The Phone!

Proofread your release, read it out aloud and have a friend or colleague do the same. Edit, check and re-check before you hit send! Once it's out there, you can't get it back.

> *Tip: If emailing to a group, always 'blind copy' their email addresses.* This is for courtesy and privacy. But it's fine to send the same release to different contacts.

Finally, follow it up. Don't be shy. Like all aspects of business, dealing with the media is about building relationships.

Decide which media outlet you would most like to run your story. The larger, higher profile media, in particular TV, will usually want to be the first to report something, or to have an exclusive on your story. If you want them to run it, follow up with them first. If they say no, then try your next preferred media on the list and so on. Follow up at least the top five on your list.

When you call them, don't simply ask if they received your media release. Instead, tell them something new and exciting – a development or angle not included in the release.

For example, your conversation could go something like this:

> "Hi John, its Kerri Pottharst, Beach Volleyball player. How are you? …. I'm just calling to confirm that you received the media release I sent to you this morning (or "yesterday", depending on the urgency of the release)
>
> ……. Great. Well, I'd like to add that since I sent that out, there's been a new development. Natalie and I have booked our tickets to the World Championships and we leave next week!

...... Yes, we qualified and we're set to join 25 other countries in the battle for the World Title. We are around all day tomorrow, training at Bondi Beach, if you'd like to send a photographer down to get some photos?"

All journalists love an exclusive, and the local press is no exception. However, they may run a version of the story even if it's been reported on TV or elsewhere.

You may get more exposure through a television journalist rather than doing an interview with your local paper. You may, however, need to work with your local paper for many years to come and so it's important to keep them on side.

If you are approached by more than one journalist interested in covering your story, be open with all parties involved from the outset. Let them know if someone else is running the story. If they aren't directly competing media or if one is very high profile, and one much lower profile, then it's possible the two stories could compliment each other and the result could be positive for everyone.

Don't Give Up

Don't be discouraged if your press release isn't used. It's not personal. You don't know what else is happening in the newsroom on any given day. The key here is perseverance.

If they say no, they don't have time or they're not interested, thank them, try not to take it personally and hide your disappointment. Try again later, when you have another interesting item of news or another angle.

It's just like when you're playing your sport. If you miss a goal or a shot, you don't give up. You try again, and again, and again, until you get it right. Trust me, persistence pays!

If you do keep trying with the media, they'll be so impressed with your persistence they may eventually cover the story – even if it's a story about how persistent you are! Their angle might be that if you're this persistent about getting media, imagine how persistent you will be in winning Gold!!

> ### LET'S TALK
>
> I lived in Perth in the lead up to the 1996 Olympic Games, and I was relentless when it came to letting the media know everything we were doing.
>
> Once, they even wrote a story about the fact that I always contacted them personally – not through a manager or a PR agent. They loved it and it made a nice story.
>
> Of course, there was a photo with the story and we made sure we had our sponsor's logos on our clothing!

Build Great Relationships With The Media

Consider the media as allies. They can help you win – sponsorship, career goals, and possibly provide opportunities for other career paths later in life. The following practices have worked for me:

- **Keep a record of media contacts and their networks.** Add your own notes so that you know who reported you fairly and got your message across and who tried to put their own spin on things. This will help with your preparation next time around or help you determine which ones to contact if you need to break a story yourself.

  You may also like to record something personal about them: how many kids they have, where they live, their interests, and so forth. This will enable you to relate to them and remind them of your relationship when you next speak to them.

- **Be friendly, positive and easy to deal with.** Journalists will be more receptive and you'll be more likely to receive coverage.

- **Send them regular updates on your progress.** This will eventually lead to more media, especially if you're in the forefront of their minds.

- **Always return phone calls and do it straight away.** If the media is calling you for a comment or a story, they will often have deadlines to meet, so be prompt in responding. It's also courteous and shows you're reliable and professional.

- **Be on time if you are invited for an interview.**

- **Contact the media directly with ideas for stories or articles.** They can't possibly know everything about you or what's going on with your sport. Let them know and at least give them the opportunity to do a story. Believe me, they appreciate it.

Bob Hart
Well Bolle me over, it's Kerri

Herald Sun, Thursday, November 9, 2000

EXOTIC attire is not unknown at Flemington. But Olympic gold medallist Kerri Pottharst will definitely elevate eyebrows when she hits the track today.

The beach volleyball champ's Oaks Day ensemble is an eye-popper — crafted from more than 250 Bolle sunglass lenses.

"I'm really, really happy with it," she told me yesterday at her final fitting.

"I spend most of my life in outfits briefer than this, so wearing it to the races doesn't bother me.

"I'm quite used to bouncing around in front of 10,000 people in a swimsuit, so this is really quite refined."

Indeed it is. The startling outfit was put together by Windsor designer William Eicholtz.

It was commissioned by Bolle, the US-owned sunglass company that has sponsored Ms Pottharst for a decade and today will sponsor a horse race — their first.

"It's very important to us," said Bolle spokeswoman Trudy Morrison.

"As far as we know, there's never been a race in Australia sponsored by a sunglass company, so we want to make it memorable."

They already have. Because in addition to paying for Ms Pottharst's racing togs, Bolle offered to fit all horses in the Bolle Stakes — an 1800m gallop for listed three-year-olds — with designer blinkers.

This generous offer was politely declined by the VRC.

So instead, to emphasise the protective qualities of their products, the company has recruited six models — three male and three female — to hand out 7000 condoms at Flemington.

"We know that's not enough for everybody," Ms Morrison said. "But we hope it will help."

Ms Pottharst, incidentally, is a turf convert.

"I went to my first Melbourne Cup this week and I loved it," she said.

"But I didn't dress up, so I think I'll like the Oaks even more."

And so shall we, Kerri. So shall we.

Eyes up: Kerri Pottharst in her Bolle dress. Picture: JAY TOWN

Ok, maybe the silliest thing I ever did - wearing a dress made out of (Bolle) sunglasses to the races!

- **Make yourself available to the media.** Become their 'go-to' person for comments about both the men's and women's side of your sport, other sports, and general sporting issues in the media. Become the authority or refer people you know who are reliable and will give them a great story. They will come back to you again for more leads.

- **Be flexible.** You don't know the priorities a journalist or their producer may have and their work is very deadline driven. They need time to fit you into their schedule, and even more time if they need to get a film or camera crew to accompany them. If you are able to adapt to their schedule and help them out, they may well run your story on another day or at another time.

- **Media craves pictures and vision.** Start your own library of good quality High Definition footage (HD – if possible 16/9 wide screen) of you in action. There are many hand-held personal video cameras available now that can shoot broadcast-quality images for TV, as long as it's in focus. This is particularly important if you are suggesting a story that has happened in the past or one due to happen locally or overseas. Offering good quality video footage for TV or stills for print media could often be the difference between the media running your story or not, even if you do have a great angle.

When the photographer for this story suggested that he bury me in the sand with only one hand and my head sticking out, I thought it sounded fun and knew it would make the papers! (I also still managed to get two of my sponsors in the shot - Bolle Sunglasses and Animal watches)

- **Feel free to contact a journalist who has written a great story about you and thank them.** They will appreciate the feedback and you will make a good contact who is more likely to report your stories in a positive light in future.

- On the other hand, **if you have been reported inaccurately or misrepresented,** report it through your manager/agent or your sports governing body. Depending on the circumstance it may be appropriate to contact the journalist in question directly, to firmly but politely discuss your side of the story. Remember though, it is the journalist's boss (the editor, sub-editor, chief of staff or producer) who will have usually have final say over what is included.

Exclusives – A Word Of Warning

If you agree to give an exclusive interview or story to a particular media company, whether print or TV, it's in your interest to ensure this story is not reported elsewhere before the exclusive has gone to print or air.

Be open and up front if someone else approaches you for a story after you have agreed to an exclusive. Ask the media that is reporting the exclusive whether they mind another media outlet covering your story (and when it would go to air).

If you do agree to an interview and then later turn them down because something better comes along, then be prepared that the initial media outlet may not want to work with you in future.

It's also worth considering the reputation of the media outlet you are choosing. Some athletes, with credibility issues at stake, may prefer an ethical programme that does not pay fees. For others, the cash incentive may be very high on the list of priorities.

If cash is being paid for a story, there will always be a contract to sign so read it carefully to ensure that you fully understand what's involved. Always get a lawyer to check it.

Be aware that if you agree verbally to a contract, but then pursue a better offer, your reputation will quickly spread to other media, who may pass on you later. Be honest, open, up front and behave professionally.

Here's a true story of exclusivity gone wrong. A high profile international athlete was visiting Sydney and his PR Company had arranged a major TV station to do a ten-minute exclusive piece on him including interviews and action footage, to go to air on Wednesday that week. It was a great opportunity and would have given him some excellent exposure.

However, the day before this piece went to air, he gave another TV station a very brief interview, and the station put those 20 seconds of footage to air that night. On seeing this, the original TV station decided to pull their ten-minute story as the 'exclusive' nature of the story was ruined – the athlete had already spoken to someone else who had put the story to air.

It would have been far better for the athlete to turn down the request from the second media outlet to ensure that the 10-minute story went to air as planned.

Media Interviews

Like public speaking, a media interview can go terribly wrong if you don't spend the time beforehand planning, and thinking through what you might say. If you know you are going to be interviewed, ask:

- Why did they choose you? This gives you a good idea of your reputation in the media.

- What time will it start? Usually the media have very tight deadlines. Allow enough time for traffic and be on time or early. Only agree to the interview if you know you can meet their deadline but be reasonable and try to help if you can, or they may not ask again.

- How long will it last? If the interview will be 20 minutes, you need to do much more preparation than if it was for 2 minutes.

- Who else is being interviewed? This allows you to prepare for who else is at the interview and also allows you to say no to the interview if there are people involved that you don't want to be associated with.

- What's the angle? Ask them to email you the details of what the story will be about and ask as many questions as you need to feel comfortable about their angle and whether or not you want to be involved.

- The journalist, researcher or producer may not give you an exact list of questions, but there's no harm in asking what the first question will be. Find out the type of questions likely to be asked.

- Who will be conducting the interview? Try to get a brief background or research them to see some of their other work and previous experience. Is their style softer or more investigative, or hard line? This just allows you to be prepared for the type of questions they may ask.

- Where will the interview take place? Get the address, and access and parking details. Ask for a phone number in case there is an emergency hold-up. Who will you meet and where?

- Will it be recorded or live? Doing an interview live can seem more nerve wracking but it allows you to get your exact message across in your own words. Recorded interviews can be easier but they will probably edit your responses and may not use much of what you say.

Practice, practice, practice! Think about how you might answer their questions. Have a friend ask you the type of questions you are likely to be asked and respond as if you were in the real interview. Write some phrases down if it helps you.

Give quality answers and expand on them so you give the interviewer more than they want, not less. However, it's important when it actually comes to the interview, to sound natural and not to read your answers.

Work on concise, interesting, sentences. The media, especially television, will often use a very short 'grab' of your response. So, if you've got a special message to get across such as when and where you'll be competing next, or a plug for one of your sponsors, keep it short and sweet, write it out, practise it and use it on air.

This following example shows how you can work a message into your answer. You want to get in a plug for your new sponsor, Jim's Electrical Services, and the question you've been asked is how you think you'll go this weekend in your National Championship. Your answer could be:

"We are really looking forward to this weekend's event at the National Championships. We have been training hard and thanks to Jim's Electrical Services, we have been able to analyse our performances using some amazing new technology they have provided. It has enhanced our training and we are looking forward to some great results."

Use 'self-contained' sentences. Sometimes due to time constraints or other reasons, the media may not want to include the interviewer asking the question every time. They might prefer to use your answer on its own. Using self-contained sentences ensures that when the final version is edited, your answer will contain enough information for your audience to understand irrespective of whether they hear the question. Responding like this also means it's much harder for your response to be edited out of context. For example:

What not to do

Interviewer: "How did the event in Thailand go?"

Answer: "Yeah, it was great, and we were pleased with our results."

This answer does not make sense unless you hear the interviewer's question beforehand. It is also very generic and doesn't promote how well you did at the tournament. Maybe you would have been pleased if you'd come 10th.

Much better

Interviewer: "How did the event in Thailand go?"

Answer: "The event in Thailand was fantastic and we were able to achieve our goal of making the Final."

This answer would make sense, even without hearing the question beforehand. It is also specific in that it talks about your goal and what you achieved.

If you are inexperienced or young, ask if you can bring someone with you – perhaps your coach, manager or a parent. They may be allowed to take a photo or two that you can use when you next update your website and social media pages.

Be honest and direct. If you don't know the answer to a question, say you will find out and get back to them. Avoid lying, making things up or exaggerating. It will inevitably come back to haunt you.

Take your time and listen carefully to the questions. We all tend to rush when we're nervous or excited, so breathe deeply before you start and slow down.

Never, ever put down your opposition. Always respect your opponents – on and off the field. Criticizing them will only ever result in you looking like a poor loser (if you do lose) or a very unappealing winner. If asked to comment on your opponent, be kind and appreciative of their efforts.

Keep your answers to the point and be succinct. Don't be afraid of silence. The interviewer may be trying to draw more out of you by keeping quiet after you have answered. If you have finished making your point, let them fill the silence, not you.

Don't be afraid to steer the interview if necessary, to bring it back to the points *you want to focus on.*

Try to appear confident even if you are feeling nervous. Shake hands. Make eye contact when you meet the interviewer and throughout the interview. Sound interested in their questions and engage them with your answers. Try to make it more conversational.

Be energetic, animated and enthusiastic. You are more likely to get asked to do more media interviews if you are engaging and easy to watch and listen to. Even if you are feeling shy or nervous, for the purpose of the interview, make a huge effort to vary the tone of your voice and appear enthusiastic about your sport and the message you want to get across.

Avoid using jargon. People listening to you may not be familiar with the acronyms for your sport's governing body or technical terms from within your sport.

Don't feel you need to answer 'what if' questions. You don't have a crystal ball and it's easy to get caught out trying to predict what may or may not happen in the future.

Try to avoid answering closed questions with just "yes" or "no". Always expand on your answer and give personal anecdotes or examples when you can. It will help your audience to relate to you.

Avoid speaking on someone else's behalf. If you are asked what someone else thinks about something, feel free to say politely, "You'll need to ask them about that."

Prepare for controversy. While you hopefully won't ever be in a controversial or confrontational interview, it's best to plan for it, so you know how you would answer if someone asks you a tricky question. Think of all the things you would not like to be asked about, whether in your personal life or within your sport. Decide how you would answer and practice your response. Think about what you will say if you are asked about drugs in your sport or another highly controversial athlete. Practice your reply. You can politely decline a question by saying "I'd rather not answer that at this time", or 'deflect' a question with a response such as "That is a really interesting point/question but did you know..." If you do deflect, be prepared for the journalist to ask you the same question again and again if they really want your answer.

Dress appropriately. If you aren't sure, ask what the dress code is. Even for radio or press interviews, you should always appear professional.

No matter how agitated you may be feeling on the inside, **always remain calm and try to avoid appearing defensive during an interview.** Just explain your side of things in clear, concise language. Some journalists will employ tactics to throw you off track or get you to say something you hadn't intended. Just keep your cool and don't take the bait!

You may also like to ask when it will be published or go to air so you can record a copy of it for your own records, website and blogs.

Dealing With Nerves

It is completely normal to feel nervous when dealing with the media, especially at first.

It does get much easier with practice as you become more aware of what they are likely to ask and how you will reply.

Role-play interviews with friends or teammates for practice, before doing the real interview. Taking it seriously and knowing how you will phrase your answers will definitely help with your nerves.

Some formal media training can also build your confidence. Many sports governing bodies have great media training opportunities. Find out what's available, and learn.

There are some great tips on dealing with nerves in the chapter: Public Speaking. The same principles apply.

> **KEY POINTS**
>
> Remember, there are many sports out there and many other athletes. You need to stand out in the crowd (in a good and interesting way – not in a controversial way!)
>
> Be creative, be different and be yourself. And we'll see you in the media.

And, sometimes you never quite know what the media is going to print! (Luckily I've never had a bad experience with the media. It's all been great exposure and lots of fun.)

Getting used to the media attention straight after our Gold Medal win

CHAPTER 18
DEALING WITH FANS

From the moment your sporting career begins to gain momentum, people will be watching you. It could be an aspiring junior player, a potential sponsor or even a talent spotter – wondering if you have what it takes to move up a level.

Before you know it, fans will start approaching you, wanting to chat, take photos, or ask for your autograph. How you handle yourself off the field will also be noticed, and you need to remember that, like it or not, you are a role model.

> *No I do not find this (signing autographs) annoying, for me this is a joy to give something back to my fans.*
>
> **Roger Federer**, Tennis Champion

By being a good role model, you can help others to achieve success in their own lives, as well as advance the success in yours.

- Be respectful and gracious at all times.
- Smile and ask their name.

- Talk directly to them and make it personal, make them feel good. They are just approaching you because they like what you do. If appropriate, ask them if they like or play your sport.

Signing autographs at a staff visit for one of my lifelong sponsors, Hamilton Sunscreen

- If they ask for an autograph, use their name and dedicate it to them.

- Always try to stay until the last autograph.

- Consider producing autograph cards with a couple of great pictures and some info about you. Fans love them! See an example of mine in the chapter: Developing your Marketing Tools.

- If you are approached when you are out with family or friends, you must still be courteous and polite. If they ask for your autograph, the same rules apply. If they want to keep chatting, politely let them know that you need to return to your group.

- Most people have a phone with camera and video capabilities. Bear in mind that while someone is approaching you, someone else might be taking a photo or videoing you. Ensure that what they capture shows you in a good light.

- If you are in a social setting, such as a restaurant, and people are glancing over and whispering, feel free to get up and introduce yourself. This takes a bit of courage, but pushing yourself out of your comfort zone is good practise for your sport! Those people will then be left with a great impression and you'll have won a few more fans.

- Thank them for saying hello and wish them luck for the future, especially if they're kids who are playing your sport.

- Consider making a promotional item as a giveaway for your fans. We had mini volleyballs made with our names, sponsors' logos and website address printed on them, and we threw them out into the crowd after matches. They only cost a couple of dollars each (which the sponsors covered anyway), and the crowd loved them.

- Set up a Facebook page and update it regularly with info aimed directly at your fans. See the chapter: Developing your Marketing Tools.

- Update Twitter so fans can keep in touch with where you are and what you're up to.

- Include a fan forum or opportunity for fans to ask you questions on your website.

- Work with the fans and be proactive when an opportunity arises. If you are getting asked the same thing over and over, post something about it on your blog, website or Facebook page.

- Be courteous but cautious when socialising with fans. Keep it on a professional level and be aware that there will no doubt be a photograph or video taken of you at some point. Think about where it could end up. Always conduct yourself professionally.

As you become more well-known and your profile grows, you will most likely become used to the extra attention. You will learn which approaches work best for you.

However, at every level of sport, there are those athletes who love being the centre of attention and those who would rather hide in the corner. The fact that people recognise you is a by-product of your success, even if it puts you outside your comfort zone. If this sounds like you, consider how much courage it might have taken the person who approached you to even come and say hi. Try and forget about your anxieties, and focus on their courage. Smile, say hello, and it will make their day.

I try to always stay until the last autograph

In his book *Jonah – My Story*, Rugby legend Jonah Lomu recalls how his life changed forever after his sudden rise to immense fame after the 1995 World Cup. He felt like his life had been abruptly ripped away from him and he wasn't at all prepared for life in the spotlight.

All of a sudden he was being recognised walking down the street or eating in restaurants and he didn't handle it well. In addition to the fans there was also the media attention, and having to deal with their constant requests. Jonah was only 20 when he returned from the 1995 World Cup and he found this extremely difficult. His manager Phil Kingsley Jones, a former stand up comedian, worked with Jonah on ways to handle the media and dealing with the fan frenzy. The senior management on the tour also kept

Jonah away from the media spotlight as much as they could, allowing him to concentrate on his playing.

There will always be someone that you can learn from to help you through difficult times. If you find yourself suddenly thrust into the spotlight or unsure of how to handle certain situations, then try to find others who have already been there, and learn from them.

> **KEY POINTS**
>
> Be a good role model.
>
> Be courteous, friendly and respectful towards fans.

200 THE BUSINESS OF BEING AN ATHLETE

Family and friends enjoy our win. My nephew says it all - No. 1!

CHAPTER 19
ON THE ROAD

Travel is time consuming and costly. But it's obviously a necessity if you want to compete on the world stage.

For many athletes, being away from home becomes the norm, and the costs associated with travelling to compete can take a large chunk out of the annual budget.

Having travelled to compete at 92 FIVB World Beach Volleyball Tour events, 20 International Indoor Volleyball events, and spending one season of Professional Indoor Volleyball in Italy, let me tell you, until you can afford First Class and Five Star, there are many ways you can make the journey more bearable.

Flights

Rule number one: Find a great Travel Agent!

This will literally save you hours of time, and potentially a lot of money. Your Travel Agent makes a commission from your bookings so it's in their interest to help you.

Booking your trips on a regular basis will allow a Travel Agent to get to know you and your schedule and the time of day you like to arrive. They can allow for jet lag, training, matches, and assist you with changing your flights. Once you know them well, it's much easier to communicate with them via email and text messages. This can make a big difference when you're in a different time zone.

So if you don't have a Manager to do it for you, find a Travel Agent who is a happy to take care of all the details. Trying to do this yourself can be extremely time consuming and expensive while you are on the road.

If your Travel Agent isn't helpful or is unable to meet your needs – then find a new one! Get recommendations from other athletes.

Luggage

We used to be able to travel with up to 32kgs or 70lbs of luggage, hassle free. A quick smile at the check-in desk was often enough to get us through. Now, however, baggage weight limits are vigorously enforced. Most airlines only allow 20kgs/44lbs. If you have Silver or Gold status, you may be allowed more weight.

The safest measure is to check each airline's website for restrictions and abide by them. Otherwise you'll be facing considerable excess baggage costs.

Usually you are allowed only one piece of carry-on luggage which must be within a certain size and weight. This is especially true for the smaller airlines that fly within Europe or the United States.

However, it is possible that some airlines will be lenient if there is a note on the system mentioning that you are representing your country at an International Sporting event. Ask your travel agent to add that comment to your booking. It may help.

I found that having the following works best:

Check-in
- 1 large suitcase with wheels

Carry-on
- 1 small rolling bag (small bag on wheels), containing my computer, all my paperwork, cameras, hard drive and other valuable items. Check airlines for maximum dimensions.
- Depending on the airline, you may be allowed an additional laptop bag as well as your small rolling suitcase. Check before you set off to the airport. You can also have one normal-sized handbag as handbags don't count as carry-on bags and they don't get weighed. Pick one with an easy to use side pocket for all your travel documents.

> *Tip: Keep a spare set close at hand*
> Always pack life's essentials in your carry-on bag: an extra playing uniform, a pair of undies or whatever you feel you can't live one day without, as your luggage can sometimes go astray for a day or two.

Travelling with any more luggage makes moving around difficult. Any less would certainly be easier, but probably not possible if you're travelling for weeks at a time.

Keep photocopies of your main passport page and credit cards in a couple of different spots throughout your luggage. If your passport and/or cards are lost or stolen, the copies will make it much easier to replace them. If your bag is misplaced, it's more likely to be returned to you if a photocopy of your passport is inside. It is also a good idea to leave a copy of your passport with friends or family back home.

Frequent Flyer Points
Racking up Frequent Flyer points is one of the benefits of frequently travelling the globe as an elite athlete. Try to book all or most of your flights within the same group of airlines such as Star Alliance, One World or a

similar group in your country. This will ensure that you can then use the miles on future bookings with the airlines within that group.

Also, and perhaps more importantly, if you reach a certain number of miles you can qualify for Silver, Gold or Platinum status, which gives you special benefits.

For the most part of my athletic career I was a Gold member with One World, which entitled me to free membership with the Qantas Club and other airline lounges in the One World group. It made waiting around in airports *so* much more comfortable as we were able to get online, check emails, update flights, contact loved ones, eat, drink and often shower for free.

With Silver and Gold status, you're also able to jump queues and check-in with Business Class passengers (unless you're already lucky enough to pay for that class ticket!) and avoid all that waiting. You'll really appreciate this when you're tired or injured after events.

Time On Your Hands
Sitting around airports, in lounges, on planes, trains or buses is an ideal time to plan, strategise, and learn. I often used this time to review how we went in the previous tournament and plan ahead for the next event.

I also used to read a lot. When I first started competing, I read fiction more than anything with a 'self development' type title. That's one regret I have – that I could have learned so much more, so much earlier. It was only towards the end of my competing days that I started to bring books on tour that actually taught me something.

In The Air
Don't arrive looking tired and haggard. There are lots of things you can do to ensure that you get to your destination in the best possible shape:

- Make sure you wear comfy clothing – track pants/leggings or loose jeans, and always take a jacket as flights can get quite cold, especially if you're sitting next to exits.

- Some athletes rave about the benefits of skin-tight compression leggings, like Skins. Skins maintain healthy circulation and minimise swelling and dehydration – the primary cause of jetlag – during forced periods of inactivity.

- Try isometric exercises while you're sitting. Squeeze and contract different muscle groups and hold for as long as you can. Do leg extensions if you have the leg room or anything you can do to keep the circulation going.

- Abstain from eating fatty foods, and drinking alcohol or caffeine while flying. Pop a few extra vitamin C's for the trip just to help your immune system fight any bugs picked up through the air conditioning.

- Drink, drink, drink lots of water. Even if it means you'll be up and down visiting the bathroom. You simply cannot hydrate enough when flying. It will aid in recovery when you land and help stave off headaches, stomach problems, cramps and fatigue.

- Try downloading a few podcasts to your MP3 player before you leave. There are loads of them around, on all different areas of interest. If you're travelling alone for a while, a podcast or two will keep you company.

Sleeping (Or At Least Getting Comfortable) On Flights

I've tried all kinds of ways to get comfortable on long haul flights.

I've tried exit rows, booking the end of the back row (hoping that no one sits next to me and I can have the entire row to lie down), aisle seats and window seats.

It only took ten years to work out the answer – bring my pillow from home!

I still try to get a free seat or two next to me, but if I can't, I just ask for a window seat and shove my pillow (normal sized pillow from my bed at home) against the wall and imagine that I'm in my bed. I have two pillowcases on it. One for travel, that can get a bit dirty at times, and one underneath for when I arrive at the hotel.

That way I also have my favourite pillow to sleep with at the hotel instead of the hard or super soft ones that are often provided. It's easy to carry as I slip it over my rolling carry-on bag handle, and hold onto the cover as I walk with my computer!

Don't forget a good set of earplugs (for those screaming kids or pesky neighbours) and an eye mask if light bothers you.

If you simply cannot sleep, then make sure bring your own comfortable headphones. The ones provided on planes are often poor quality and if you have your own noise-cancelling headphones, you'll probably fall asleep anyway as they are so comforting!

Avoid Catching An Airline Cold

Most commercial airlines fly in an elevation range of 30,000 to 35,000 feet, where humidity typically runs at 10 percent or lower. At very low levels of humidity, the 'natural defence system' of mucus in our nose and throat dries up, creating a wonderful breeding ground for germs. This protective system is your first line of defence against harmful germs and bacteria, so you need to be on guard, and keep the nasties at bay.

- **Stay hydrated.** Drinking plenty of water will actually strengthen your natural immune system. Sip water regularly throughout the flight. Nasal mists have also been found to be very effective in hydrating the nose. Hot drinks are another good way to keep your protective mucous membranes working – firstly, to assist in keeping you generally hydrated; secondly, by triggering the system into gear; and thirdly, by directly providing moisture in the form of steam. Note that this is not a treatment it's just a suggestion to keep your defences strong and functioning.

- **Keep your hands clean.** Your hands are the most consistent first point of contact with the common cold, flu and other germs. Research shows that the type of virus that causes the common cold and the flu has been found to survive for up to 3 hours on your skin or on objects such as armrests, TV remote control handsets, tray tables and similar surfaces. However, the simple act of washing your hands with hot water and soap guards against you carrying these germs to your mouth and nose.

  If possible, wash your hands before all meals and after your flight as well. There are many anti-bacterial wipes and cleansers on the market that don't require water. Keep one handy in the seat pocket in front of you.

- **Take your vitamins.** It's not proven that taking large doses of vitamin C will prevent colds, but it may reduce the severity or duration of symptoms.

- **Wear a facemask.** If you're really serious about not catching a cold and your sport depends on your exact state of health, then the most proven way to avoid a cold is by using a facemask. It might be uncomfortable, but so is losing the opportunity to stand on the podium!

Recovering From Jetlag

As soon as you board, try to adjust to the time zone that you're landing in. Change your watch. If it's night time there, try to sleep. If it's daytime for a few more hours, rest, eat lightly, read and sleep when you normally would if you were there. You might even start preparing for the new time zone in your last couple of days at home if that's practical.

If you arrive in the morning, resist the urge to nap. Try to stay awake until evening mealtime, at least.

Do some light exercise and get lots of fresh air outside, in daylight. If you can't survive without a nap, have one for an hour, no longer.

Insurance

Don't leave home without travel insurance – whether you're travelling within your own country or overseas.

Over the years, I've had cameras, jewellery and even some beach volleyballs stolen while in transit or staying in hotels. One of our coaches was held up on the beach in Rio while going for a run and had to hand over his wallet. You never know what, when or where you could lose something or have something stolen.

It will also cover you for illness, accident and injury (but not while competing in your sport).

You can get single trip insurance or take out a yearly policy, which I did most years as I was travelling so much. And, don't forget it's tax deductible so you'll get part of it back.

Eating Well

Those of you with specific diets might find eating on the road challenging. The best thing you can do is to take as much of your special food with you and research ahead of time what you can buy at your destination.

Examples of this may be recovery food, especially food high in protein. Pack your suitcase with tins of tuna, nuts and protein drinks. They were amongst my favourites.

I've included many more tips about eating whilst on the road in the chapter: Nutrition.

Accommodation

There are plenty of options for accommodation, and the Internet makes it easy to research them before you go. Depending on your needs and your budget, consider:

- Where are the other athletes staying?

- How far is your accommodation from the airport you are flying into? Does your accommodation or the event provide free transfers from the airport? If not, how will you get there? What are the travel times and costs of public transport or a taxi?

- How far is your accommodation from your training and competition grounds?

- What transport (if any) is provided to/from your accommodation to matches/practice and how often? If no transport is provided, what are your alternatives? Car hire (check out parking options at your accommodation and parking at the event venues) or public transport?

- Are there secure areas to store valuables?

- What part of town is your hotel in? Will you feel safe getting to and from your accommodation early in the morning or late at night?

- If you are worried about how noisy your accommodation will be, ask how busy it will be at the time you will be there. There is no harm in asking if your room could be situated in a quiet area of the hotel, as far as possible from any major noise sources such as reception, restaurants and dance floors.

- Is food provided at the accommodation? Ask to see a menu and ask them to clarify dishes if you don't know what they are.

Here are some of the pros and cons of the different options:

Type of accommodation	Advantages	Disadvantages
Self catering	<ul><li>Cooking for yourself allows for more flexible meal times.</li><li>You can meet specific nutritional needs in making your own meals.</li></ul>	<ul><li>Buying ingredients (possibly in a foreign language) and cooking in an unfamiliar kitchen, can be more time consuming. If you are tired after training or matches, it may increase the temptation to grab fast food on the run.</li></ul>

Hotel	• All or most meals are cooked for you.	• The hotel restaurant food may not be suitable to your needs as an athlete. • Your stomach may not be used to local ingredients. • Can be a more expensive option. • Meal times are usually fixed, unless you use room service.
Staying with friends	• Usually free! • Can be great to relax after training and matches with good friends, especially overseas. • Friends can often help you get around the city and/or sightsee.	• Shortage of space. • Inadequate rest, particularly due to the temptation to socialise more than sleep.
Backpackers/Youth Hostel	• Cheap	• In-house cooking facilities can vary widely. • Check safety. • Can be noisy and distracting.

Working Out On The Road

Working out and maintaining your peak fitness (power, speed, strength and agility) is one of the challenges you'll face travelling as an athlete. Apart from being able to visit a gym, swimming pool or use your field/court or track as a place to do extra physical exercises, there are lightweight tools you can take with you that will enable you to have a decent workout. For example, swiss balls, resistance bands, jump ropes, and the TRX Suspension Training system.

We used a swiss ball, resistance bands and our own body weight and often improvised in hotel rooms, corridors and occasionally in airports if we were delayed. It was fun coming up with different exercises and we sure had a lot of people wondering what we were doing!

The best option these days is the TRX Suspension Training system. It's versatile and becomes a complete training system that you can work with anywhere just using your body weight. It's lightweight, rolls up to the size of a shoe and builds core strength, balance and flexibility. If I were still competing I'd be using this and nothing else.

Find out more about the TRX Suspension Training system – www.fitnessanywhere.com

Another option is practising Pilates or Yoga, both of which require no equipment and can be done anywhere. Make sure you've been to classes before you travel, and get your instructor to help you prepare a good program of exercise specific to your needs and level of skill.

Be careful not to do anything new or too difficult as it could result in injury or muscle soreness. You don't need that when you're competing.

Travelling Around

Local transport varies dramatically from city to city. Plan ahead, research the different options, and work out the distances between your accommodation and training/competition venues. Then you can establish (before you arrive) the best way to travel between them.

The main options will be:

- Event transport if provided
- Hire car
- Public transport – train, bus, tram, monorail, underground train
- Taxi
- Walking

In some cities, using public transport is extremely safe, economical, efficient and often the best option. Whilst in others, using public transport can be confusing, time consuming and not always the safest way to travel.

It is far better to feel safe and relaxed, so that your mind can focus on your competition, rather than worrying about your own safety or whether or not you will get to the venue on time.

Be A Tourist!

Although the daily grind of training and matches can be tiring, make sure you take time out to enjoy your surroundings, sightsee and have fun. Include time for this in your schedule and enjoy being a tourist. It's a healthy break from your physical preparations and you never know if you will ever have the chance to visit these places again.

Research points of interest before you arrive so that you have an idea of what you'd like to see and where the venues are in relation to where you are staying.

Once you're there, ask your hotel or local tourist information centre for suggestions. They will point you in the right direction, and will be able to recommend activities, places to see, and best times to visit.

KEY POINTS

Find a great Travel Agent.

Pack well.

Try to stay healthy.

Choose the best accommodation for your needs.

Enjoy the trip!

CHAPTER 20
NUTRITION

The food you put into your body can have a critical effect on your ability to train and compete.

Athletes need to be more aware of the type and quantity of nutrients they are getting from their diet including carbohydrates, proteins and fats along with essential vitamins and minerals – in order to achieve peak performance.

To find out what is best for you, get professional advice from your doctor or dietician specific to your age, your sport and your level of competition. Chat to your coach or trainer. Your sport's governing body will often be a great source of information, as they will understand the unique nutritional requirements of an athlete in your sport. The requirements for a weight lifter will be very different from those of an endurance athlete.

There are so many good books and websites you can read to find out more on nutrition for athletes. I have included here a very basic guide that I've found invaluable. Much of this information and more can be found on the Australian Institute of Sport website which is a great reference for all athletes.

The Basics

You need to work out an eating plan that can be adapted as needed for specific situations such as travelling overseas, competition or changes in training goals or weight.

Setting yourself a good basic diet will enable your body to get the essential nutrients to enable optimum training and recovery. If you're training more intensely, you will need additional nutrients in the form of carbohydrates, proteins, vitamins and minerals.

What Is GI?

You'll often hear nutritionists mention 'GI'. GI stands for Glycaemic Index and refers to the amount of time it takes the body to break a carbohydrate food down and release it into the blood stream as glucose. You should aim to eat low GI foods, as they produce a longer, more sustained energy source and are much better for general good health, especially important for an athlete. Good low GI foods include legumes, grains, and vegetables (preferably not white breads).

High GI foods, on the other hand, give a rapid energy burst initially, quickly followed by a slump. Avoid them as much as possible – high sugar and often highly processed foods such as cakes, biscuits, french fries, sweets/lollies, chips, crisps.

Whole Wheat And Whole Grain – Are They The Same?

There are similarities but they are not the same. The main difference is that whole wheat flour has gone through a refining process that removes some of the nutrients. Whole grain has not been through this refining process so all nutrients should be intact.

Whole wheat bread will feel lighter – sometimes almost as light as a bleached white loaf.

Whole grain bread can make you feel fuller due to its increased nutritional content and you can eat less and still feel satisfied. So where possible, choose whole grain bread.

	Why	Good examples	Avoid
Protein	At least 50% of the dry weight of your body is protein Helps control appetite and blood sugar Helps speed recovery Helps provide satiety	Less than 5% fat Fish (not fried) (flounder, sole, scrod, cod, halibut) Shellfish (clams, lobster, scallop,) Turkey breast (skin removed) Egg whites 5 to 20% fat Prawns, Tuna, Sardines and Salmon Chicken breast (skin removed) Lamb or Veal Ricotta Cheese 97% Lean red meat (top round, fillet, sirloin) Dairy (Low-fat cottage cheese) Legumes & Grains (must be combined to form complete protein) see best carbohydrate sources below) Soy beans, black beans, kidney beans, chick peas and lentils, tofu, tempeh, soy burgers	High fat cuts of meat (beef burger, pork roast, frankfurts, bacon, Pork sausage Most high fat cheese (cream cheese)

	Why	Good examples	Avoid
Fats	Good fats in your diet play an important role in maintaining a healthy body	Polyunsaturated fats: Sunflower, corn, soybean, and flaxseed oils, and also foods such as walnuts, flax seeds, and fish (omega 3). The best sources of Omega 3's are fatty fish such as salmon, herring, mackerel, anchovies, or sardines, or some cold-water fish oil supplements. Monounsaturated fats: Extra Virgin Olive Oil Canola Oil, Peanut Oil Other good sources Avocados, nuts (almonds, hazelnuts, and pecans) and seeds (pumpkin and sesame).	Saturated fats (usually solid at room temp) such as: Animal fat Most Cheeses Butter Biscuits Pastries Trans Fats – mainly found in commercially produced foods
Carbohydrates	Primary energy source Provides fibre	Under 5% fat, over 70% carbohydrate Rolled Oats Potatoes Vegetables Fruits Brown/Basmati Rice Wholegrain Cereals Whole wheat Whole Buckwheat	Soft drinks White bread Highly processed sugary carbs Fruit Juices (high in sugar)
Calcium	Builds strong bones Helps protect from injury	Dairy products Milk (low fat) Yoghurt Cheese	Avoid eating too much high fat dairy. Takes longer to digest, so don't eat just before physical activity.

	Why	Good examples	Avoid
Iron	Helps oxygen get to muscles Helps prevent fatigue Boosts stamina & immune system	Red meat (trimmed of fat) Green leafy vegetables such as: spinach, asparagus, broccoli Iron-fortified cereals Figs Apricots	Red meat that is high in fat such as low quality mince and burgers.
Vitamins & Minerals	Stimulates healthy body and mind	A wide variety of fresh fruit and vegetables every day	
Fibre	Curbs appetite Regulates digestive tract Prevents heart disease	Whole grains Apples Berries Legumes Rolled oats (porridge)	

Quick Snacks

Sometimes it can be really difficult to meet your nutritional needs around training, competition and other commitments. It's easy to grab something at the last minute from the local shop which might be more convenient but not so healthy. Instead, by planning ahead you can ensure you are getting a good mix of nutrients in some simple easy-to-prepare snacks. Try one of these:

- Peanut butter on wholegrain bread or toast.

- Baked beans on toast.

- Hummus and vegetable sticks.

- Baked potato with tuna or salsa.

- Vegetable sticks or fruit slices with peanut butter or low fat cream cheese.
- Porridge with low fat milk and fruit.
- Fruit and yoghurt with cottage cheese.
- Smoothies made with low fat milk, fruit juice, yoghurt, frozen or fresh fruit.
- Wholegrain crackers and cheese.
- Mix of seeds, nuts and dried fruit.
- Sliced banana into plain yoghurt containing probiotics (helps aid recovery).

When To Eat And How Much?

Finding the balance of what to eat and when is a mixture of research, experimenting with what works for you (outside of competition) and good planning. Here are some very basic suggestions of what to eat, and when.

- Five small meals a day, or three meals and two small snacks is preferable, but they all need to be healthy and planned around your training schedule. This can become challenging if you are training twice a day or have sustained periods of activity such as triathlons or track meets.
- Plan your meals for the week in advance so you can buy the right foods at the supermarket. Buying in bulk will also help keep costs down.
- Prepare healthy snacks in advance to avoid grabbing a quick sugar fix at the last minute when you are really hungry.
- Try to eat before you get too hungry. This will help curb your appetite and lessen the likelihood of over-eating at meal times.
- Adding lean protein to carbohydrates (for example, lean chicken breast with whole wheat pasta) will help ensure that you feel full and not crave that extra bowl of pasta. Combining protein and carbs is also a great way to enhance recovery.

- Avoid food high in fat such as burgers, french fries, ice cream and soft drinks before exercising. These foods are harder to digest and although they can give you a short term burst of energy, your blood sugar levels may drop quickly while you are exercising leaving you light headed and feeling weak or tired.

- Eat foods that you are used to eating when you are competing. Everyone's bodies react differently to food – make sure you trial new foods on a non-competition day.

- Allow 1 hour to digest a small carbohydrate snack, 2-3 hours to digest a small meal before competing and 3-4 hours to digest a large meal. See the table below.

Time	Description	Suggestions
3-4 hours prior to training/ competition	Main meal	Pasta with lean protein and tomato sauce Baked potato with tuna or salsa Toast/bread with lean meat, cheese or peanut butter
2-3 hours prior to training/ competition	High carbohydrate snack	Any fresh fruit Bread, bagel or pasta Baked beans on toast Yoghurt Water Rice Cakes Rolled Oats
1 hour prior to training/ competition	Small carbohydrate snack or drink – mainly fluid based	Apple Watermelon Grapes Peaches Oranges Sports bar 1.5 cups of sports drink

Time	Description	Suggestions
During training/competition For activities less than one hour	No food. Fluid only.	Water only
During training/competition For activities 90 minutes or more	No food. Fluid only.	Water plus sports drink containing glucose and electrolytes
During training/competition For activities 3 hours or longer	Small carbohydrate snack or drink – mainly fluid based	Water, sports drink plus some gels, energy bars and/or banana
Within 15 mins of completing training	Small carbohydrate snack or drink – mainly fluid based. To replace glycogen stores.	Water Fresh fruit or fruit juice
With 2 hours of completing training	High carbohydrate + protein snack. To replace lost glycogen and stimulate insulin response.	Sports bars Yoghurt Flavoured milk or fruit smoothies Breakfast cereal and milk Toast/bread with lean meat, cheese or peanut butter Baked beans on toast 4:1 ratio of carbs to protein based on 1g carbs + 0.25g protein per 1kg body weight For example, if you weigh 80kg you might eat 80g pasta with 20g lean chicken or fish.

Nutrition While Travelling

Planning your nutritional needs ahead of time and working out how best to meet them while you are overseas can make a huge difference to your performance. Before you go:

- Research whether the basic food types and snacks you are used to eating are available in the country you are visiting. You can do this via

Google, or by asking athletes in that country or the governing body of your sport in the country you are visiting.

- Actively make an effort to drink extra water and ensure you remain hydrated throughout the entire journey. This is especially important if you are travelling by plane where the humidity in the cabin can cause you to lose additional water. Choose bottled water if you have any doubt about the local tap water.

- Contact Immigration to find out if you are able to take certain foods with you from home – either in your checked luggage or by mailing it ahead if appropriate. Be wary of how much it will add to your overall luggage weight, as you don't want to pay for excess baggage. Repackage into smaller or plastic containers if possible, and seal well. These could be used as back up meals if food availability or food safety is an issue – such as canned meals (spaghetti or baked beans), dried fruit, two-minute noodles, flavoured rice, powdered milk, juice concentrate, spreads such as jam, honey or vegemite/marmite, dried crackers, biscuits or rice cakes, long life cheese or powdered meal supplements and sports bars/gels.

- Consider taking some basic kitchen items such as snap-lock bags or plastic containers, a plastic bowl, herbs and spices to add flavour, and a single cup heater to boil water.

- Take nutritious snacks for the journey such as grains, nuts, seeds, muesli bars and dried fruit so that you have a better chance of meeting your required calorie intake and arriving at your destination able to train and perform at your best. Don't fall into the trap of overeating when you are bored – arm yourself with books, journals, and music for distraction.

- Find out before booking your accommodation, the kinds of food the venue serves. Are you better off in self-catering accommodation so you can prepare your own meals and snacks, or will the hotel food be appropriate for you and you will only need to supplement it to a small degree?

- Educate yourself before your trip about the local food, and whether it will be appropriate for your training needs.

Eating Out

Although preparing your own food is cheaper and you have total control of the ingredients, sometimes when you are on the road, it is inevitable that you will need to eat out occasionally.

Ask for recommendations when you arrive at your hotel or apartment. This saves aimlessly wandering around an unfamiliar town then choosing the worst option because you are so hungry!

> *I educated my palate and my brain about food – taking the opportunity to taste your way around the world is one of the wonderful benefits of being a good athlete.*
>
> **Nici Andronicus,** International Tri-athlete

Tips On Eating Out

- Drink water continually throughout the meal. Sports drinks or fruit juice can be good options to include some extra carbohydrates.

- Base your meal on complex carbohydrates such as rice, noodles or pasta.

- When you need more fuel, order a side of plain bread, rice or baked potato.

- Choose a medium size portion of protein – lean meat, fish or poultry.

- Choose sauces that are tomato or vegetable based and avoid cheese or creamy sauces.

- Choose options that include a variety of vegetables or order additional steamed vegetables or a salad on the side to ensure that you are getting enough vitamins and minerals.

- If you need something sweet to finish off, choose a fruit salad or skim milk hot chocolates. Desserts with more carbohydrates can include rice pudding, bread and butter pudding or fruit crumble and custard.

See These On The Menu? Steer Clear!

- Anything deep-fried or battered
- Bacon, fried eggs, french fries
- Cheesy dishes, cheese platters
- Creamy sauces such as carbonara, side serves of cream or sour cream
- Buttery sauces, side serves of butter, or dipping oil
- High fat desserts and cakes
- Mayonnaise or creamy salad dressings
- Flavoured breads such as garlic and herb bread – they can be high in fat
- Caesar salads and quiches – they can also be high fat choices

Tempting Take-aways

Although many take-away outlets offer food that is high in fat and low in nutrients, some options are better than others.

- Try to find salad bars, which allow you to make your own order, rather than having to take something that is pre-prepared.
- Avoid 'meal deals'. They may seem like value for money, but they are really just tempting you to eat more than you need.
- Read the nutritional information that the major take-away chains provide, and choose wisely.

- Select your own pizza toppings, including lots of vegetables and lean meat such as chicken. Don't be afraid to request no processed meat or half the normal quantity of cheese.

- Sandwiches or baked potatoes can be another good option but choose lean toppings and fillings such as tuna or chicken with plenty of salad. For a baked potato, try baked beans, salsa, chilli con carne or Bolognese sauce. Steer clear of butter, extra cheese or sour cream.

- Kebabs or souvlaki can be a good take-away choice if they don't include high fat meat and creamy dressings.

- Instead of deep fried fish and chips, choose grilled fish and salad.

> **KEY POINTS**
>
> The type and quantity of nutrients that you put into your body, will have a profound effect on your ability to train and compete.
>
> **Eat wisely.**

CHAPTER 21
HYDRATION

We all know that you need to keep hydrated during exercise to replace lost fluids.

Rehydrating effectively after exercising can also result in a more effective recovery, ensuring your body is in form for your next work out.

Hydrate properly, and you will be able to train harder and for longer, and this can ultimately mean the difference between winning and losing.

But how much fluid should you be drinking? When should you drink? And what is the best drink for that moment?

Most of us drink during exercise when we are feeling thirsty, but thirst is actually not a great indicator of dehydration as exercise can in fact suppress thirst. Some athletes only start to feel thirsty after a 2% loss in body mass, but losing this amount before you start to replace it can lead to a 10-30% loss in performance!

Research has also shown that many athletes are replacing less than half the fluid they are actually losing while they are exercising. If you aren't drinking enough (or conversely, although rare, drinking too much), this can have a detrimental effect on your physical and mental performance and ultimately could lead to some serious medical problems.

Very few people bother to do it, but the only real way to determine how much fluid you are losing during exercise is to measure your own personal sweat rate. This is so individual to each person and is affected by many factors including your weight, gender, level of fitness, local temperature and humidity, the clothing you are wearing along with the intensity you are working at and the duration of your workout.

While there are many sites online that can give you some reasonable estimates of sweat rates for other athletes in your sport (or a similar sport) across various temperatures and exercise intensities, if you really want to know what's right for you, you need to take the time and effort to measure for yourself.

I could never get enough water

How To Measure Your Sweat Rate

To measure your sweat rate in kilograms per hour, you need to weigh yourself in the same clothes, before and after exercising, while taking into account how much fluid you drank (or losses if you went to the toilet) while you were exercising. All weights should be recorded in kilograms (kg). This is how you do it, step by step.

1. Weigh yourself immediately prior to exercising in light clothing (Weight A)
2. Keep track of any fluid you drink during exercise (1litre of fluid = 1kg of weight) (Weight B)
3. Keep track approximately of the amount of urine passed if you use the toilet during exercise (Weight C)
4. Immediately after exercising, towel yourself dry and weigh yourself in the same clothing and in the same location as you weighed yourself before (Weight D)
5. Make a note of how long you exercised, in hours (Time T)

Formulae

Next, use the following three formulae to work out your sweat rate:

Formula 1: A + B − C − D = Total weight lost while exercising (Weight E)

Formula 2: E/A x 100% = Percentage of body mass lost

Formula 3: E/T = Sweat rate per hour

For example:

1. Pre-exercise weight   68kg   (Weight A)
2. During exercise, drink 1litre of water   1kg   (Weight B)
3. Urine passed (approx 500ml)   0.5kg   (Weight C)

4. Post exercise weight   66.5kg   (Weight D)
5. Time of exercise   1.5hrs   (Time T)

Using Formula 1 above:

A + B − C − D = 68 + 1 − 0.5 − 66.5 = 2kg (Weight E)

2kg of weight has been lost during exercise, which is equivalent to 2 litres of fluid

Using Formula 2 above:

E/A x 100% = 2/68 x 100 = 2.94% of body mass has been lost during exercise

Using Formula 3 above:

E/T = 2/1.5 = 1.33 litres per hour

Under these conditions, this athlete is losing 1.33 litres of sweat per hour and therefore should drink at least that amount per hour in order to remain fully hydrated and maintain peak performance.

Urine colour is also a good indicator of hydration. Urine should be almost clear or very pale yellow. A darker colour indicates some level of dehydration, with darker colours being more serious.

Hydration Table For Body Mass Loss Percentages

The following table reveals how different percentages of body mass loss indicate the level of dehydration.

Level	From	To	Outcome
Well hydrated	+1%	-1%	Able to continue to train at optimum levels. Body responds well and can maintain peak performance.
Minor dehydration	-1%	-3%	Possible 10-30% loss in performance.

Significant dehydration	-3%	-5%	Further reduced performance including noticeable impairment of concentration, judgement, reaction time and decision-making.
Serious dehydration	>-5%		Significant medical consequences possible. Recovery time massively extended. Possible inability to continue competition or training for a period of time.

How To Keep Well Hydrated

- The body can only absorb so much fluid at one time, so lots of smaller sips before, during and after exercise are better than having big drinks once or twice. However, there's no benefit to drinking more than you need and there's even a chance of becoming over-hydrated which can also be dangerous for your body. Learning your sweat rate is the best way to ensure you are getting the right amount.

- It is especially important to continue to drink after exercise with lots of small sips in the few hours after you finish, as your body will continue to sweat and rehydrate. Your urine should be clear or pale yellow and there should be plenty of it.

- Studies have shown that adults typically lose 2.5-3 litres per day, even without exercising. You need to replace all this in addition to the fluid lost while you are exercising, in order to remain in peak condition. Some of this lost fluid is replaced by foods eaten but many athletes are only drinking 50% of what they are losing while exercising. Work out your sweat rate to ensure you are really drinking enough as it is so variable from one athlete to the next.

- Different athletes can tolerate different amounts of dehydration before beginning to lose the edge on their performance. You are much more likely to be affected by dehydration in hot conditions than in cold ones. Exercising at altitude can also increase the likelihood of dehydration.

- If you are exercising for over 1.5hrs, choose a sports drink that contains carbohydrates (usually as glucose) and sodium (salt). In the majority of cases, any sodium loss will be replaced in your normal post-exercise meal, but for endurance sports longer than 4 hours, you need 0.5g-1g of sodium per hour. It may help to consume salty snacks such as pretzels, salted crackers or even salt tablets. The addition of sodium can also help stimulate thirst to aid recovery.

- Studies have shown that typically men do sweat more than women, even when expressed as a percentage of body weight. But this doesn't necessarily mean that women are controlling their body temperature more efficiently. Women may need to ensure their body has other ways to regulate temperature such as wearing loose clothing that doesn't retain heat and splashing the body with cool water.

- Elite athletes sweat more. You may think the opposite would be true but studies have shown that as the body becomes more highly trained, it also becomes more efficient at cooling down through sweating. However, this also means you need to replace the additional fluid loss.

- Research by the Australian Institute of Sport across 30 sports has shown that sweating does increase with the intensity of exercise. So sports such as volleyball or short to middle distance runners will sweat more than say, long distance runners or cyclists. However, overall sweat loss might be similar at the end of the day as the long distance athletes will typically exercise for a longer period of time.

What Are Electrolytes?

Electrolytes are mineral salts carrying an electrical charge, which are naturally present in the body and are needed for the regulation of muscle contractions and other functions. Sports drinks are marketed as having a critical effect on an athlete's performance, and contain varying amounts of electrolytes.

Sports Drinks – The Pros And Cons

Are sports drinks a con – is there any advantage to be had in drinking them, or are you really better off with plain water?

The manufacturers would have us believe that we need the added carbohydrates and minerals in their drinks to ensure maximum performance.

They loosely claim that by consuming the sports drink, you'll get a quick boost of energy through carbs (in this case in some form of sugar) and the added electrolytes will replace the lost minerals (salt being the only one of significance here) and allow absorption of the glucose.

However, the actual benefit you receive depends on your sport and the duration of your workout. For sports that involve training or competition for less than 1.25 hours, sports drinks have not been shown to provide any benefit. However, for training or competition over 1.5 hours, and in particular for endurance type sports, they can be extremely useful.

Remember, what you are trying to do while exercising is to stay hydrated, not treat dehydration. That means drinking enough in regular small quantities before, during and after exercise – not waiting until you are already struggling, then taking in a whole load of fluid with a few huge gulps.

Before Splashing Your Cash, Beware!

Commercially available sports drinks are high GI sugar for quick absorption during training. However, some of them contain up to 17% sugar, which also helps to mask the taste of the added salt. These drinks can be beneficial but only if you are competing in events longer than 1.5 hours.

Studies have shown that over 8g of carbohydrates per 100ml of fluid can cause stomach upsets and are too 'heavy' to digest during exercise. Check the ingredients and ensure that your chosen drink doesn't contain more than 8% carbs.

You are unlikely to deplete your body's stores of sodium and potassium unless you are competing for very long events such as a marathon or an iron man event. Electrolytes in your sports drink are only really needed for these high endurance events.

Studies have claimed that if sports drinks are sipped continually over long periods of time, they may cause tooth decay as they contain a large amount of sugars, acids and additives – a toxic combination for your teeth. There have been reports of athletes spending thousands of dollars on dental work following years of sipping sports drinks in their youth. To minimise the possible effects:

- Don't make sports drinks your regular drink of choice. Water is much better for you overall and kinder on your teeth. Keep your sports drinks only for training or competition.

- Don't drink them in lots of small continuous sips – drink more at one time.

- Drink through a straw to minimise contact with your teeth.

- Rinse your mouth with water after drinking.

If used correctly, sports drinks can help you replace lost fluid and electrolytes. Use them sparingly and only when you need to.

DIY Sports Drinks

If you do find that you can drink more sports drinks than water, and they seriously help keep you hydrated, why not make your own and save some cash? There are plenty of websites that feature recipes. It's just a case of trial and error.

Cheers!

KEY POINTS

Keep well hydrated during and after exercise.

Measure your sweat rate to understand how much fluid you need to replenish.

CHAPTER 22
SPORTS RECOVERY

The greater the intensity of your workout, the greater the recovery required.

Sports recovery is about taking positive action towards helping the body return to its optimal state for exercising. This is particularly important at the elite level where you might be training twice a day at an intense level and for long periods.

Allowing enough time for recovery is just as important as training and competition. Continuous training can damage even the strongest athlete and also increase the chance of injury. And without sufficient recovery, your body will not have the ability to reach peak performance.

While you are exercising, you use up your body's energy stores (glycogen) and the protein in your muscles breaks down. Whilst in recovery, the muscle protein repairs and builds up again and it's actually this repair process, following the exercise, which makes the muscles stronger.

If there's not enough time between exercise sessions for the body to rebuild protein and restock glycogen stores, then more muscle protein will be destroyed before your body has had the chance to fully recover.

If you skimp on recovery, thinking that more workouts must be making you stronger – think again. Additional workouts without additional recovery, is in fact is making you weaker.

Recovery is important for your wellbeing:

1. **Physically** – so your muscles can repair and rebuild to increase your strength and endurance, and

2. **Psychologically** – to ensure there is some balance and variety in your life and you don't end up lethargic, unmotivated and with reduced physical ability. Over training can then lead to poor sports performance. Insufficient recovery can also hamper your mental sharpness, which may be the very edge you need in a tough competition.

During competition, particularly when you have to compete in multiple events throughout a day or a series of days, allowing sufficient time for recovery can be extremely challenging. It's easy to pay little or no attention to short-term or long-term recovery, and focus solely on the actual training.

Short-Term (Micro) Recovery

Short-term recovery takes place in the immediate hours following intensive training or competition. This not only includes recovery from the physical exertion, but also from the mental stress, adrenaline and even the travel to the event, all of which puts additional strain on your body. Your body is rebuilding muscle protein for up to 24 hours after you finish exercising.

Studies have shown that the way you use the hours immediately after exercising can have a dynamic effect on your recovery. You need to be doing some, or all of the following:

- Cooling down and stretching

- Eating the right foods to enable protein build up, glycogen replacement and allowing soft tissues (muscles, tendons and ligaments) to repair

- Using recovery therapies – ice bath, compression garments

- Undertaking treatment – massage, physio, osteopathy, chiropractic and so on

Long-Term (Macro) Recovery

Long-term recovery varies from sport to sport, but it is generally a period of time specifically built into your schedule following an intensive season of training or competition. The purpose is to alleviate the accumulative effects of many weeks or months of training and competition, and it may range from a few days to a few weeks. It could involve cross training in another sport, or taking part in another kind of activity such as:

- Walking
- Swimming
- Stretching or yoga
- Changing intensity and/or duration of work-outs
- Specific activity using different muscle groups

Allowing sufficient time for recovery is really important and essential to maintaining good health, preventing injury and ensuring muscles are allowed to develop to their full potential.

It's a good idea to reduce the intensity of your training for the days immediately following a big competition. Use this time to catch up with equipment maintenance – shoes and clothes, along with actual mechanical servicing and repairs, or equipment replacement.

When you next come to compete, both your body and your equipment will be in A1 condition. Sufficient recovery time should form an integral part of your program and be scheduled into your weekly, monthly and annual training and competition calendar both at the macro and micro level.

Sleep

When we are short of time and trying to squeeze a few more things into our day, sleep seems to be one thing that is easy to cut back on. Don't!

Sleep is perhaps the single most important component of successful recovery. This is when your body does its best repair work. Losing a few hours one or two nights occasionally won't make a huge difference but long periods of insufficient sleep can definitely affect performance and recovery, and consequently strength and endurance capabilities.

Cool Down And Stretching

Undertaking a purposeful cool down can benefit you on a number of levels:

- Allows the heart to return to pre-exercise heart rate levels
- Helps your body recover
- May help ward off injuries and help prevent muscle soreness
- Helps to lessen the build up of waste products in the muscles that build up during exercise

Stretching can help to prevent injury, warm up and cool down muscles, and assist in rehabilitation after injury.

Recovery Therapies And Their Benefits

According to a recent presentation at the Australian Institute of Sport, recovery strategies should be carried out in the following order (where possible):

- Cool down and stretch
- Nutritional snack (sports drink, small carb/protein snack) (within 45 minutes)
- Hydrotherapy
- Compression garments
- Nutritional meal (within 2 hours)
- Massage

SPORTS RECOVERY

Here are the relative benefits of a few different recovery therapies:

	Ice baths	Contrast water therapy	Compression
Increases range of motion		✓	
Decreases stiffness or muscle soreness		✓	✓
Stimulates central nervous system		✓	
Decreases pain and muscle spasm	✓		
Increases blood flow	✓	✓	✓
Decreases swelling	✓	✓	✓
Decreases metabolism	✓		
Decreases core temp	✓		
How long and when	10-15º for 15 mins or up to 20 mins in cold tap water straight after training or competition (Post training soak in the sea or local river with fellow team mates!)	2 mins hot, 2 mins cold x 3 repeats (finish with cold to bring core temp down)	During and after training and competition as well as during airline travel and long drives
What is it?	Body is submerged up to the waist in a bath containing water and ice, or, just cold water	Body is submerged in bath or shower alternating hot and cold water	Using compression garments eg. Full length tights to pump blood back up to the heart
Therapy	Ice baths	Contrast water therapy	Compression

EEEEK! Don't Like The Idea Of An Ice Bath?

Let's face it, no one really actually wants to jump into an ice bath! But many elite level athletes swear by them and it's definitely worth a try as part of your recovery program, particularly to help stimulate blood flow and ward off injuries.

If you don't have an ocean or river handy to make the activity more social, make yourself a cup of tea/coffee/hot chocolate, grab a woolly hat if you like and a towel for your shoulders, maybe a good book or magazine that you've been dying to read. Jump in up to your waist (include the hips) and the next 15 minutes will fly by (honestly).

If you feel better the next day, include it in your schedule as a regular recovery therapy after major workouts.

MMMMMassage!

The good news about massage is not only does it feel great, it is actually doing you some good at the same time. The aim of massage is to relieve the tension that has built up in the muscles while exercising, as well as to help to remove chemical build up in the cells. Many top athletes have their own masseur who travels with them around the world, who knows their body and how to treat it.

Even if having your own personal masseur is still on your wish list, regularly using a properly qualified sports masseur near your home (preferably the same one each time) can also reap huge benefits in the short and longer term.

If there are additional aches and pains that persist after massage, then it's an indication that further medical assistance may be required such as through your chiropractor, osteopath or doctor. This will ensure that when you return to training, your body is in peak condition.

Recovery Nutrition

Recovery nutrition is important for a whole range of reasons including:

- Getting enough carbohydrates back in to refuel the muscle and liver glycogen stores.

- Taking enough of the right fluid on board to replace the fluid, minerals and electrolytes lost in sweat.

- Allowing sufficient time for the body to manufacture new muscle protein, red blood cells and other components as part of the repair process.

- Allowing the immune system to handle the damage caused by intense exercise. Ensuring your body has sufficient carbohydrates has been shown to help here.

For every sport, the amount you are affected by each of the above points will vary. Really think about;

- How much energy you've used and so how much food is needed to replace it?

- How much sweat you've lost? (See the chapter: Hydration, for how to measure sweat loss).

- How much muscle damage has occurred?

- How you can stimulate muscle protein rebuild?

The best time to replace glycogen (carbohydrate) stores is within the first hour after exercising when the rate of glycogen synthesis and storage is highest. Storage is still high within the first 3 hours after exercising and remains slightly higher than normal for 24 hours (but not at the same rate as the first 1-3 hours).

However, refuelling within an hour of exercising can prove hard if you don't usually feel hungry so soon after exercising, *or*, you don't have the correct food and fluids with you.

So if you are serious about optimising your recovery, it's worth doing something to address the situation:

- Prepare the right food in advance and take it with you.

- Consider alternatives such as protein and carbohydrate fluid meals if you know you struggle to stomach food straight after an intensive session.

- Experiment with different things, but make sure you do something to find a solution that works for you and fits well within your overall diet.

Refuelling

After exercising, you need to take on enough carbohydrate to replace the glycogen broken down from your muscles. This will of course depend on how hard you worked – the harder the session, the more to replace.

Studies have shown that by including a small amount of protein with the carbohydrate in your post exercise meal, you will helps promote protein rebuilding and can rapidly increase the rate of glycogen absorption. This basically just means that you are maximising your chances of faster recovery and getting stronger by eating carbs and proteins together after exercising.

The best ratio seems to be around 4:1 carbohydrate to protein. That is, for example, 80g carbs plus 20g protein. (Around 1g of carbs per kg of bodyweight is a good guide.)

Note – if you have low body fat, you need to also consider including fat along with the carbs and proteins.

Training Or Competing In The Evening

Many athletes, especially those who have to work, need to fit their training sessions into the evening. Or they compete in a sport that holds evening or night matches.

The same basic recovery principles apply and the post-training meal still needs to be packed with nutrients, carbs and protein. Key difference – make the meal smaller. Plan to meet the bulk of your nutritional needs earlier in the day. It may just take a little more planning to ensure that you still get your full intake of nutrients earlier in the day but it will mean that you don't need to refuel with a large meal late in the evening.

Eating a big meal just prior to going to bed, will take your body longer to digest. It could lead to an uncomfortable night and may mean that some of the nutrients may not be absorbed as fully and therefore be stored as fat.

Real Food Versus Supplements

Supplements such as liquid meals or sports gels and bars, are good for emergencies or occasional use, but it's far better to meet your dietary needs through real food, rather than supplements. Plan ahead and ensure you have the right type of foods available to ensure the best possible recovery.

KEY POINTS

Some athletes pay more attention than others to sports recovery, but it should be an integral part of your training schedule.

It really can make a huge difference in your training and competition outcomes if you allow your body to recovery sufficiently.

You will then be in peak physical and mental condition every time you exercise.

More Info?

For further information check out your own national sports institute website. They usually contain a wealth of information. The Australian Institute of Sport's website has some great ideas on foods to meet nutritional needs.

SECTION III

BELIEF

Building The Mindset Of A Champion

You want it, with every fibre of your being.

You've mapped your plan and laid the groundwork.

So what's missing? What is the last, most critical component – without which you will never achieve your Ultimate Big Picture?

Some people say I have attitude – maybe I do...but I think you have to. You have to believe in yourself when no one else does – that makes you a winner right there.

Venus Williams, Tennis Champion

When you have the passion and have done the preparation, the only piece of the puzzle left is the belief. Without a winning belief and mindset it won't matter how good your preparation has been. Managing your mind and your emotions play a huge part in winning.

Research into the psychology of sporting performance has proven a link between the mind and the body. Simply put, what you think and believe will affect the way you behave and perform, and will therefore shape the outcome.

Belief in my ability and not afraid to show it

What's exciting is that you have the power to control your thoughts and develop your 'winning' beliefs. Every time I have asked a successful person, whether they were an athlete or business person, what they felt initially stood in the way of success, resoundingly the answer has to do with their own thoughts, their own beliefs.

Once they resolved to change negative or debilitating thoughts, their results quickly improved and they went on to achieve great success.

At the top end of your sport, the only difference between the best and the rest is what's going on between your ears! Have you ever heard the saying, it's 90% mental and 10% skill?

Here's a simple explanation of how it works. There are essentially two parts of your mind. Your unconscious (which makes up 95% of your mind) and your conscious (the other 5%).

If I asked you: What did you have for dinner last night? ... You could answer quickly, using the information stored in your unconscious mind. You use your conscious mind to answer, but draw on your unconscious mind for memories, facts, beliefs and your values.

So as an athlete, the beliefs you hold deep in your unconscious mind actually determine all your sporting results.

Poor results occur when your conscious mind decides it wants something but your unconscious mind rebels, because of past programming based on your life experiences. These experiences were developed during your youth and impact your attitude, beliefs and values.

For example, you may really want to qualify for the next Olympic Games, but every time the pressure is on and you have a chance, you blow it. That's because part of you (your unconscious mind) doesn't believe that you can do it.

You're not alone. Deep down many people don't believe they deserve success. They don't think they're worthy of success. They long for it, they imagine it. They do all the preparation and training, but they will forever struggle to reach that pinnacle.

Here's the key. You need to re-programme your unconscious mind. You need your unconscious mind to be aligned with your goals and dreams.

How? I'll guide you step-by-step in the next chapters. Essentially, by using a range of techniques, you communicate to the unconscious via your conscious mind, feeding it clear directions, pictures, sounds, feelings and positive self-talk.

> *Man is what he believes.*
>
> **Anton Chekhov,** Author, Playwright, Physician

KEY POINTS

You must truly *believe* you can achieve success.

To make it happen, learn to align your unconscious mind with your goals and your dreams.

CHAPTER 23
THOUGHTS BECOME THINGS

Thinking creates.

Everything that was ever created by a human being, whether it was out of need, or for comfort, luxury or amusement began as an idea, a concept…a thought.

The most powerful influence in your life is the information fed to your mind. This is what creates your thoughts. Unfortunately, one of the misconceptions that most people have is that you get what you want in life solely by what you *do*, or through the actions you take.

It's not your action that makes things happen, it's your intent, your focus and your thoughts.

> *Nothing can stop the person with the right mental attitude from achieving his goal; nothing on earth can help the person with the wrong mental attitude.*
>
> **Thomas Jefferson,** Third President of the United States

If you focus on what you want instead of what you don't want, you will know when it is time to take action. And when you do, it will seem effortless. Doors will open and it will seem like the entire universe is on your side, collaborating to help you achieve your goals!

We have about 60,000 thoughts each day and most of them are the same thoughts we had yesterday and the day before. Thoughts are like small grains of sand, sticking together to form a sand castle. This sand castle is your reality.

If you want to produce different results in your life you have to **think differently**.

> *We cannot solve our problems with the same thinking we used when we created them.*
>
> **Albert Einstein,** Theoretical Physicist, Philosopher, Author

Whatever you're thinking about, you create. That's why all the best personal development books focus on how you think: *Think and Grow Rich, As a Man Thinketh, The Power of Positive Thinking, The Power of Focus* and so on. Learn from these books, as I did.

You need to be conscious of what you are exposing your mind to, and the feelings and thoughts that you are letting seep in. We are surrounded by negativity, fear, and worrying situations. Everything that goes into your mind matters. It will shape your view of the world and yourself.

So how can you control the sort of information you allow in? For a start, watch less TV!

It is estimated that the average person watches just over 4 ½ hrs of TV per day, which equates to almost 1,700 hours of TV a year. Now you may not be one of the averages, but if most of what you watch revolves around news, current affairs and violent movies, be aware of all the negative stuff that you're feeding your mind. Garbage in, garbage out.

News and current affair programs tend towards sensationalism. Try to eliminate them from your viewing, or at least be a little more selective.

What else could you be doing? How about feeding your mind with something positive and uplifting? Or something that will help contribute to achieving your goals.

Set up RSS feeds* on your computer. This will bring you information that specifically relates to your interests and your goals.

If you don't mind giving your email address, sign up to newsletters or blogs written on websites that interest you. At any time you can unsubscribe if they are not on track with what you're after. But at least you're now starting to fill your mind with information that aligns with your goals.

> **Tip: Set up a few email addresses**
> Have a separate email address for newsletters and blogs. Use hotmail or Gmail. If the spam then gets too much, you can always delete that email address and create another one.

How Do Successful People Think?

It's often been said that highly motivated and successful people spend most of their spare time on education rather than entertainment.

Could you do that? If it sounds a bit extreme, and you think it would be too hard to change now, then how serious are you about achieving success?

Unsuccessful people also tend to think about what they don't have most of the time. They listen and talk about problems.

Successful people think about what they want and how they can get it. They are engrossed in specifically focused thoughts to do with their goals.

Do you drive to and from training or work? Are you on public transport often? How many of these hours could you turn into productive learning hours? Feed your mind, by listening to powerful and uplifting audio books and podcasts, using your car CD player, iPod or MP3 player.

---

*RSS allows you to stay informed by retrieving the latest content from sites of interest. You save time by not visiting each site individually. You protect your privacy, by not needing to join each site's email newsletter.

Feed your mind wisely. Realise that you can choose the input. Maximise your time and you'll get closer to your goals every day.

> ### BEWARE OF LIMITING THOUGHTS
>
> After having competed in three Olympic Games with a vast number of athletes, I have noticed that some are happy just to get to the Olympics – because that's their goal. That's the limit of their thinking. They've capped their belief to 'just making the Games'. Then, once they're there, they under- perform because they've basically already reached their goal.

Widen Your Scope

All throughout this book I have suggested doing things that may be a little out of your comfort zone. Things that you may *think* you can't do or achieve.

If you really want to win in sport and in life, you have to push yourself outside your current boundaries. You must start *thinking* beyond those boundaries.

We've all had moments of self-doubt. Self-doubt is created because we start to focus on all the negative things that can go wrong. "What if we lose? What if I hurt myself? What if I can't finish the race...?"

Your thoughts have the ability to affect you in either a positive or negative way. Try thinking about and imagining the feeling of winning and finishing strong. Focus on what you *want* to happen. Discard all the other thoughts. Remember, you can choose the thoughts you keep.

I like the analogy of driving a car. Where do you look when driving a car? Out the front window, of course. If you were always looking in the rear-view mirror, you'd get nowhere (and you'd probably crash). But, if you drive your car looking out the front window, looking to the road ahead, you'll get to where you want to go, steering yourself along the way.

If we apply this idea to sport, why not make the decision *before* you go out on the field that you're going to steer yourself over the finish line, and win the game. Focus on what you *do* want to happen, despite the distractions and obstacles, rather than on what you *don't* want.

It seems so easy, yet most people can't do this. They allow their circumstances to determine how they feel and this creates their results. They blame everything on others; their family, their upbringing, and their teammates. They refuse to take responsibility for being at cause. They are *victims* of their circumstances. *Victims* of their own thinking.

Others, who are able to use their will to steer their thoughts, their mind and their beliefs are more able to control who they are and what they create. They are the *victors* in the game of life.

I don't think of myself as a poor, deprived ghetto girl who made good. I think of myself as somebody who from an early age knew I was responsible for myself, and I had to make good.

Oprah Winfrey, Host, Producer, Philanthropist

So, which are you? If you've been believing yourself to be a victim of circumstance, then stop blaming and start taking responsibility for the thoughts you keep. It's not what happens to you that matters, it's how you choose to think about it and then deal with it that counts. No one but you controls your mind. Think on purpose, not by accident.

If you're a victor – congratulations! Keep feeding your mind with great thoughts.

Watch your thoughts; they become words.
Watch your words; they become actions.
Watch your actions; they become habits.
Watch your habits; they become character.
Watch your character; it becomes your destiny.

Anonymous

You can see how important it is to first become aware of your thoughts, rather than be caught up in them, and then learn to take control of them. Our choice of thoughts, beliefs, emotions and actions creates our results.

What Are You Focused On?

Whiners see the glass half empty; *winners* see the glass half full.

The ability to control your thoughts, especially under pressure, is what creates champions in any field.

Tennis legend John McEnroe explains in his book, *Serious*, how he had to learn to improve his focus, and as a result, his game became better and better. At aged 18, he recalls how a noisy heckler threw his concentration so much that he ended up losing the first round Wimbledon qualifier. The heckler turned out to be his opponent's wife. He says: "As you play better people in different circumstances, more and more things will start to happen that you have never experienced before. You learn to adjust. At the time, I was just flabbergasted."

KEY POINTS

Everything you feed your mind will have an effect. Be selective.

Take responsibility for the thoughts you keep.

CHAPTER 24
BELIEVE TO ACHIEVE

One of the most crucial elements of a champion mindset is self-belief. It's your belief that gets you started on your journey, it's belief that keeps you going in the face of adversity and it's that last ounce of self-belief that completes your journey to the very top.

Belief is not fact – I repeat, belief is not fact! (Although we often act as if it were.) Belief forms your reality based on what you feel and perceive of your experiences.

FIRE IN THE MIND

The Brazilian team we faced in the final of the Sydney 2000 Olympics was, on paper, the best team in the world at that time. They'd won almost every event and most teams thought they were unbeatable.

In the three year lead-up to the Games, we'd only beaten them once out of 17 matches.

Without a doubt, everyone thought the Brazilians were going to win and they thought that there would be too much pressure on us at home to win that match.

To help strengthen our self-belief, our Success Coach got us to do some crazy things that would push us out of our comfort zone, things that we were originally afraid of, like walking on hot coals and broken glass.

Afterwards, we'd look back and say to ourselves, "Wow, I didn't think I'd be able to do that, but I did."

We then transferred that to our initial belief (that we couldn't beat the Brazilians), and bit by bit we started to realise that beliefs can be changed. When we finally made it to the Gold Medal match, there was no fear, no doubt, and no distraction. Just a sense that this match would be ours.

Sometimes we under-estimate what we can do. We might initially be afraid of something, but with courage, we step out and take the risk. You need to put yourself in situations that push your limits ¬— that will help you identify your fears and doubts. Attack your limiting beliefs and say "Look, this is really not that scary," or just take that first step towards something you fear. You'll find that once you take that first step, you'll then take the second step and the third.

If you ever have the chance to walk on hot coals or broken glass (under correct supervision) I encourage you to try it. It's an unbelievably empowering experience.

Walking on broken glass

So What Exactly Is Belief?

Belief is a generalisation that we make about others, about life in general and *especially* about ourselves.

Your belief forms a set of rules by which you conduct yourself. For example, if you believe that life isn't easy, you must therefore believe that life is hard. That is the way you act, and in turn that attracts more hardship.

Muhammad Ali once said: *"To be a champion, you must believe you are the best."*

In his early days Ali's belief in himself drove him to get right back up each time someone knocked him down – simply because he *believed* he was the heavyweight champion of the world. Champions don't just lie there and give up. Champions fight on and on and on.

Now, it's easy to say you *believe* you are going to do something or become someone. But if you are to be truly honest with yourself you need to admit if these are just words or if you truly *believe in your belief.*

Do you perhaps have a genuine lack of inner conviction? It's OK to admit this to yourself now, because we will work on that in the next few chapters. Start by being really honest with yourself.

Are You All Talk and No Belief?

In *The Winners Bible*, Dr Kerry Spackman gives a great example of an **Optimist** versus **One with Unshakeable Belief**.

Dr Spackman explains that an optimist says the stone in her running shoe isn't going to bother her as she climbs the mountain. This optimist often fails.

The runner with unshakeable belief is more of a realist and says the stone is hurting her feet and she needs to get it out. The mountain is long and high and she is hurting badly. But, she *will* get to the top and she *will* enjoy the view when she gets there.

Yes you do need to be optimistic and maintain a positive approach, but if you don't have the underlying belief, it's really all just empty talk.

Do you really believe that you can achieve the goals you set out in the front of this book?

Yes or no?

If you said no, despite the best intentions and the most methodical planning, when the going gets tough you'll lose confidence in yourself. You'll get dispirited and downhearted when you lose. Your feelings and emotional happiness will depend on your most recent success or failure and your life will be a roller coaster. You are not alone. Many people cannot even set goals because of their underlying lack of self-belief. Rest assured, you can improve your belief. Keep reading and I'll explain how.

If you are a true believer you'll probably display an air of confidence. One that is natural and not put on. It's not arrogance, but quite a different way of being. A great sporting example is Roger Federer. He just gets on with the job, because of his unshakeable self-belief.

However, he wasn't always like this. As a teenager, his athletic prowess was matched by his feisty temperament. He constantly berated himself – for the smallest mistake, or when dissatisfied with a (point-winning) stroke.

Perhaps his conscious mind was telling him how good he was and how much he wanted to win. And, at the same time, his unconscious mind may not have believed it, thereby causing friction and frustration. Federer was able to resolve this conflict, and today, is recognised as one of the world's greatest tennis champions.

Self-belief is a learned skill that any of us can improve upon at any time.

How Do You Develop This Unshakeable Belief?

Some athletes seem to be born with an 'unshakeable belief' in themselves. Some have had it instilled in them by their parents, teachers and coaches.

If you're not fortunate enough to fall into either camp, is there any hope?

The simple answer is: yes. You can train yourself. You can instil in yourself the unshakeable belief that is needed to reach the ultimate prize. Trust me, I did, and I know of many other successful athletes who have done the same.

Just like you train to hit a golf ball or kick a football – if you follow the advice in this section, do the exercises and practice over and over and over again, you will feel it. A belief like this is more than words or thoughts, it's a *feeling*. A positive feeling of power.

Setting your goals (Section One) was your first step in developing that belief. If these goals excite you and drive you to jump out of bed each day, they will fuel your unshakeable belief system.

INSPIRATION FROM TRUE BELIEVERS

In 1996, at the Atlanta Olympic Games, Natalie and I lost the semi-final to a team that we had every chance of beating, as we had done so a few times in the year leading up to the Games.

However, we'd gone into that semi-final with a 'fear of losing' rather than a 'will to win'. We were focused on what would happen if we lost. And we did!

That evening, Nat and I were devastated but we had to try to regroup and regain our confidence. Our playoff for the Bronze Medal was scheduled for the next morning.

Nat decided to get a massage and have some down-time. She wasn't doing well, mentally or emotionally. We'd had what we call a 'beat down' by the Brazilians and our Coach and I were worried. If we couldn't get her 'up' again it was going to affect our playoff for Bronze.

Off she went, to get her massage.

Expecting to walk into the Australian Medical Centre in the Olympic Village and see the many massage tables, packed with athletes being rubbed down from the day's events, Nat was greeted with an almost empty room. Where were they all?

About to leave, she just caught the end of a cheer and the rumble of voices around the corner. She decided to see where everyone was and found the therapists and athletes crowded around a small TV screen watching the live feed from the Olympic Swimming Centre.

The Men's 1500m Freestyle final was about to start. Swimming in lane 8, the outside and worst lane of the pool, was the Australian Gold Medallist from the previous Olympic Games, Kieran Perkins.

Kieran was already an Australian hero in the pool. Everyone knew him and was excited to see how he would go, but they weren't very confident in his ability to win another medal in this race.

You see Kieran hadn't had a great lead-up to the final. He was obviously struggling and had only just qualified by a fraction of a second. Barely a finger length!

The media and all the people standing around Nat that night had already written him off, saying how lucky he was to have even made the final.

The gun went off. Kieran, determined not to listen to the negative talk, started ahead and stayed ahead until he hit the end of the pool and won his second consecutive Olympic Gold Medal.

The massage room exploded. For the 15 minutes of the race, their enthusiasm and confidence in Kieran had grown until he finally hit the wall in first place. The atmosphere was unbelievable.

In Nat's words from her book, Go Girl:

> "I clearly remember the sight of him getting out of the pool, veins protruding like the veins of a racehorse. He said to the interviewer that he didn't feel comfortable at all in the water, but was determined to push through it and win, even if his arm fell off. And there I was thinking, "No one believed he could do it. But it didn't matter. All he needed to do was believe in himself." If he'd listened to the press, and everyone else who was amplifying that little voice he probably had in his own head, he would have lost. From that moment I realised "I'm the only one who decides! It's up to me to paint the picture." At that moment I made the

decision that we would win a Bronze Medal the next day. I walked back up the stairs. I'd got just the attention I needed! I didn't need physio.

Looking back on that event, I now know that I was seeking inspiration when I went down to watch Perkins swim to that unlikely Gold Medal. In that respect, it wasn't a chance event. My mind was prepared to be inspired, but only on a subconscious level. And there's the difference.

If there's anything to learn from that little incident in retrospect, it's this: knowing what I know now, I wouldn't have left it to chance. I would not have hoped for inspiration – I would have deliberately sought it much earlier! Today this is one of the most valuable pieces of advice I could possibly give: deliberately seek to be inspired and it will happen! The rest will take care of itself. Have the radar out, and look to be stimulated, stirred and moved by the successes you see around you all the time. Then find out how they do it."

Meanwhile, I had been roaming around the village seeking my own inspiration to bounce back in the play-off for Bronze.

I found it in the players of the Australian Men's Field Hockey team. They recalled how they had felt, back in 1992 at the Barcelona Olympics, when they'd finished fourth. They described how they could have also won their semi-final, but didn't. They then took that feeling of loss into their play-off and played nowhere near their best, lost and were out of medal contention.

They explained how their lingering emotion crippled their ability to perform. They made it pretty clear to me that I had to let go of what had happened that day so I could go out and win the next day.

Both Nat's and my experience couldn't have happened at a better time. We managed to overcome our earlier disappointment and come out with all guns blazing against the USA in our play-off for Bronze. And we won! Thanks to all the amazing athletes around us (the Men's Field Hockey Team also won Bronze that year), and our true belief in ourselves.

260 THE BUSINESS OF BEING AN ATHLETE

Over the years, having spoken to many athletes about self-belief, I've found two key strategies that will nourish and grow an unshakeable self-belief:

1. Actively Seek Inspiration

   Surround yourself with other inspiring people. Try putting pictures up in your room or in your Winner's Toolbox, of other amazing athletes that have shown remarkable belief in themselves.

   Consider Usain Bolt, the 100 metre world record sprinter. He often raises his forefinger in victory before he even finishes the race!

Our first Olympic podium – Bronze in Atlanta 1996

Surround yourself with success. The company you keep, the books you read, the movies you watch, the pictures and words you have on the wall. It will sink in.

2. Remove The Beliefs That Limit You

   Limiting beliefs can be crippling. They can stop you from ever succeeding. You must eradicate them if you truly want to develop an unshakeable belief system.

   Many of the limits you perceive are not really limits at all. They're simply boundaries that you've placed around yourself. You must step out of your comfort zone to get beyond these self-imposed limitations.

   The size of your success is determined by the size of your belief.

   Dr David J Schwartz, Motivational Expert

Back in 1954, it was considered preposterous to believe that a human could run a mile in less than four minutes. However, on May 6 1954, English athlete Roger Bannister became the first person to break the four-minute mile barrier and smashed the widely held belief.

Within the next twelve months, dozens of athletes went on to break that four-minute mile. Bannister had broken a belief in the limit of a human's ability to run at such a pace and opened a floodgate. What was once deemed to be impossible is, today, commonplace.

Doctors and scientists said that breaking the four-minute mile was impossible, that one would die in the attempt. Thus, when I got up from the track after collapsing at the finish line, I figured I was dead.

Roger Bannister, Champion Runner

Before I explain how to eliminate limiting beliefs, I'd like to digress and get a little technical.

I was amazed when I found out about this biological process – what I had previously thought of as 'co-incidence'. Your Reticular Activating System (or RAS) is the part of our brain that constantly prompts us to take notice of what is relevant to us at that time in our lives. Whatever we focus on, or believe, or identify with, will trigger the RAS, which then literally points things out to us to help us 'get' that object or goal. Things that were there all the time, suddenly appear more often.

Think of when you decided you wanted to buy a particular car, or any high value item, and how suddenly you seemed to see that car everywhere, notice more advertisements for that car, become aware of dealers selling that car. I can remember this happening to me at 17, when I desperately wanted a Volkswagen Beetle. I thought about this car every day, constantly, and dreamt up many ways to earn money to buy one. I truly believed I was going to get one. Over the coming weeks it seemed every second person was driving that VW Beetle.

Now, it wasn't exactly true that there were suddenly more Beetles on the road, it was just that my RAS was finding the evidence that supported my thoughts and beliefs and pointing them out to me.

Evidence in this sense is just another name for 'opportunity'.

I believe that the saying *"make your own luck"* simply means that you should focus on what you want and the opportunities will be made obvious to you, courtesy of your RAS.

When you add self-talk to your RAS, the 'evidence' becomes even stronger.

Can you see the danger in thinking negative and limiting thoughts? Your RAS will support your thinking by sending more 'evidence' to support more negative thoughts and limiting beliefs. More bad luck!

So, how can you use your RAS and your conscious mind to eliminate your limiting beliefs? Try the next exercise. It will help you to identify, clear and replace your limiting beliefs.

Even if you're not entirely convinced yet, please give it a try. You have nothing to lose. If it helps in just a small way, you'll be one step closer to your goals.

Clear Your Limiting Beliefs

On a separate piece of paper (not in your Winner's Toolbox) write down all the limiting beliefs that have stopped you from achieving your goals up until now. For example, "I'm too short," "I'm not strong enough," "I only train part-time" and so on.

Next, ask yourself this: Will hanging onto these beliefs hold you back from achieving your goals?

Now, write down how much has it cost you in the past to have these limiting beliefs? Write down the pain and the lost opportunities.

And, write down what is it going to cost you in the future if you continue to have these limiting beliefs.

Finally, (in your Winner's Toolbox under the heading of 'My New Empowering Beliefs') write down the beliefs you need to have in order to achieve your goal. Start feeding your mind powerful pictures with new and empowering thoughts and pictures. Get creative – find or draw pictures that represent the new beliefs. For example, if your new belief is that you are strong and powerful, draw muscles or paste in a picture of dumbbells. Whatever works for you. Remember, the more descriptive, the more emotion it will evoke and the more powerful it will be.

(Read how I used this exercise to my advantage in the lead up to qualifying for the 2004 Olympic Games in Chapter 29 - Attitude is Everything.)

Tip: Send them on their way
Don't forget to rip up that first piece of paper with all your old limiting beliefs. Or burn it, and watch the negativity go up in smoke!

Review your new beliefs, at least daily. As your thoughts become actions, take notice of all the things that just seem to show up, that re-inforce your New Empowering Beliefs. The more you immerse yourself in them the more you will become them.

> *Whatever the mind can conceive and believe it can achieve.*
>
> **Napoleon Hill**, Philosopher, Author

Use affirmations to help you, even pin them up on your walls. Do whatever you can to remind you that these are the beliefs you want to uphold.

Breaking out of a limiting belief is like opening a door to another world – a door to a world you haven't yet discovered.

When your beliefs are in harmony with your goals, then you will easily achieve whatever you desire. That's why it's important to ensure that your goals are *your* goals and not someone else's and that they are what you really, really want.

Story Time: The Chicken (Author Unknown)

Once upon a time, there was an eagle's nest, perched high up on a mountain summit. The eagle's nest contained four large eagle eggs. One day an earthquake rocked the mountain causing one of the eggs to roll down the mountain to a chicken farm, located in the valley below. The chickens knew that they must protect and care for the eagle's egg, so an old hen volunteered to nurture and raise the large egg. One day, the egg hatched and a beautiful eagle was born. Time passed, and the eagle was raised to be a chicken. Soon, the eagle believed he was nothing more than a chicken. The eagle loved his home and family, but his spirit cried out for more. While playing a game on the farm one day, the eagle looked to the skies and noticed a group of mighty eagles soaring above.

"Oh", the eagle cried, "I wish I could soar like those birds". The chickens roared with laughter, "You cannot soar with those birds! You are a chicken and chickens do not soar".

The eagle continued staring at his real family up above, dreaming that he could be with them. Each time, the eagle would let his dreams be known, he was told it couldn't be done and that is what the eagle learned to believe. The eagle, after a time, stopped dreaming and continued to live his life like a chicken. Finally, after a long life as a chicken, the eagle passed away.

Moral of the story: You become what you believe you are.

Many people are supposed to fly like eagles but they live like chickens because they think like chickens. Many eagle-people don't fly because they allow chicken-people to influence and convince them that they cannot do it.

Soon they begin to think like chickens and live in a yard scratching for worms all their lives They die like chickens even though they were engineered to fly like eagles.

So be careful who you associate with. If you mingle with chickens, you will think, live and die like a chicken.

> *Can you imagine what I would do if I could do all I can?*
>
> **Sun Tze**, Ancient Philosopher

KEY POINTS

Setting goals will fuel your 'unshakeable belief' system.

Surround yourself with inspiration.

Use your **RAS** and your conscious mind to eliminate your limiting beliefs.

CHAPTER 25
FEARS AND DOUBTS

I learned that courage was not the absence of fear, but the triumph over it. The brave man is not he who does not feel afraid, but he who conquers that fear.

Nelson Mandela, former President of South Africa

To overcome your fears, you need courage. It doesn't mean that you will no longer have those fears; it just means that you move forward, *despite* those fears.

In the introduction to his book *Seb Coe – Born to Run*, David Miller says, "Fear runs through sport. Fear of the opponent. It is there all the time, whether seen or not. It is there in losers; yet it is as likely to be there in the mind of a winner during some phase of victory. Fear can be both a motivation and an inhibition. Fear exists in the conspicuously physical sports such as boxing or rugby, and every Olympic downhill racer will tell you they encounter fear on the face of the mountain. Yet fear also stalks the competitor in something as unaggressive as golf. So much of sport at its pinnacle is played in the mind."

Like all negative feelings and emotions, fears will crop up in your life, day in and day out. What moves you forward is how you deal with them. You can let the fear crush you or you can stand up to it with courage and face it head on.

I'm not just talking about the shaking-in-your-boots, paralysing kind of fear. I'm talking about the everyday, commonplace fears.

Here's a list of the types of things that I've been afraid of or had doubts about at certain times in my career. You might find that you have similar fears:

- Being judged
- Looking silly, stupid or being laughed at
- Being humiliated
- Having your reputation tarnished
- Being teased or called names
- Losing or ruining a relationship
- Losing money
- Being injured or other physical pain
- Getting into trouble
- Failure
- Rejection
- The unknown

Wouldn't life be great if we could avoid all or some of these fears? But, quite frankly, the biggest rewards and greatest successes come from actually taking risks, facing these fears head on and moving past them.

Keep Fear in Perspective

It's time we changed our perspective on fear. I like to think of fear as neither good nor bad, but instead, an *aid* to help us develop.

Once you acknowledge them, then you can start to deal with them. Sit still and listen to your fears and doubts. Are they real? Are they worth worrying about? Take time out to analyse them.

Respond to them accordingly. Don't just react. Acknowledge, analyse and respond. Be brave.

If you don't think you can face the possibility of losing or making mistakes, you'll never, ever come close to your potential.

Being successful means being brave, over and over again. Having courage to take risks and step totally out of your comfort zone is what's going to propel you toward reaching your dreams.

Are Your Goals Big Enough?

It takes guts to set big goals. If your goals aren't big enough, it probably means you're afraid of failing.

Remember, even though you've already written them down, you can always change them. Do you need to go back and make them bigger? If so, do it now.

> *The only people who never fail at anything are those who don't try anything.*
>
> **Earl Nightingale**, Author

No one ever said that being successful is an easy or comfortable ride.

Acknowledge Mistakes

Research shows that successful people, from all walks of life, make more mistakes than unsuccessful people. They first realise their mistake, then they learn from it, fix it and try never to repeat it – instead of giving up.

You can't win Gold unless other athletes have beaten you down, in your climb to the top.

> ## TURNING DOUBT INTO POWER AND PRECISION
>
> Many years into my Beach Volleyball career I had developed one of the fastest serves in the world. However I still made lots of mistakes during training and competition. I had the courage to stick with it, though, as it made our team many points.
>
> When Kurek started working with me, one of the first things I asked him to help me with was my serve. I felt that even though I had one of the fastest serves in the world, I couldn't control it. Basically, I totally doubted my accuracy and therefore made the mistakes that I expected of myself.
>
> Kurek's first advice was to change the way I thought about my serving. He told me to release the doubt and change my self-talk to something more positive. I changed it to "I am the fastest and most accurate server in the world." I wrote it down, I read it often and I said it over and over to myself.
>
> The results of releasing this doubt and then adding positive self-talk and affirmations were astonishing. Within a few weeks, my accuracy had improved 100% and I was still serving the ball just as hard, if not harder.
>
> My serve became one of our most valuable weapons in defeating the Brazilians for Gold.

If you take a risk, you may fumble, you may fail. It may be a mistake. But think of risk as your friend. And learn and grow from the outcome.

He who is not courageous enough to take risks will accomplish nothing in life.

Muhammad Ali, Three-time World Heavyweight Champion

Jump serving with force on the Australian National Tour

Expect Criticism and Doubt

Criticism usually stems from jealousy. Sometimes, it will come from people you trust and look up to. It will hurt, briefly. But, if you can see it for what it is and learn from it to move closer to your goals, then it's a gift.

Doubt is nothing but a thought, and is often instilled in you by others. When your experience proves them wrong, doubt will quickly disappear.

Shelley Taylor-Smith (seven-time World No.1 Women's Marathon Swimming Champion) was tagged as 'nothing above average' with 'no natural ability' at the age of 12. But she never let others' opinion and doubts affect the way she thought about herself. She just swam on and on and on until she made history. Imagine if she'd given up in those early days. Imagine if she'd let other people's doubts encroach on her beliefs. She would never have achieved such amazing results in long distance swimming.

How to Move Beyond Doubt

The best way to annihilate your doubts is to simply:

1. Acknowledge the doubt.
2. Reframe your thoughts about the situation in a positive way.
3. Frequently reaffirm your thoughts.
4. Take action.

Think about some of the people you admire most. Think about their accomplishments. Do they seem to possess that unshakeable belief in themselves?

When they have to make a decision, they don't hesitate. They think positively and they have a clear picture of where they want to go. They have no fears or doubts.

So, what's stopping you from doing the same, and thinking as they do? Nothing.

Remember, the thoughts you keep are your choice. It's time to stop yearning to be like others. It's time to *become* a success story yourself.

> *Success is not final, failure is not fatal. It is the courage to continue that counts.*
>
> **Winston Churchill**, Former British Prime Minister

FREE FLOW BANISHES DOUBT

This is one of my own journal entries from 13 August 2001, where I reflected on some tough times. It shows how I talked myself out of my doubts until I felt back on top of my game. This was all written over a period of about 20 minutes.

I've just been through a 'dark patch'. It started after Nat injured herself and I felt I had to do more.

I played with Ang and couldn't play 'above' myself to get a good result.

Then with Nat again, our whole game changed back to her being served every ball.

I tried to do more, but when it didn't work, I got frustrated and ended up doing less and worrying more about my mistakes.

I felt like I was failing her and our team.

My confidence hit an all time low. My serving was lousy.

Then, as Nat became better, our opponents began serving me again.

Austria was a nightmare. I let my personal problems interfere with my enthusiasm and my mood.

I tried, in vain, to dig myself out of it but it didn't work.

In our match against Italy at Maria Worth, I played possibly the worst game of my life – my mental state was disgraceful. My confidence so low that remembering that I'd won a Gold less than a year ago meant nothing.

Now (a month later) after Japan, I am bouncing back.

We (as a team/unit) are on our way up.

I am being served again and will probably continue to be.

This is GOOD. I can control the game.

It gives me 'touch' for my serving.

Unfortunately my first game/tournament 'back', I just tried to hit everything down.

I will now ask for my sets off the net a bit, continue to hit, HIGH and hard.

I will open up my angle with a fast line shot and GO TO cut shot.

I MUST TAKE RISKS to improve.

I am the strongest player out there.

I have 'touch' – touch is relaxation and belief.

If I get blocked again, then 'smile' and say 'thanks for reminding me to hit HIGHER and deeper.

TRY BODY FAKES – Everyone is so used to seeing how I hit so change the picture.

RELAXATION – CLEAR MIND – BELIEF

SUPER "K" – PLAYER OF THE DECADE

KEY POINTS

Don't just react to fear – acknowledge, analyse and respond.

Choose to learn from criticism, and don't take it personally.

CHAPTER 26
DEALING WITH CHALLENGES

There are often one or two specific life changing moments when the reaching of goals hangs in the balance. It's tempting to turn back, give up or say, "This is all too hard".

Be thankful for the hand of cards you've been dealt and work with them. Don't let those cards work you. Remember, it's not about what you've been dealt, but which cards you choose to play.

Pain is temporary. It may last a minute, or an hour, or a day, or a year, but eventually it will subside and something else will take its place. If I quit, however, it lasts forever.

Lance Armstrong, Seven-time winner of the Tour de France

Athletes who succeed in reaching their goals have more often than not overcome greater obstacles than they had anticipated, experienced more crushing lows than they could have imagined and paid a higher price than they had ever planned.

I don't wish to discourage you; I just want to prepare you. The journey may be rough, but if you stick at it, the benefit at the end is priceless.

FREAK ACCIDENT BECOMES A TURNING POINT

I've experienced my share of setbacks. I've suffered serious injuries, broken relationships and even lost money from bad investment choices. These were all extremely difficult times, but each time I was 'knocked down' it simply made me work harder to get back up again.

The most significant hurdle I faced within my sporting career was toward the end of 1992. An injury to my right knee. One jump, and the way I landed and twisted my leg, changed my life forever. It was at the height of my Indoor Volleyball career, and I had ruptured my crutiate ligament, my medial ligament, and wrecked a significant amount of cartilage and meniscus.

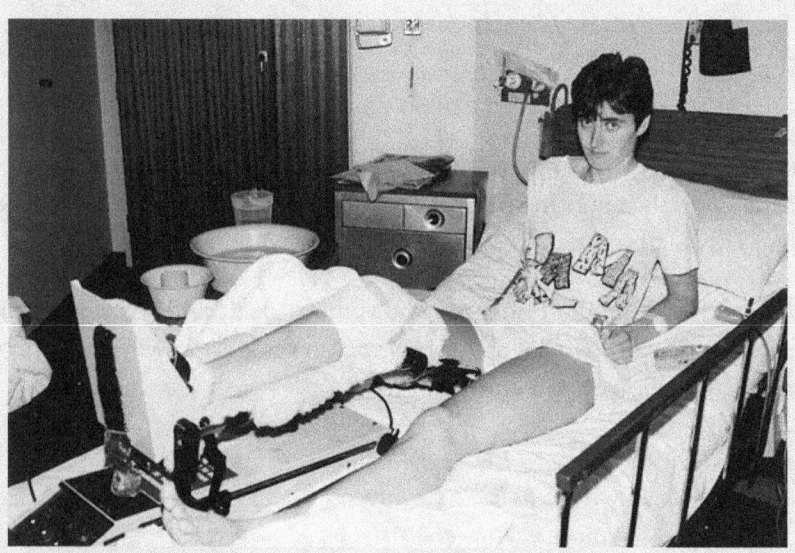

In hospital after my second surgery in 2 months, Dec 1992

I believed, during the painful and lengthy rehabilitation, that I would never be able to play Indoor Volleyball again. This was an incredibly difficult time for me as all my friends, my boyfriend and my family were all involved with my Indoor Volleyball career. I had been one of the best players in Australia and felt I could still improve so much more. I was 27 years old and had played for the Australian National Team for the past 10 years. I had also recently been made the Captain during one of our last tours.

I fell into a type of mild depression, smiling on the outside but often crying myself to sleep. Volleyball was my life. What would I do now? How will I ever even be able to walk again, let alone run?

Then came the turning point. The moment that was going to change my perspective, and lead me towards a positive future once more. My boyfriend at the time, Jeff, brought home a brand new white volleyball. He passed it to me and said:

"On each panel of the ball I want you to write a goal. Then, date that goal and bit by bit I want you to work out how to get back on the court again."

Now I must say here that no one had actually told me that I couldn't play again, I just assumed it because the surgeon had told me it was one of the most serious injuries he'd ever seen.

I had also never written down any goals before.

That afternoon, with little else to do, I started writing on the ball. Bit by bit, I filled in each panel. I started with 'running in water' then 'jumping in water' then 'riding a bike', and so on, until I had added each volleyball skill. I completed the last two panels with: 'practice match' and 'competition match.'

It was such an exhilarating feeling to all of a sudden see the path I needed to take to get back to playing. And, it was written on something that represented my sporting life – a volleyball!

Bit by bit, I followed each step and eventually tried to play again. Unfortunately, it wasn't to be as my original assumptions were correct and I wasn't able to handle the hard floorboards.

However, there was still one small step on my ball that I had yet to try. Written in small print on one side was beach volleyball – and even smaller, underneath, I'd written Atlanta 1996.

The rest is history!

My Indoor Volleyball covered with goals to give me the inspiration to get back on the court

Obstacles are a part of life. There's just no avoiding them. If I hadn't have written down the steps to making a comeback, I may have given up right then and there, and never played sport again.

This is also why I believe goal setting is so powerful. And truly life changing, particularly when you're facing rejection or serious setbacks.

So, what do you do when you are faced with a seemingly insurmountable obstacle?

Start By Thinking Deeply, Asking Questions

- What does this 'challenge' mean?

- How can I make it better?

- What can I do to get back on course straight away?

Studies have shown that the most effective people solve challenges within milliseconds. No yelling, no crying, no feeling sorry for themselves, no delays. Just straight away. Great inner dialog, they ask the right questions and they get the right answers to move forward.

> *I can't control my opponent, but I can master the ball and this will impact on my opponent.*
>
> **Steve Anderson**, Gold Medal Beach Volleyball Coach

Look Ahead – To Where You're Going. Do this, and you'll be much better able to deal with where you are right now. Challenges will make you stronger and the distractions won't seem so distracting if you're focusing forward.

Remember – look through the windshield and not your rear view mirror. If you focus on your worries, your losses, your injuries and your anxieties, those are the things that will grow.

> *I skate to where the puck is going to be, not to where it has been.*
>
> **Wayne Gretzky**, Ice Hockey Champion

Remind Yourself Of Your Purpose. Remind yourself *why* you want to achieve your goals. Go back and read your 'Purpose' in your Winner's Toolbox, to help give you the motivation to overcome your frustrations. It will set you back on track with a renewed energy. It will remind you to see, hear, feel and taste the end of your journey. The more you visualise the Ultimate Big Picture, the more energy you'll have to keep going.

> *Obstacles are those frightful things you see when you take your eyes off your goal.*
>
> **Henry Ford**, Industrialist, Founder of the Ford Motor Company

It's up to you to decide how to deal with a challenge. Time will pass whether you do anything or not.

Have a strong positive attitude. When you hit a roadblock, try not to think of it as the end of the road. Think of it rather as a bend in the road. Treat it as an opportunity to learn. Turn the negativity of it into something positive. It's a chance to make adjustments and improvements to your plan.

Be ready to adapt. When things change, you need to be able to change with them. You never know what's in-store. One of the greatest skills you can develop is adaptability. Be ready to change your course at any given moment. If you're not going to be flexible, you may as well stop right there in your tracks. Reinvent yourself and expand who you are.

> ## ONE SMALL CHANGE FOR VOLLEYBALL, ONE GIANT WIN FOR AUSTRALIA
>
> Since the invention of volleyball in 1895, one rule stood firm: the ball was not allowed to hit the net on serve. If it did, then it was deemed a fault and the ball was turned over to the opposition.
>
> Then, at the beginning of the year 2000 and only a few months from the Sydney Olympic Games, the International Federation decided to change the rule. From that moment on, it was acceptable for the ball to be able to touch the net on serve. Even if the ball hit the net, then dribbled over, unplayable, it was deemed OK.
>
> Upon hearing this, players from all around the world complained. They said it would damage the game, make it ugly to watch, and so forth. Even I stood up in a player's meeting and said, "What happens if, during the Gold Medal match at the Olympic Games this year, the ball hits the net on match point and dribbles over for the win? How awful would that be for our sport? What a horrible way to win the match."
>
> Well, it didn't change the minds of the powers-that-be, and the new rule stayed. We all simply had to learn to adjust. We had to learn new habits and ways of dealing with this rule.
>
> In the Gold Medal match, less than six months later, Natalie and I reached set point against the Brazilians. Nat had the ball in her hand. She made an aggressive serve and her serve hit the top of the net and dribbled over! Just as I had pictured. Maybe not match point, but it gave us the set and one huge advantage in the best of three sets.
>
> To top that off, when the Brazilians served one that hit the net, Natalie dove forward, dug it in the air for me to play it over and we won that point. An almost unheard of play by Natalie, but only because we were willing to adapt.

> I now have the players that I coach deliberately try to hit the top of the net with their serves. We have all survived the change and adapted. I now even like the rule!
>
> Be ready and willing to adapt and this may very well be the difference between coming 2nd or 1st!!

Persist. The power of persistence is significant. One small effort may not have much of an effect, but if that same effort is repeated over and over again, the results can be dramatic. Soft drops of water can wear away the hardest of stones. Tiny trees burst through the floor of the forest and grow into skyscrapers. With persistence, things that may seem impossible can be achieved.

Persistence doesn't require a massive effort or special skills and resources. All you've got to do is keep on going. Bit by bit, step by step. Learn from each effort.

When you've done what you think needs to be done, go ahead and do some more. That will put you ahead of the rest.

Did you know that Abraham Lincoln lost eight elections before he became president?

Did you know that Colonel Sanders suffered 1000 rejections before he sold his first chicken recipe?

Have courage. Courage doesn't mean you're not afraid, it means that you move forward, in spite of your fears and challenges. There will many on your journey who will question what you're doing, question your purpose and even question your goals. They may try to dim your vision and it will feel like they're trying to trip you up as you stride toward the finish line. Often, they are either afraid *for* you or afraid that you will succeed, and that will make them look weak. Don't listen, and be brave.

Take Responsibility. It's so easy to blame. Blame others, blame your surroundings, blame your opponents, blame your coaches, blame your

CIAO BELLA! ... HEY, I'M NOT GOING ANYWHERE!!

By 1990 I was one of the best Indoor Volleyball players in Australia, but I still wanted to improve. I looked into the possibility of playing as a foreign player in another country's National League. Players in these leagues were earning good money and I realised that this was a way I could take a year off work, get a whole lot better at Volleyball and actually earn money for playing Volleyball for the first time in my life! I was lucky to get a really good position in Bologna in the north of Italy in a Division I team.

Warming up for my first match with Italian Indoor Volleyball team – San Lazzaro, 1991

However, it wasn't long into the season, our team wasn't doing as well as expected, and they sacked the coach. Then, the following week they sacked me! I was one of the two foreign players allowed per team and was easily replaceable. It didn't matter that I was playing the best volleyball of my entire career, what mattered was that they needed an even better player, so they decided to bring in a Brazilian girl to take my place.

I had a choice to make at that point. I could give up and go home. Cut my losses, feel sorry for myself and say "Oh well, I tried but I failed". Or, I could stay on, train with the team, but not play matches.

I decided to stay. I dug my feet in and I trained really, really, really hard because I just couldn't give up.

By the end of the week they called me back into the office and said, "Well Kerri, you've amazed us this week. We want you to stay. We're going to sack the other foreign player!"

I stayed on to complete the season and we managed a few more wins to keep the team in Division 1.

This experience taught me the true value of persistence and to never, ever give up. Success could be just around the corner.

With my Italian team mates Maria Cristina Lesa (L) and Luisella Milani (R) just after we'd been told I was staying on!

upbringing, and so on. We all do it from time to time. It's the easy way out. Learning to take responsibility was probably one of the biggest things I had to learn as I was developing into an elite athlete. It didn't mean that I thought every bad experience was my fault, it just meant that because I had something to do with it, I could also have something to do with *changing* it.

A champion takes responsibility for everything. They don't have a victim's mentality and blame others. You don't hear champions saying, "Oh, I could have won that, but...." or "If the wind wasn't so strong I would have...."

If you're getting negative results, rather than thinking that it's someone else's fault or the fault of circumstance, ask yourself, "How did I create this result?" If you still think you did everything possible, then ask yourself, "What can I learn from this to become better?"

Instead of saying "I can't..." teach yourself to ask "How can I....?" It's not your fault; it's your *responsibility*.

Forget the pain. Pain is hard enough to deal with when you're in the moment. Forget the pain once you've learnt from it and replace it with the joy of knowing you've broken through the barrier. Don't hold onto it – let it go.

The key to dealing with a lot of challenges and setbacks is not focusing on what's happening to you, rather, focusing on how you can deal with it.

> *If you hit a mountain of a roadblock, start climbing.*
> *If you hit a river, start swimming.*
> *If you don't know what to do next, go and learn more about it.*
> *If you need others to help you, go out there, ask and persuade.*
>
> Anonymous

So, find a way. Find the courage, commit, and persevere. View every challenge as an opportunity.

Upsets, setbacks and failures are all tests. They are opportunities to help you build the mental and physical strength that will take you through your sporting career and through the rest of your life.

DEALING WITH CHALLENGES 285

Whether it is injury, poor form, worries over selection, media intrusions or conflicts – they are all part of the life of a professional athlete. The world isn't perfect, and you can't change it. But you can change yourself.

When you change the way that you're looking at the challenges in your life, the challenges that you're looking at will change.

Kurek Ashley, Peak Performance Coach

Never give up!

KEY POINTS

The journey may be rough, but never ever give up.

Constantly remind yourself of your 'purpose'.

Instead of focusing on a setback, focus on how you can deal with it.

CHAPTER 27
SELF-CONFIDENCE

I am the greatest.

Muhammad Ali, Three-time World Heavyweight Champion

Self-confidence is not just the absence of doubt. It's the complete certainty in your ability and/or the outcome. Muhammad Ali believed he was the greatest, and told anyone who would listen. He said it so often and with such conviction that even his opponents started believing it.

Self-confidence comes from experience, encouragement, preparation, desire, imagination and courage. All of these things you can work on and improve.

In some people it is so obvious you can almost touch it. It's the way they look, the way they talk, the way they enter a room.

Now, I'm not saying that the solution is to go around yelling, "I am the greatest!" But if you do suffer from even the occasional self doubt

– and I know I sure do, then it's time you put your gloves on, and stepped into the ring.

Why Is Confidence So Important?

When confidence is high, sporting potential turns into sporting performance.

Self-confidence gives you the ability to work well under pressure. High achievers are risk takers and have the courage to take on tasks beyond their skill set. They are often willing to put themselves in an environment that requires more of them than they appear to be able to do. They find a way and they do it with confidence.

Most people need evidence that something will work, before they try. Successful people believe it without proof.

How Does It Affect Your Performance?

When confidence wanes, pitfalls and problems are magnified and poor or under-performance is inevitable. Loss of confidence can be as bad as a broken leg and can even take longer to heal.

On the other hand, being confident will bring with it a higher level of motivation and an ability to persist in the face of challenges.

I've read about athletes involved in experiments who were told that their opponents were weaker than they actually were. They then went on to beat those seemingly 'weaker' opponents during arm wrestling contests and other strength tests. Psychological barriers come down when athletes are more confident.

I know that whenever I went out on the court with the feeling that we were stronger than our opponents, and that we were the better team, we almost always won.

When you lack confidence in yourself, other people are likely to agree with you. They figure you know more about yourself than they do – so if you're down on yourself, they probably will be too. Not only is this the wrong picture to be giving your opponent; if you're in a team sport your team will feel it too. Your coach will also get this impression and be less inclined to put you on the field or use you during important points.

When you project energy of confidence and self-assurance, the opposite is true.

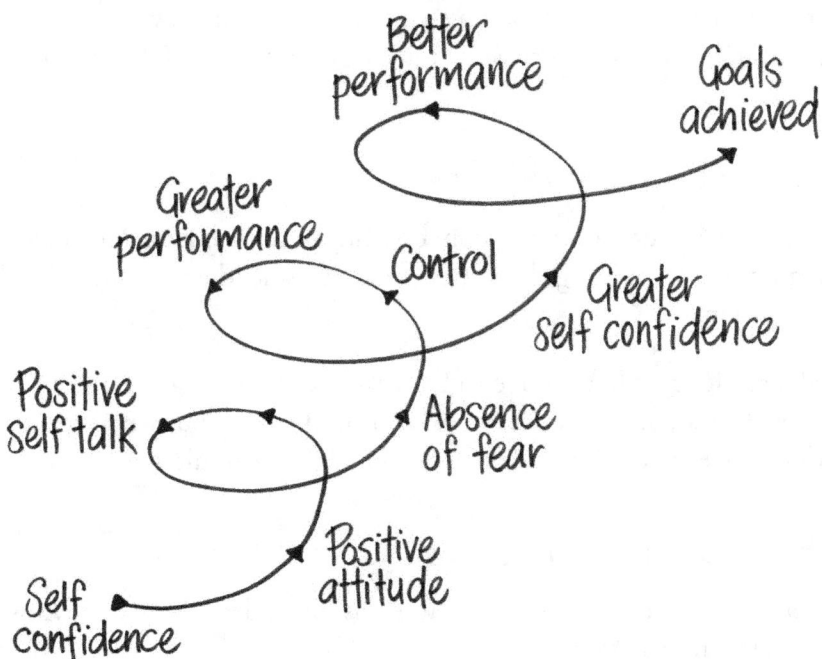

At some point in your career, you may progress to the level where you'll get to play against your idol, your role model or mentor. This is when your self-confidence can really be tested.

In his book *Serious*, John McEnroe describes how his lack of self-confidence affected his early game. At the age of just 18, against all odds he had made it to his first Wimbledon semi-final. He was scheduled to play Jimmy Connors – one of his idols, and first saw him in the locker room before the game. He says, "I walked up and tried to say tried hi to Connors. He wouldn't even look at me. He wouldn't even acknowledge my existence. It was a very short moment.... I certainly felt intimidated.... And so at that moment, I pretty much decided I did not want to win this match. *Don't want to win*, I thought. *Can't handle it*. (Not that I could've won if I *had* wanted it.) He had won the initial battle of wills." He goes on to describe how if he had beaten Connors, he would have played Borg. "Borg was a poster on my bedroom door (right next to Farrah Fawcett). I just wasn't emotionally capable of thinking about beating any of these guys yet."

Picture a scene like this happening to you, and imagine how you'd respond. Do this and your confidence won't take the beating that McEnroe's did that day.

What Is Real Confidence?

Real confidence doesn't come from boasting or talking it up. It comes from listening, understanding, learning from fears and then moving ahead in spite of them.

Real confidence is like a force to be reckoned with. It can't be stopped. It may be dented, or it may get knocked around a little, but when combined with positive action, it will deliver truly impressive results.

What Happens When You Lose It?

When you lose confidence in yourself as an athlete, it's like having the control taken away from you.

It can feel like time is rushing by. You feel hurried and helpless. Your attention and focus wander and nothing seems easy anymore.

When you have great confidence, you feel the opposite. You seem to have lots of time to work on each skill, and everything may even be in slow motion. You feel happy and things seem easy.

>
> ### Building Self-Confidence
>
> Everyone has a certain amount of self-confidence — that's part of what makes up your personality.
>
> Yet there are many areas of confidence that are not related to personality, but are dictated by circumstances. These are the areas that you can learn to control and improve.
>
> Let's start by determining what confidence means to you — what it looks and feels like. In your Winner's Toolbox write down the name of any person, animal, object or word that you associate with confidence. It can be whatever you like.
>
> For example, confidence to me means: Roger Federer, a lion, staring eyes, smiling face, knowing, raised arms, great posture.
>
> Next, work out which of these words best describes confidence to you. Mine is the lion.
>
> Now, find a great picture of that word and put it straight into your Winner's Toolbox. Write the words 'Ultimate Confidence' above or below that picture. Look at the picture at least once a day, and 'meditate' on the feeling of confidence it gives you.
>
> Use this picture to help create the unshakeable belief you have in yourself.

One Step At a Time

Confidence can be built one step at a time. A small achievement brings with it the confidence to take it to the next level. Each time you succeed, you gain the confidence to reach higher.

Start with a realistic attitude towards your performance. Know that bad performances will happen from time to time and strengthen your resolve to learn from them.

Confidence in your physical condition will have a significant impact on your performance. If you feel strong, agile and prepared, you will naturally feel more confident.

Physical preparation can feel extremely tedious. I know. I wasn't a fan of all the conditioning work we had to do in the gym and in the pool. However, the time and effort you put into learning, practising, developing your skills and lifting those weights lays the groundwork for self-confidence.

> *I figure practice puts your brains in your muscles.*
>
> **Sam Snead, Champion Golfer**

Then, when you compete, you *feel* more prepared, more ready to battle the opponents, knowing that you've done all the hard work.

So prepare to achieve. Be ready for every type of game situation. Play those situations out at practice, in your head. So, when and if they happen, you'll know what to do and how to deal with them.

IN JOYFUL STRAINS

I often joked to Natalie that the reason we won Bronze in 1996 was because I didn't know the words to the Australian national anthem!

When I was in school, Australia sang a different anthem, and I grew up knowing all the words to God Save the Queen.

So, as part of my preparation leading into Sydney 2000 I made absolutely sure I knew Advance Australia Fair, word for word! I even stuck it up on the back of the toilet door in our Olympic accommodation so I could sing it at every chance. Nat loved that, especially first thing in the morning!

For me, it was about making sure each piece of the jigsaw was in place. That I'd done all the work.

And, when I stood there on top of the podium with the Gold Medal around my neck, I felt so proud, and belted those words out like a rock star!

Singing the Australian National Anthem on the podium at the 2000 Olympics – one of the proudest moments of my life

There are several other techniques I've found invaluable in building my self-confidence:

1. **Breaking It Down**

    For me, this approach was critically important, particularly in regaining lost confidence. You break down a particular skill into a series of tasks, and master each step before going on to the next. You'll have that skill perfected in no time.

    This approach not only helps you develop complex skill-sets, but it can also help you re-learn a skill if you've hit a low point in your confidence level, and believe you can't perform that skill anymore.

> ## GOING BACK TO BASICS
>
> For whatever reason, there were times that my confidence in certain aspects or skills of my game would be so low that I could barely win a point with that skill.
>
> I even talked myself into believing that I had never even possessed that skill, which was totally untrue. It was just that my confidence had been shaken whilst using that skill.
>
> Fortunately, I had a great coach who was quick to remind me that the skill was there, I just wasn't 'seeing' it. We went back to doing a very basic break down of the skill until I was able to put it back in my game.
>
> It was never gone; it was my confidence and my negative self-talk that was stopping me from performing. Going back to basics was an ongoing process throughout the 25 years of my playing career. You're never too old or experienced to go back to working on the foundations.

2. **Being Involved With Other Successful Athletes**

   Getting to know other elite athletes, and watching them perform, can give you a massive boost in confidence.

   Being part of a large group, even if you're an individual competitor, also has its advantages. I found travelling with the Olympic Games teams to be an incredibly powerful confidence booster.

   You're able to feed off your fellow athletes' successes, just as Natalie Cook did in watching Kieran Perkins win Gold at the Atlanta Games.

   If you're not at Olympic level yet, then get to know and travel with the best athletes in your sport. It might lead to great times, and even greater inspiration.

SELF-CONFIDENCE 295

Being inspired by Lawrie Lawrence (Legendary Swim Coach and Master Motivator) just before the Sydney Games started

Natalie and I spending time with the late and great Peter Brock (Australia's most successful motor racing driver) in the Olympic village

In our official uniforms for the ..... From left, Basketballers: Andrew Vlahov, Paul Rogers, (me), Luc Longley and Hockeyroo: Juliet Haslam

Sailing legend, John Bertrand (who skippered Australia 2 to victory in the 1983 America's Cup) visits our room at the Olympics with the "Gold" theme

Finally meeting Peter Robertson, Olympic triathlete, at the Sydney 2000 closing ceremony. I'd read about Peter's struggle to qualify for the Games in the newspaper and it had inspired me so much that I hung the newspaper story in my room during our qualification period.

Enjoying the closing ceremony with swimming legends Grant Hackett and Michael Klim

3. **Using Verbal Persuasion**

   Using verbal persuasion is a fundamental way to change an attitude or belief, in order to achieve greater self-confidence. I'm essentially referring to the use of positive self-talk and affirmations, which I cover in detail in Chapter 11: Affirmations. Repetition is critical to reinforce the positive messages.

   'Verbal persuasion', whether it comes from your coach, your peers or your own inner voice, can be very successful in just keeping you on track (at the very least).

4. **Controlling Negative Emotions**

   The emotional response to your circumstances – how you feel and your overall emotional state, can build or destroy your confidence. I cannot stress enough, the importance of realising this.

   For instance, if you become anxious about a particular event, your confidence will almost certainly plummet. If you are scared of losing, you most likely will. If you're returning from injury, and feeling apprehensive at performing, self-doubt will result.

Your emotions are often triggered by your imagination. Your interpretation of events (on and off the field) is personal. But, it is also something you can choose to control.

Instead, use your mind and your imagination to highlight your strengths and search out your opponent's weaknesses.

5. **Calming, Relaxing Through Breathing**

    Learning relaxation and breathing skills can help control your thoughts and emotions, leading to greater self-confidence.

    Here is a simple breathing technique that can be done anywhere – in the car, on a bus, waiting at the airport, at work or before a big game.

    - Sit, stand still or lie with your hands resting comfortably in your lap or by your side. Use soft music to help reduce distractions.
    - Gently close your eyes and focus internally on your breathing.
    - Breathe in through your nose and out through your mouth.
    - Keep the tip of your tongue in contact with the top of your mouth, just behind your top teeth.
    - Start inhaling slowly, smoothly and deeply to a mental count of 4 seconds. Fill your lower lungs first (by pushing out your abdomen), then your middle and upper lungs.
    - Hold your breath for a mental count of 7 seconds.
    - Slowly and smoothly exhale for a mental count of 8 seconds.
    - As you exhale, try to let go of all your fear, doubt or negative thoughts.
    - Have a brief pause, without inhaling, and then do it again.

    Try doing this about 10 times until you start to feel stronger and more relaxed. It should calm your mind and balance your emotions.

6. **Visualisation**

   Visualisation is a powerful tool you can use for many areas of personal growth, and works wonders in creating confidence.

There's nothing like replaying the movie of achieving your goal in your mind ... High fiving the spectators as I run down the finishing shute, standing on the dais to collect the gold medal with a flag draped around my shoulders, an excited phone call from my parents telling me they had seen my win on TV, my children jumping into my arms to share the moment – all of the reasons that you get up on those days when you wake up so exhausted that you literally cry tears at the thought of getting up and working out again. I would remember that someone, somewhere in the world, would be trying to train harder and smarter than me to beat me to my goal.

There's no motivation like reminding myself of the sweetness of a win.

Nici Andronicus, International Tri-Athlete

Try creating a 'winning' soundtrack to play before competing:

Have someone read this out to you:

It's time to re-live your best ever sporting moment. The performance where you had supreme confidence....

- Relax and close your eyes.

- Bring to mind that moment of complete confidence.

- See yourself preparing to compete.

- Notice your surroundings, the sights, the sounds, and the atmosphere. See what you're wearing, the colours and feel how it fits. Hear the noises and smell the air.

- Look over to your opponent. How does he/she look? How does he/she make you feel?

- Now you're off. You're playing really well. Zone in on each point, each minute of the game. Pick out all your good touches on the ball or steps in the race.

- Notice the score, the time, the way you're moving, the way you feel.

- You're playing the best you've ever played. You're feeling extremely confident. No one will beat you when you're like this.

- Notice how focused you are, how well you're concentrating. Notice how relaxed your body is.

- Keep on imagining how you're performing. Feel each movement. Pick out details where you're performing the skill at its best.

- Who do you remind yourself of when you're playing like this?

- ….Slowly return to now, and open your eyes.

Next grab your iPhone, MP3 or laptop, and voice record what you just saw and felt in your own words. Describe exactly what happened and how you felt. Use the questions above to remind you.

You now have a soundtrack that you can take anywhere, anytime, and play to re-invigorate your confidence to perform at your very best.

Never Give Up

Never let your head hang down. Never give up and sit down and grieve. Find another way. And don't pray when it rains if you don't pray when the sun shines.

Leroy Paige, Legendary US Baseball Player

Sometimes we can feel so low, so depleted of confidence (especially after sporting losses), that we need a boost to bounce back.

Before this happens to you, I suggest you create a Personal Confidence Booster that you keep in your Winner's Toolbox.

Some refer to this as a strategy to 'fake it till you make it', a way to get back on top on low confidence days. You imitate confidence (even if you don't 100% feel it,) and as that confidence produces success, it will develop into *real* confidence.

Boost The Juice

Take some time to create a Personal Confidence Booster, by working through the following:

Write down what you are good at. Write down all your talents, skills and competencies. Make a long list and refer to it often so you can to remind yourself how good you are!

Reflect on your achievements. Write down all the things you have achieved so you can remind yourself of your successes.

Read testimonials. If you've gathered positive feedback from your coaches, teammates or clients, take time occasionally to read what they have said about you. Keep it in the one place; so you see at a glance, how many have said you are exceptional.

Surround yourself with VIPs (Very Inspiring People). Get rid of VDPs (Very Draining People) and only spend time with people who inspire you to achieve more, become more, give more and want more from life. Write their names in your Winner's Toolbox, and the reasons each one is good for you.

List things that make you feel good. Refer to this list when you don't feel 100%. They can be simple things like walking the dog, watching a funny film, playing a certain game with the kids. Just remembering those times will make you feel good.

Remember you are unique. There is no one on the planet with the same qualities, experiences, fingerprints or ideas as you. Embrace your uniqueness.

Trust and believe in yourself. Rely on your instinct and past experiences to guide your decision-making and remember it's up to you to be your biggest fan. When you believe in your own capabilities, others will too.

Watch Your Language

You might be unconsciously talking yourself down. We often take on the expressions used by our parents as we learn to speak. Try to use positive phrases instead.

Replace "I'll try" with "I will". I'll try means: "I feel compelled to do it, but I really don't want to do it".

Banish these words: should, could, ought to, and have to. They just increase your stress and your feelings of guilt.

Start accepting compliments and praise. This is a tough one for many. Instead of protesting that you don't deserve them or firing off some lame comment, just say a big 'thank you' and nothing more.

When asked how you feel (even in passing), say "great" or "fantastic" – not just "fine", "OK", or worse still – "not bad"!

Never say, "I'm too (stupid, fat, short, inexperienced, weak or afraid) to....." because someone will believe you. Don't expect them to disagree, particularly if you are saying it in a roundabout way to gain a positive affirmation.

Helping Others, Helping Yourself

When you focus solely on your gloom and despair, you can't help but feel negative and down. Yet if you turn to someone else and help them with their challenges, you will naturally feel more positive, more powerful. In talking to them, you may even start to work through your own confidence issues.

Give It Your Best Shot

After so many years of sport, I have simply developed the habit of giving my best in everything I do. I can't imagine being any other way. I can't imagine doing something half heartedly or with 50% effort. What's the point?

As an elite athlete, you're always learning, always improving. You'll have times when you're up in confidence and times when you're low. Keep your Winner's Toolbox around you. Type out your confidence boosters, laminate them, hang them up on your walls and take them on tour. But most importantly, just like your goals, read them every day.

If you constantly give your best in everything you do, your self-confidence will become effortless.

Do You Think You Can Win?

You can if you think you can!

If you think you are beaten, you are,
If you think you dare not, you don't.
If you like to win, but you think you can't,
It is almost certain you won't.

If you think you'll lose, you're lost,
For out in the world we find,
Success begins with a fellow's will.
It's all in the state of mind.

If you think you are outclassed, you are,
You've got to think high to rise,
You've got to be sure of yourself before
You can ever win a prize.

Life's battles don't always go
To the stronger or faster man.
But soon or late the man who wins,
Is the man who thinks he can.

C. W. Longenecker

> **KEY POINTS**
>
> Confidence can be built one step at a time.
>
> Create your own 'Personal Confidence Booster'.
>
> Fake it – till you make it.

CHAPTER 28
NEGATIVE SELF-TALK

Internal negative chatter creates stress. It can seriously impact your ability to achieve success (and certainly won't help in overcoming challenges).

Negative self-talk results from perception, not reality.

Understand that the words you use to describe who you are and how you perform as an athlete are self-fulfilling. You are what you say you are.

If you say that you're a great defender, but your offense isn't so great – it won't be! If you say that you can drive the golf ball further than anyone on the course, but you're not that accurate, you won't be!

I used to always say how bad my memory was. And, surprise, surprise, it was. As soon as I realised that I was just giving myself an excuse to 'forget' things and started saying that I had a *great* memory, I began remembering a lot more information than ever before.

Next time you talk to someone about your performance, whether it's your teammate, your coach or the media, listen to how you describe yourself. Is it all positive or are you putting yourself down?

Empowering Yourself With Positive Self-Talk

It can sometimes feel impossible to overcome negative thoughts. My advice is to just give it a try. Use some of the following tips, and persist. You'll find that you can change the way you think and talk about things. This will in turn, help you achieve the success you may have been telling yourself was out of your reach.

1. **Recognise The Negativity**

    The first step is to become aware of how often you say negative things in your head. When you hear yourself say something negative, say "stop" out loud (try not to frighten the cat). Or, put a rubber band around your wrist and snap it every time you say something negative in your head. This will certainly make you aware of how often you are negative.

2. **Re-think It Rationally, Not Emotionally**

    Once you've identified when you do it, ask yourself these questions, and try to give rational answers:

    - Is there another way I can look at this situation?
    - Is there another meaning to this situation?
    - If I had to turn this into a positive, what would that be?
    - Is this situation really that bad?
    - What's the worst that could happen? Is that likely to happen?
    - What's the best thing that could happen?
    - What's probably going to happen?
    - Will it really matter in six months, one year or five years time?

3. **Learn From Your Mistakes**

    If you've made a mistake, don't waste valuable time reminding yourself how stupid you are or regretting the fact that you've ruined any further opportunity in that area. State it in a positive, rational way by telling yourself what you've learnt for next time.

"Next time, I'll take into account more of what my opponent has just done, so I can be better prepared for where his next shot may go."

or

*"Now I know how **not** to do it and how I can fix it. Next time I will succeed."*

> ## THANK YOU SO MUCH!
>
> As one of the most powerful spikers on the World Tour, it was often quite hard for me when my opponent blocked out my spike, thus losing the point. It would knock my confidence and I would then become distracted and often lose a few more valuable points before I got my focus back on track.
>
> One day, my Coach said to me "Kerri, when you get blocked out, why not thank your opponent for reminding you to hit higher, harder and deeper?"
>
> I took this on board and it worked wonders. I stopped focusing on what had happened and looked ahead toward how I could make it better.

Every strike brings me closer to the next home run.

Babe Ruth, Baseball Legend

4. **Resist Sharing Your Self-Doubt**

    We often put ourselves down when talking to other people in the hope that they will refute what we've said.

    Resist the urge to show yourself in a bad light, even slightly. That doesn't mean that you lie. You can still tell a story about having made a mistake or the wrong choice in a certain situation. Just make sure you turn it around and explain what you've learned from it (or how it can be turned into a positive).

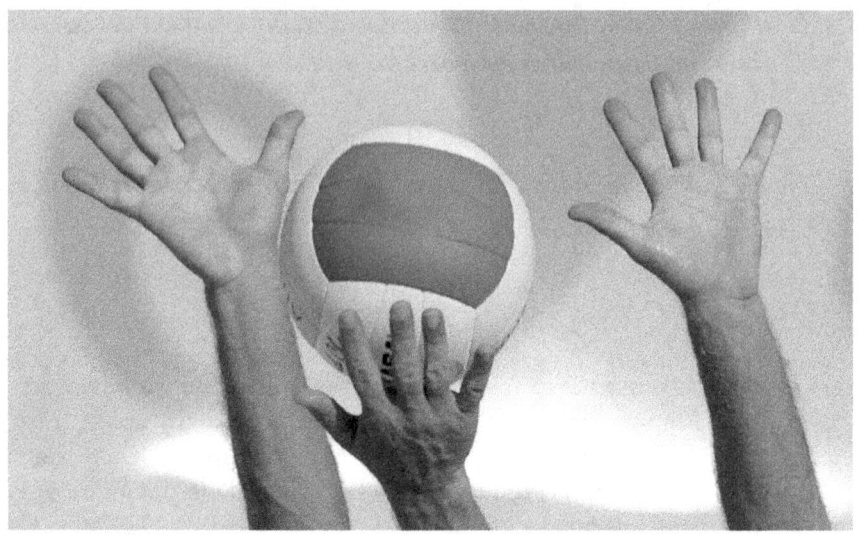

There's always a way through

5. **Stay Focused On Your Outcome**

   How often have you woken up for an early morning training session feeling tired, sore and lacking energy? Your inner voice tries to convince you to stay in bed and do the workout later....such a nice warm bed....

   While you know something's good for you, you also know that if you wait, you will keep putting it off until you eventually skip it all together.

   What do you do? Simple – focus on the outcome. Focus on the fact that by doing the training you not only feel fabulous for the rest of the day, but you'll be one step closer to your goals (ignore the fact that you're tired, and your bed is so cosy).

   By focusing on your outcome, you'll create positive thoughts and feelings, which will in turn create positive self-talk.

   You can apply the same technique to any work situation. Instead of lying awake at night, worrying about all the work that has to be done for a proposal due the next day, focus on all the great things that will result from handing in this proposal. If you commit 100% to changing your thoughts, not only will you get a good night's sleep, but the next day you'll have much greater energy, and feel much more positive – boosting your ability to get it done in time.

Trust me. Changing what you focus on, how you're thinking and talking to yourself will have an immediate impact on your life.

Don't let your success suffer by the way you think, feel and talk to yourself.

Natalie Cook describes in her book *Go Girl*, how, early on she learnt the value of positive self talk: "When I was a kid and wanted to be a champion swimmer, I kept losing to a girl who was half my size. I would say to myself, "She's too good; she's too quick. I can't do it". One day, for some reason, I changed it. I started saying "I'm too big to let her beat me". I didn't lose to her again from that day on. It was a change in my self-talk; a change in the way I viewed myself and my ability. There was not one physical change. It was all in my mind."

Saying that you can do something may not guarantee your success, but saying you can't, will most definitely guarantee your failure.

In his book *Open*, Andre Agassi talks about how being alone on a tennis court can lead to self-talk and for him, self-talk starts in his afternoon shower before a night match. "I step into the shower again but this shower is different from the morning shower. The afternoon shower is always longer – twenty-two minutes, give or take – and it's not for waking up or getting clean. The afternoon shower is for encouraging myself, coaching myself.... This is when I start to say things to myself, crazy things, over and over, until I believe them."

I am....

Do you want to improve your self-talk? Try creating a new identity – a few new words that you use to describe yourself.

Write down exactly how you'd *like* to be described as an athlete. The type of athlete you'd like to be and need to be to achieve your goals and dreams.

In your Winner's Toolbox start a new page and give it the title – "I am …"

Now, write down the type of person you'd like to be, in order to reach your goals and dreams. What characteristics do you need to uphold? What skills do you need and how good do you need to be? How can you be totally and utterly happy? How will you be feeling? How will you act? What will you be doing? It's not just the material things you want from this journey; it's the person you want to be because of this journey.

If you're stuck for inspiration, go back to Section One, where I described how one of the rings on our Gold Medal Excellence plan was all about the characteristics that we felt we needed to become champions. You could also jump ahead to the Chapter 11: Affirmations, to see the list of "I am's" that I wrote out and read each day to affirm who I wanted to become (and thus be able to win the Gold Medal).

Just think, if you were to start acting like this right now, would it take you further toward your goals?

Tip: Good morning new you

Start your day by reading your new identity out loud in front of the mirror! It may sound corny but why not indulge a little? It will build your self-esteem and make it difficult to do anything but positive self-talk.

You won't **become** this person the moment you reach the top; you have to **be it** in order to get there.

> ### NO TIME FOR LOSERS, 'CAUSE WE ARE THE CHAMPIONS
>
> Kurek Ashley, our Success Coach in the lead up to the 2000 Olympic Games, says "Your identity creates your beliefs which become your behaviours. Behaviours are transmuted into your actions and actions produce your results".
>
> He had us proclaim to ourselves and those around us (in a fun way) that we were Gold Medallists. We did this for an entire year before the Games.
>
> It felt kind of weird, but eventually our subconscious mind started to believe it and we started to behave like Gold Medallists. And, eventually, 12 months later, we became Gold Medallists!

> ### KEY POINTS
>
> Practise positive self-talk.
>
> Changing the way you think and talk to yourself will bring immediate results.

312 THE BUSINESS OF BEING AN ATHLETE

Becoming Gold Medallists with Dawn Fraser leading the cheering!

CHAPTER 29
ATTITUDE IS EVERYTHING

The more I talk to athletes, the more convinced I become that the method of training is relatively unimportant. There are many ways to the top, and the training method you choose is just the one that suits you best. No, the important thing is the attitude of the athlete, the desire to get to the top.

Herb Elliott, Three-time Gold Medal Middle Distance Runner

If you were to put in place everything that you've learnt in this book so far, you may have a chance of being successful. However, if you add the right mental attitude to the mix, there is absolutely no way you can lose. Attitude is everything!

Every negative event, whether a sporting loss, a heartbreak or a job frustration, brings with it an opportunity. Rather than wallow in the pain, pick yourself up and look for ways to make it better. You get back what you project. You're a mirror of what life brings you.

You may not be able to choose the challenges that life throws at you, but you can *always* choose your response. And in the long run, success in life is not dependant on luck; it's dependent upon the quality of your response.

FROM PINING TO SHINING

In 2002, two years after having won Gold in Sydney, I decided to retire at the age of 37. My boyfriend and I had been together, off and on, for the past seven years and he'd finally decided that he was ready to settle down and start a family.

I announced my retirement to Natalie and we sadly parted ways. She took on a new partner for the next Olympics and I settled into what I thought would be a 'normal' life.

Little did I know that my boyfriend's change of heart was to be short-lived. Within three months of supposedly starting our new life together, he left!

As you can imagine, I was devastated. I'd finally got what I thought I wanted. The idea of starting a family was special to me and I really thought he was the one.

Over the next few months I was at the lowest point I'd ever been in my life. Lower than when I'd wrecked my knee and assumed I'd never play again.

It was like a death in the family. I was 37, alone and had just given up my chance of continuing on to another Olympics with Natalie Cook.

I definitely wasn't much fun to be around, I can tell you that. All I could do was talk about him, and cry a lot. Then came the moment that changed everything for me.

I was in Melbourne, trying to have some fun with friends out on a ski boat off St Kilda beach. I was once again moaning about how bad I felt when my friend just looked at me and said "Kerri, it's a long time in a pine box!"

At first I didn't get it. And then it sunk in. The longer I had this attitude, the longer my life would remain exactly as it was. I would be lonely, miserable and blubbering all the time!

No one wants to be with someone like that. And, it is a long time that we'll all be lying in our coffins. Our time on earth is pretty short, so we've got to make the absolute most of it.

Thanks to my friend, I started to pull myself out of this black hole and decided I would be happy once more. At first I had to fake it, but eventually I made it.

Not long after, I started seeing my wonderful husband, Max. I then decided I would make a brief comeback to compete in the 2004 Olympics with another partner. After that I finally retired and we had our beautiful son, Tyson.

Celebrating Tyson's 4th birthday

There's always a happy ending if you have the right attitude!

Controlling Your Emotions

Emotions, like thoughts, are a choice. You can choose to be annoyed by the wind, the sun, the venue that you're competing in or you can choose to feel OK about it.

You can choose to be annoyed by all the traffic on your way to practice or you can choose to use the time to breathe, and think about all the great things you're going to improve upon once you get there.

Next time something annoys or frustrates you, choose to see it in a different way. Learn to control your emotions.

Your emotions will determine your actions. So, if you're filled with negative emotion, it will translate to negative action, which will in turn become a negative result. Is this the way you want to play sport or live life?

Now, some athletes seem to achieve more when they're a little aggressive or fired up. This is different to simply reacting in a negative way. They have learnt a state that drives them, and they are controlling that emotion – using it to help them win. They are in the zone that works best for them.

I encourage you to try different states. Find one that works best for you and 'bottle it', from 'calm and relaxed' through to 'aggressive and charged'. Learn to let go of other emotions that interfere with this state.

Perhaps you can develop an anchor that helps remind you of this state. We'll talk more about this in Chapter 31: Handling Competition Nerves. An example might be a fist pump or a hand slap. When you see Tennis Champion Lleyton Hewitt yelling "Come on!" and he's doing his 'cobra', you just know he's in his perfect state.

Don't Worry, Be Happy

In the following diagram, you can see where an unhappy person's emotions and thoughts begin: look at the star that says 'Start'. Unhappy people focus on current results. This creates negative thoughts, which then create negative emotions. Negative emotion turns into negative actions and behaviours and this creates more negative results. And so the cycle continues.

Negative/Unhappy person

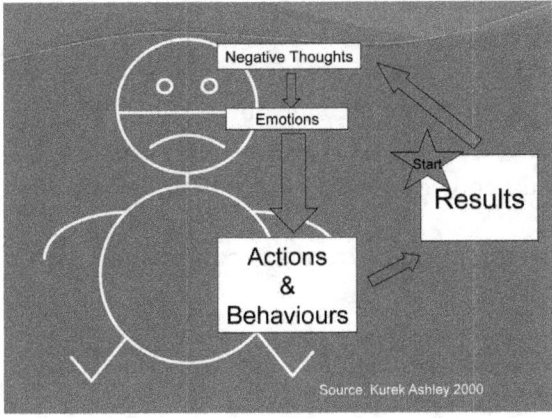

Now look at where the happy person's focus begins. He starts with happy, positive thoughts. These become positive emotions which create positive actions and behaviours, and ultimately positive results.

Positive/Happy person

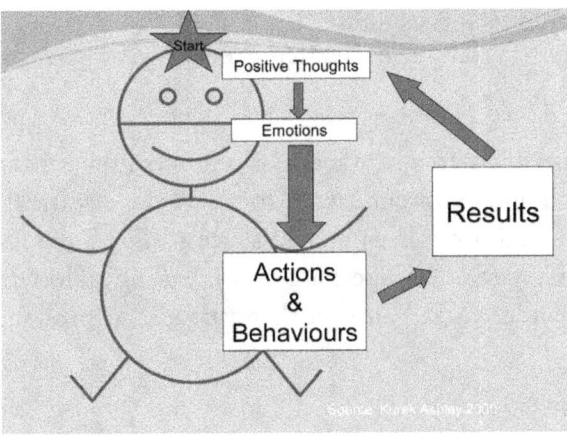

Quite a simple theory, really. But it works wonders. Try it!

Your attitude is the easiest thing to change at anytime. You don't need to practice it for hours and hours, like a sporting skill. You can choose to change it right now. All by yourself!

You Are Not Your Attitude

It may at times seem an insurmountable challenge or you might feel too close to that attitude.

Let me remind you that you are *not* your attitude. You can create, control and maintain any attitude. No special skills required. All you need is a willingness to take control and choose the attitude you want.

You may have allowed your emotions to control you in the past. Who's the boss?

Consider this – What's the difference between an exciting experience and a terrible ordeal? Attitude!

Consider this – What's the difference between gratitude and bitterness? Attitude!

Some people choose to feel bitter about life, while others choose to be grateful. They see problems as opportunities. It's the difference between winners and whiners!

Consider this – What is the difference between success and failure? Attitude!

Inventor Thomas Edison was asked by a reporter how it felt to have failed thousands of times (in his endeavour to create the electric light bulb). He replied that he had not failed; he had successfully eliminated a thousand ways that hadn't worked and because of this was now closer to discovering the one that would work. Without that attitude, he probably would have given up.

HIGH SEAS, HIGH ADVENTURE

One of my first ever International Beach Volleyball trips was to a remote Island called Boracay in the Philippines. There were no cars on the island and we had to take a rickety old boat across some pretty deep waters to get there from the mainland.

I loved it and was relishing in the adventure of it all. But, some of the other players I was travelling with were petrified. They were convinced we were all going to drown.

I enjoyed the trip, they hated it. Same circumstances, different attitude.

The rickety boat out to Boracay Island in The Phillipines, 1989

Lucky things happen to all of us all the time, but that isn't true unless you orient yourself to see situations, conversations and circumstances as fortuitous. As with most things in life, it begins with a mindset or an attitude. You cannot see what you don't look for, and you cannot look for what you don't believe in.

Sir Richard Branson, Entrepreneur

Why Are We All So Different?

Some people have a tendency towards a positive outlook on life; others the opposite. This may be a result of their upbringing or even their culture. Regardless, they still have in each and every moment, the capacity to choose an attitude.

Newspapers, TV, radio, magazines and other influential media focus on the world's disasters and tragedies, and the darker side of human nature. When we are young and impressionable it's easy for this to be accepted as the norm and to believe that this is all life has to offer.

Converting negative thoughts in day-to-day life to positive ones takes quite a bit of energy. If you are stressed by your career, finances or your personal life, it's likely that you're not eating or sleeping well. Under these circumstances it's easy to simply feel too tired to change your thoughts – so you give up and go back to the familiar way of thinking.

Some people think that if they change and become more positive, others may tease them or mock them. Think about those types of people. Are they constantly complaining about their lot in life? Are they going nowhere fast? Hmmm...most likely.

At the end of the day, having a good positive attitude all comes down to choice. You choose the attitude you have towards circumstances in your life.

I love the story from a tennis match between Bjorn Borg and John McEnroe early on in their careers. McEnroe describes in his book, *Serious*, how he felt when Borg went out of his way to show him respect:

"The second or third time we ever played, in New Orleans in early 1979, it was 5-5 in the third set, and I was getting all worked up and nutty, and Bjorn motioned me to the net. I thought, *Oh God, what's he going to do? Is he going to tell me I'm the biggest jerk of all time?* And he just put his arm around my shoulder and said, 'It's OK. Just relax." This was at 5-5 in the third set! But he was amused by the whole thing. 'It's OK,' he told me, 'It's a great match.' It made me feel really special. He didn't look at what I was doing as something I'd done to affect him. It was just my own nuttiness."

Borg obviously had a great positive attitude that day and enough grace to even offer some to his opponent (known for quite the opposite attitude!).

Changing A Lousy Attitude

If you sway towards being a person with a negative outlook on life or on yourself, or if you keep company with negative people, chances are your thoughts about most things will also be negative. As a result, your life will be moving at a snail's pace toward your goals and dreams.

Ask yourself whether this attitude is taking you towards your goals or *away* from them.

If the answer is 'away', then practice changing your attitude in the same way you would practice your sport.

Do it next time you're delayed in peak hour traffic, when you start to feel agitated and angry towards all the other drivers. Ask yourself: "Is getting angry going to get me to my meeting any earlier?" No, it won't. It will just make you have a more stressful journey and when you get there you'll arrive in a bad mood.

Instead, realise that you're getting agitated and remind yourself that there's nothing that you can do about the situation. Then, think of ways that you could have avoided this and what to do better next time, like leave 20 minutes earlier.

Now you've taken the pressure off yourself, you can turn on some music, sit back and breathe.

Maintaining A Positive Attitude

Life is not a dress rehearsal. We have 83,000 seconds per day and we can choose to make that time happy or miserable.

I know that being positive doesn't always come naturally. We all have to work at from time to time.

So, here are some tips on how to set your orbit to bliss:

- **Surround yourself with positivity.** Hang out with positive people, read motivational books, watch uplifting and motivational movies, listen to motivational MP3's while driving, commuting, waiting for appointments. Definitely, definitely avoid negative people. They will drain all the happiness out of you.

- **Make your environment fun and inspiring.** Hang up posters, motivational sayings and pictures that inspire you.

> ### ALL FIRED UP
>
> In 1998, two years before the Sydney Olympics, I realised that I had to move north to Brisbane to train with Natalie and our coaches, who all lived there. I loved my home on the Northern Beaches in Sydney, but knew that I had to make this sacrifice to reach my goals.
>
> I moved to a small suburb close to the city of Brisbane, and we began our training in the new environment. Luckily I had two amazing housemates, but I still felt far from happy.
>
> The biggest issue I had was the sun coming up around 4.30am during the summer months!
>
> I decided that if I was to be lying there awake each morning, waiting for the alarm to go off at 6.30am, I needed to do something positive to enhance the situation.
>
> So I typed up, in large font, my favourite motivational sayings. I put each one on a piece of A4 paper and added pictures to them to make them fun. I then stuck them up all over my room so I couldn't possibly lie there in a stink each morning.
>
> By the time I got out of bed, I was often already pumped and raring to go!

- **Dress for success.** Always make sure you look great, because that way you'll feel confident and happy. Even go so far as to have a makeover. If it makes you feel good, just go and do it.

- **Greet people with gusto.** If our Success Coach Kurek met someone during the day, and they asked him "How are you today?" he would answer "outstanding" every single time. It not only made him feel good, it always put a smile on the other person's face.

- **Compliment someone every day.** Make someone else feel good. What goes around, comes around.

- **Only talk about happy things** to everyone you meet. See the best in your day, and see the best in others.

- **Smile often.** Be aware of how you feel and *choose* to be happy. Put a smile on your dial right now!

- **Have the attitude of gratitude.** You have so much to be grateful for. Let people around you know that.

- **Laugh a lot.** There is so much around us to make us laugh. Look for the joy in life, and laugh – it's addictive.

- **Give away as much love as you can.** Your love can never run out. Be affectionate, appreciative, warm and friendly to those around you. It will all bounce back to you.

- **Fill your life with happy moments.** Cuddle a pet, play with kids, do some community work. Do whatever makes you smile and feel great.

- **Share your wins and happy events.** At the end of the day share the good stuff with your partner and family.

Having a positive attitude shouldn't just be a one off burst of emotion, it should become a lifestyle.

Why A Positive Attitude Will Take You To A Better Place

Let the sun shine in, and **you'll simply create a much nicer atmosphere around you.** Your journey will be enjoyable and enlightening. Positive people will be drawn to you and together you'll make great things happen. People love to be around positive people. It's an indicator of high self-confidence, which almost everyone is attracted to.

Your first impressions will make people *want* to spend time with you. These can turn into relationships that last a lifetime.

You'll be more productive. It's a lot easier to get things done when you remove the obstacle course of negative thoughts and attitudes.

You will attract more good things. The Law of Attraction states that whatever you think about, you attract into your life. So, if you replace a negative attitude with a positive one you will start to attract more positive opportunities and people into your life.

You'll be healthier! According to Michael D. Lemonick in his book *The Biology of Joy,* "People who rate in the upper reaches of happiness on psychological tests develop about 50 percent more antibodies than average in response to flu vaccines. In addition, happiness or related mental states like hopefulness, optimism and contentment appear to reduce the risk or limit the severity of cardiovascular disease, pulmonary disease, diabetes, hypertension, colds and upper-respiratory infections."

Being negative has absolutely *no* advantages, so why choose to live your life like that?

You had the opportunity to do the very same exercise, as Summer and I did in Athens, back in Chapter 24, Believe to Achieve.

Did you write down the types of thoughts and attitudes that you need in order to be the person who can achieve that Big Ultimate Picture? Well, if you did, my question to you now is: Why not be that person *right now?*

Roger Federer didn't decide he was a great tennis player *after* he won his first Grand Slam, he *knew* he was great before that – and that's how he won.

Nat and I became Sydney 2000 Olympic Gold Medallists in 1998!

If you want a loving relationship, be loving and lovable *now*. If you want success, act positively successful. If you're acting poor now how will you ever become rich? If you're constantly complaining about where you are now, that's where you'll stay until you start acting like you're where you want to be.

Find someone you trust to partner up with so you can keep tabs on your thoughts and attitudes. Two minds are better than one, and you'll help each other stay on track.

Live each day as if it's a precious gift – because it is.

NEVER SAY NEVER

In 2002, just as I was starting to feel good about myself again after the devastating breakup with my boyfriend, a young up and coming player by the name of Summer (perfect name for Beach Volleyball, huh?) came to me with a hesitant request.

She wanted to play the Australian summer with me as her partner, with the idea of maybe trying to qualify for the 2004 Olympic Games in Athens.

At first I was quite amused at the thought of a comeback. So many athletes do it and I really wanted to be sure when I retired that I'd really retired.

My new boyfriend, who is now my wonderful husband, encouraged me to get back out on the sand and at least give it a try.

So, off I went, travelling around the world once more. This time, I had a new partnership with Summer and we had an almost impossible task of qualifying for the Games.

We had six months to accumulate enough points to make it to Athens. All the other teams around the world had accumulated their points over a two-year period. To top that off, our second to last event in Norway saw us finish stone cold last! Our worst result in all seven events we'd played so far.

Our last chance was the final qualifying event in Spain the following week. We had to finish in the top 13 and ahead of another Australian team who we were competing neck and neck with for the 2nd Australian spot (Natalie Cook and her new teammate had already qualified in the 1st spot for our country).

By the time Summer and I arrived and checked into our hotel room the pressure had hit its peak. Everything we said, thought about or focused on was negative. We could barely think, feel or relate to each other in a nice way. Things were looking pretty bad and we were wondering if this whole thing had been worth it.

I knew that somehow we had to pick ourselves up and start feeling positive again, so I took Summer out onto the balcony of our small hotel room and did the following exercise.

On one piece of paper we wrote absolutely every single negative, horrible, soul-destroying thought that we had in our minds. We completely purged ourselves of this feeling of doom that we'd been carrying around.

Then, on another piece of paper, we turned each of those negative thoughts and feelings into a positive one. For instance, if I'd written something like: "My serve is soft, I'm not making any points" I'd change it to "My serve is still the best in the world and I make many points per match with it."

We continued to do this until each negative point had its opposite. Then, we crumbled up our negative sheet of paper and set it alight! We watched as all the smoke from those horrible thoughts and feelings blew off into the sky.

Every morning and every night we read our list and to this day I believe it saved us.

We ended up 4th in that event and beat the other Aussie team by one placing. We had qualified in less than six months and were heading to my 3rd and Summer's 1st Olympic Games.

In every successful person's journey there are often one or two specific life changing moments when the reaching of their goal hangs in the balance. It's tempting to turn back, give up or say this is all too hard. I could have done that with Summer. Our egos could have ended our journey to Athens right there.

It's during these times that you have to stop, take a step back, revisit your purpose, your goals and your dreams; remind yourself why you're in the game. Then you can take a step forward.....

I've learned that either you control your attitude or it controls you.

Relaxing after training before the 2004 Athens Olympic Games with my new team mate Summer Lochowicz

Natalie and I were still close friends, even though we were on opposing teams. (Me), Summer Lochowicz, Natalie Cook and Nicole Sanderson (Nat's Athens team mate.)

You had the opportunity to do the very same exercise, as Summer and I did in Athens, back in Chapter 24 Believe to Achieve.

Did you write down the types of thoughts and attitudes that you need in order to be the person who can achieve that Big Ultimate Picture? Well, if you did, my question to you now is: Why not be that person *right now*?

Roger Federer didn't decide he was a great tennis player *after* he won his first Grand Slam, he knew he was great before that – and that's how he won.

Nat and I became Sydney 2000 Olympic Gold Medallists in 1998!

If you want a loving relationship, be loving and lovable *now*. If you want success, act positively successful. If you're acting poor now how will you ever become rich? If you're constantly complaining about where you are now, that's where you'll stay until you start acting like you're where you want to be.

Find someone you trust to partner up with so you can keep tabs on your thoughts and attitudes. Two minds are better than one, and you'll help each other stay on track.

Live each day as if it's a precious gift – because it is.

The Pursuit Of Happiness

Winning isn't just about achieving goals. Winning at life makes you genuinely happy.

Being happy not only makes life gratifying and enjoyable, it also gives you the motivation and energy to achieve greater success. (Did you notice that we had 'Have fun and enjoy the journey' in four out of the five Olympic rings on our Gold Medal Excellence plan?)

Just to be clear, I'm talking about real, deep-seated happiness. Not the superficial, temporary kind that some people pretend.

What Makes You Truly Happy

This is a very simple, yet extremely powerful exercise that I urge you to do, even if you're feeling good right now. You never know when you'll need it.

Start with a blank sheet of paper and brainstorm all the things that make you happy. Include family, friends, pets, your home, holidays, books you've read, past experiences, past achievements, music, movies, events that you're proud of, parts of your body, and so on. Think outside the square a little and just write whatever puts a smile on your face.

Once you've got your list together, I want you to compile some pictures or phrases that you can cut and paste onto a double page spread in your Winner's Toolbox.

Next time you're feeling down, immerse yourself in these pages and put that smile back on your face!

> **KEY POINTS**
>
> You can create, control and maintain any attitude.
>
> Choose to be positive – it will take you personally and professionally to a better place.

CHAPTER 30
EXCUSES – TAKING RESPONSIBILITY

The price of greatness is responsibility.

Winston Churchill, Former British Prime Minister

Excuses may temporarily make you feel better, but they certainly will not bring you success.

What excuses have you been giving yourself so far whilst reading this book?

Too hard? No time? Wouldn't work for me? I've already tried that, and it didn't work?

It is much easier to find a reason *not* to do something. Am I right? And when it comes to commitment, these days, many will give their word with no real intention of following through.

Be different. You are so much better than the average person. Committing to something is not hard. It just takes discipline. You already know you have that from your sporting life. Transfer it to your entire life and change will happen.

Is there something that always seems to happen to you on a regular basis? No more excuses – take responsibility, and work out how you can deal with the issue.

For example, are you *always* late? Just sit for ten minutes right now – yes *now*! – and write a list of all the things you could do to be on time. I'll start you off:

- Prepare everything you need the night before. Make a list if you need to.
- Have all the instructions of how to get there.
- Get up earlier. Set your alarm.
- Depending on how late you usually are, set off at least 15 minutes before you think you need to.
- Allow for traffic relevant to the time of day and route you're travelling.
- Allow for public transport delays.

Add more things…

- _____
- _____
- _____

- Relax. You will get there on time.

If for some reason something goes wrong and you're late again – **don't make up an excuse!**

Instead, review what really happened. What was the *real* reason for it? Did you follow the steps on your list? Were you late because of a random traffic accident or did you just leave the house half an hour later than planned?

Whatever happens, take responsibility.

Anthony Robbins, Self-Help Author and Success Coach

You already know you are exceptional on the field of play. Be exceptional off the field as well. Rise above the rest.

The difference in your commitment will affect every aspect of your life as a professional athlete. Don't be average, and stop finding excuses to change.

Excuses – Busted!

I've put together a list of common excuses you may have used and explained how to work with them. The answers aren't the be all and end all, but they just might help give you the motivation needed to take responsibility.

1. **What Would Other People Think?**

    Why are you concerned with what other people will think? That's their problem, not yours.

    You obviously know what you need to do. What will really make you look foolish is if you continue to sit around and make excuses. Giving your best is nothing to be ashamed of.

    People who achieve their dreams, stand out. You can't be part of the crowd and expect to achieve far greater things than the crowd that you are part of. If you want extraordinary results, you've got to do extraordinary things.

2. **I'll Never Be As Good As Her/Him.**

    The only person you should compare yourself with is yourself. Everyone is unique, and has their own set of strengths and weaknesses.

    If you decide before you even try something, that you'll never be as good as someone else, then you'll miss the opportunity to really find out.

    Winners learn from those currently better than they are, they don't envy them.

3. **It'll Take Too Long**

   Then you better get started straight away!

   If you keep moaning about how long it will take, it will take even longer. Get going.

   Success takes time and effort. If it were easy, everyone would be successful.

4. **I Can't Do That!**

   My basic philosophy is, if someone else can do it, so can I.

   You just need to really want to do it. Then do all the hard work. And believe that you can get there. My theory: Passion + Preparation + Belief = Success.

ALWAYS DREAM AND SHOOT HIGHER

At the 2004 Athens Olympics I met a remarkable 56-year-old woman by the name of Annette Woodward. She was an Australian Shooter competing in her second Olympics. I sat next to her on the bus, as we travelled out to see a rowing event, and we exchanged stories.

She told me that she was often referred to as the pistol-packing grandmother. She was Australia's oldest Olympian in 28 yrs!

At an age when most of her compatriots are starting to slow down, Annette told me "I think it just shows what self-belief can do. Because of my age I didn't really think I could make the team so I'm pretty pleased with what I've done."

She'd come out of retirement to make the team that year and was a mother of six!

She went on to explain how she'd started shooting. "I'd never held a gun, let alone fired one, when I suddenly became interested in the sport after watching 52-year-old Patricia Dench win bronze at the 1984 Olympics in Los Angeles."

She decided she too wanted to be an Olympian. She first tried archery but didn't really like it as they put her in the corner and asked her to watch. She then went down to her local shooting club and asked if she could have a try. They gave her a gun straight away.

"Like a lot of people I was frightened of guns, I thought it was all cops and robbers stuff," she said. "But I hit the target with my very first shot and I was hooked straight away."

Woodward quickly set about making up for lost time. She made the Victoria State team a year later but it was not until 1990, when the last of her children had been enrolled in school that she started to take the sport seriously.

A natural talent, she won two gold medals at the 1994 Commonwealth Games in Canada and represented Australia at the 1996 Atlanta Olympics, finishing 20th.

She won a third gold medal at the 1998 Commonwealth Games in Kuala Lumpur but retired immediately to nurse her husband who had been diagnosed with cancer. He died in 1999.

"I couldn't do it any more when I lost my husband," Woodward said. "I just didn't have the ability to concentrate any more. I couldn't even stand on the line without thinking about him so I had to give it away."

Not long after her husband's premature death, a thief broke into Annette's home and stole her shooting medals, though they were later discovered in a rubbish bin.

To help her deal with her grief, Woodward poured her energies into her job as a radiographer but after missing the Sydney Olympics and the 2002 Commonwealth Games she decided to make a comeback.

"I really needed to make a comeback. I didn't want to leave the sport the way I had," she said. "I knew I had to learn to start dealing with things and getting back on the line was an important part of it."

Woodward finished 18th at the 2004 Athens Olympics – a better placing than her 1996 Atlanta Olympics result. She is a tremendous example of courage, focus and determination. Setting her sights high, no excuses, she earned her place in history.

5. **It's All Too Hard**

    This excuse is similar to: "It'll take too long". Nothing great was ever achieved easily.

    If it's worth having, it's worth the effort. Remind yourself of your goals and dreams and your reasons for wanting them. Surround yourself with the vision of your journey. Take one step at a time. Build a great team around you. Many hands make light work.

6. **It's No Fun**

    Focus on the end result, not on the tedious task you're doing now. Change your focus, and just do it. Remember, that tedious task is helping you get closer to your goals, your end result.

    Is it possible that you are doing this task because you've taken on someone else's dream? If that's the case, then of course it's not fun. Perhaps it's time to reassess your goals. Trying to achieve this dream will in fact become a nightmare.

7. **What If I Fail Or Lose?**

    If you lose, there is always something you can learn from that event. Choose to learn from your mistakes so you've got a better chance of winning next time.

    Ask yourself – how can I make it better? What can I work on for next time?

> *I've missed more than 9000 shots in my career. I've lost almost 300 games. 26 times, I've been trusted to take the game winning shot and missed. I've failed over and over and over again in my life. And that is why I succeed.*
>
> **Michael Jordan**, Basketball Legend

8. **I'll Do It As Soon As I ....**

    If you wait for conditions to be perfect, let me tell you something – that time will never come! Perfection is the ultimate illusion.

    So why bother waiting? Waiting will only make it worse. Stop procrastinating, and crack on towards your goal.

9. **I'll Do It Later**

   Ok, so you can do it later, but when *is* later? And if 'later' ever comes, you'll probably say the same thing then. The timing will never be perfect for you to start and nothing will ever get done by putting it off.

   When you make a decision to embark on your journey, any action that is not taken straight away will likely never get done. Ask yourself now: "What can I do today to take me one step closer to my goals?"

   Make that phone call, do that paperwork, go to the gym and improve your strength. A little bit now will translate into great things later.

10. **I Tried Before And It Didn't Work**

    Trying isn't good enough. If at first you don't succeed, you can at least learn something about how not to do it next time!

    Appreciate the opportunity to learn from your failure, and try, try again.

11. **Just Too Busy**

    What are you really *getting done* with all that busy-ness?

    Everyone is busy these days. It's about setting your priorities. What are your priorities right now? Those things should be on top of your 'To Do' list.

    Get up earlier. Stop watching reality TV. Get off Facebook. Check your email less often. Bonus = more time for the really important stuff.

12. **I Can't Decide What To Do**

    If you're having trouble deciding on something, then there's probably not all that much difference between the choices.

    Write a list of pros and cons. Be honest and objective. If you still can't decide, just choose one. You can always change paths later.

    Moving forward is much better than analysis-paralysis. The decision you need to make is: make a decision and go for it.

13. I Don't Know Where To Start

Start small. Make your 'To do' list and prioritise the tasks. It feels gratifying to accomplish a task, and cross it off the list. By writing things down you will remember what you need to do and it will be a visual aid to help you focus in on one task at a time.

As much as we all think we are multi-taskers, our brains are not wired to focus on several things at once. It is important to give full concentration to one task at a time so that each task gets the full care and attention that it deserves.

KEY POINTS

Stop making excuses – they're holding you back.

Focus on the end result. That will help you overcome the 'excuse'.

CHAPTER 31
HANDLING COMPETITIVE NERVES

I'll be nervous probably the night before the match. And then, yeah, when I get on the court, you know, I'm sure I'll be nervous at the start. But being nervous is one of the best things for a sports person. You know, it shows that you care, that you're ready to play. If there's no nerves, that's when I get worried. If I don't have that adrenaline... I feel like I play my best tennis when I have the adrenaline, when I'm nervous.

Andy Murray, Tennis Champion

Managing nerves takes practice. All athletes feel nervous, and you need to learn how to channel your nerves to play your best.

THE WEIGHT OF A NATION IS LIFTED

It was day one. Natalie and I were the first Aussie team to hit the sand at Bondi Beach in the Sydney 2000 Olympic Games. The crowd was excited and boisterous.

We knew we were meant to be here. We had prepared ourselves for absolutely everything. Our coach had told us numerous times that we'd done all the work. Now it was our time to shine.

But…and that's a huge BUT…we had no idea what it was going to be like, playing in front of 10,000 people in our home country, my home town, that were all cheering for us!!!

We'd played in Brazil where thousands of locals had cheered loudly against us. We'd played in the Atlanta Olympics, four years earlier, against the Americans, where the crowd was screaming "U…S…A"

But we had never played with so many people on our side. We felt like they were willing us and expecting us to win every point!

The game began. My nerves were at an all time high. So were Nat's. You could almost hear my knees knocking together with nerves. I needed to go to the bathroom, badly (and I'd only just been minutes before).

That day we were up against the Mexicans. Somehow we managed to win that first game. I often wonder how we did it. Maybe the Mexicans were nervous too.

We then had two days to prepare for our next match. How were we ever going to overcome the nerves? It felt like each time we lost a rally we were disappointing the entire country! When 10,000 people express a collective "ahhhhh", it is incredibly loud!

I suggested to Nat that we find some other Australian athletes that may have experienced the same when playing in their home country.

Pat Rafter, 1997 and 1998 US Open Champion and one of Australia's most loved tennis players seemed to me the ideal person to chat to. As it turned out, our physical trainer knew his physical trainer and they arranged a meeting. We were lucky enough to be able to spend about an hour with Pat. We also spent some time with Lleyton Hewitt (Former World No. 1 Tennis Champion) and Renee Stubbs (Grand Slam Doubles Winner).

Pat had some great advice, especially about coming together as often as we could and really maximising our eye contact during matches. It's so loud when you're down on the sand surrounded by a 10,000 seat stadium that you sometimes can barely hear each other speak.

He told us to hear the crowd, but not to listen to them. He said to play for each other, not for the crowd.

From that moment on, I started to imagine a sort of 'glass cone of silence' around Nat and I. When I look back at the video, I can see how focused I was. I was totally and utterly in the zone, thanks to that cone of silence and thanks to Pat.

Renee Stubbs had some great advice for Nat. She said 'when the crowd goes "ohhhh" after you've lost a point or made a mistake (they're just feeling sorry for you), turn it around in your head to make it seem like "ahhhh, they love me so much!"

We also spent some time with the Olympic Sports Psychologist, Phil Jauncy, who gave me some advice that I learnt to live by and always try to pass on to those I now coach:

- When you're nervous, acknowledge the nerves. Feel them. But, don't act nervously. Act confident and superior. Also, simplify things. Think about each task, one at a time. Each skill.

- Don't over complicate things with lots of information when you're nervous. This is a good tip for coaches, too. If you feel your players seem nervous, use the K.I.S.S principle. Keep It Simple Stupid!

After speaking to the athletes and Phil Jauncy, this is what I wrote in my journal: "Nat and I are going to stay in our little bubble. Do what I normally do, hear but don't listen. Concentrate on the 18 square metres of sand. Enjoy the crowd and let them lift me in the air. Get up there and meet the ball – smack it! Hand high! And watch the ball – focus on the ball."

The rest is history. Each game we became more and more comfortable with the amazing Aussie crowd until the final match – the match for Gold. By that time we felt like the court and the stadium were ours and the Brazilians were on our turf!

342   THE BUSINESS OF BEING AN ATHLETE

Spending time with Patrick Rafter in the village

10,000 people cheering for us at Bondi Beach in 2000

Practice dealing with your nerves outside competition. Visualise an up and coming event, and see yourself as the star player. Feel the nerves coming on, acknowledge them and then practice dealing with them.

If you've felt that in the past your nerves have negatively affected your performance, be honest and ask yourself whether you were anxious because you *knew* deep down that you hadn't done all the work and preparation that you were supposed to do.

The obvious solution to fending off these nerves is to DO ALL THE WORK before the competition!

> "Nothing gives an athlete confidence like knowing they have done everything they possibly could have done to their best of their ability in training and preparation."
>
> **Lawrie Lawrence,** Australia Swim Coach

State Management and Using Anchors

State management is another trick many athletes and business people use to help them prepare for important events. It simply refers to the process of managing how you feel (your state of emotions) at any given time.

Instead of shaking with nerves, wouldn't it be better to feel confident, calm, focused yet energised?

Well, the best way to harness nerves is to use anchors. An anchor is a type of stimulus that reminds you of a previous event and it can evoke the state that you were in, during that event.

In this case the best stimuli to use would be something you feel, see or hear. It can be internal, such as a visual image in your mind, or external like a piece of music or a fist pump that reminds you of that feeling of your best performance.

Some of the feelings that you'll want to anchor to help you with your nerves: confidence, power, excitement, as well as the thrill, the elation, and the steely calm you experienced during your best moments.

Here's how to set up your anchor:

1. **Remember a past experience** where you felt invincible. You were playing your absolute best with total confidence and power. You were also so relaxed and calm that you almost knew what was going to happen before it actually happened. You were reading the game really well.

   The more intense the memory, the more powerful the anchor will be.

2. **Relive that experience** as if you were there, right at this moment. Feel the strength and determination. Feel the heat of the sun on your shoulders or the floor beneath your feet. See your opponents and see yourself dominating them with ease.

   Feel it all, rather than just thinking about it.

3. Now, at the peak of your memory and when you are totally engrossed in that feeling – **apply your chosen anchor** (examples: fist pump, squeezing your thumb and forefinger together, your hands slapping together, maybe it's a word or a phrase that you like to use).

   Whatever it is, make sure you apply it at the emotional peak of your memory.

4. Next, **have a break** of a few minutes or so and think of something totally neutral.

5. Now, **repeat** steps 1 – 4 five times.

6. Finally, when you've done that five times, **test the anchor**. Think of something neutral and then fire it off. If it's not working well, do steps 1 – 4 again until it really feels right.

C'MON!!

Natalie liked to use a fist pump and I used a strong hand clap. These were both quite explosive movements that channelled our nerves, and got us into our ultimate state.

My anchor developed early on in my career. To pump myself up and to celebrate a great point, I would often slap my hands together.

I also had another anchor that sort of developed on its own. After I'd made a mistake or if I started to feel frustrated I lifted my sunglasses a little and wiped the sweat (whether it was there or not) off my eyebrows. With a quick flip of my fingers, I flung the imaginary frustrations off my head onto the sand. Gone, and back to concentrating on the moment.

> **KEY POINTS**
>
> Channel your nerves to win.
>
> Create your own anchor to harness your nerves.

CHAPTER 32
AFFIRMATIONS – BE LOUD AND PROUD!

> *Sow a thought and you reap an action; sow an act and you reap a habit; sow a habit and you reap a character; sow a character and you reap a destiny.*
>
> **Ralph Waldo Emerson**, Philosopher, Poet

Emerson said it beautifully. "Sow a thought and you reap an action." The easiest way to 'sow a thought' is to simply use affirmations. Affirmations are positive thoughts, wishes or desires, said as if already true, over and over again.

Affirmations are a great way to create positive change in your life. The catch is, to get the most out of them; you must honestly believe them on some level.

They need to become part of your subconscious. Only then will you *believe* it to be true, rather than just *want* it to be true. To be accepted as truth by your subconscious, you must use constant repetition combined with strong emotion.

But, before we go into exactly how to do this, try the following exercise and write down your thoughts on a separate piece of paper.

Use Your New Identity To Create Your Daily Affirmations

Have a good look at what you wrote down when you did the "I am..." exercise (Chapter 7: Negative Self-Talk). Remember, whatever you attach the words "I am" to; you become.

Did you write something positive? Did you write something that was a stretch of where you are today? (When I started writing this book, I added the words – "I am an international bestselling author" – to my description of myself. At first it was fun, my friends and family would smile. Now, I believe it wholeheartedly and know it will come true!)

Hopefully your description matches your goals. Now, by saying this to yourself everyday it will give you the best possible opportunity to *become* your new identity.

You are sowing a new thought into your subconscious, and by doing this, it will create the actions necessary to get you on track to reaching your goals.

It may feel weird at first, but I guarantee that it will add a sense of self-confidence to your daily actions and get you where you want to be a lot quicker.

Be Realistic, Then Raise The Bar

If you are currently winning local or regional competitions, one of your affirmations might be: 'I am National Champion in my sport'.

Gradually, as you truly believe your current affirmations, then raise the bar bit by bit until you are affirming your ideal goals and scenarios. Your affirmation might then become 'I am World Champion in my sport'.

If your goal is related to weight loss – you currently weigh 85kg and you want to be 65kg, it may seem too far away to affirm, "I am 65kgs and loving my new body!"

So your initial affirmation might be "I am 80kgs and feeling great!" Once you reach that goal, your affirmation would change to "I am 75kgs and looking fabulous!" Using smaller steps like these allow you believe little by little and gradually you will make those huge changes.

Some people love affirmations. Others are sceptical, and wonder if it will really make any difference. If you want to achieve some lofty goals, you need to change how you think and sometimes that will mean stepping outside your comfort zone.

If you go into it with a doubting mind and don't fully apply the technique, chances are it won't work for you. Give it a go and believe it will work – you've got nothing to lose.

How To Create The Affirmations You Need

Affirm the new you

Write down your affirmations using some or all of the points from the "I am…" exercise that you did back in Chapter 28. Keep them short, sweet and to the point.

Write them in the **present tense** as if they are already achieved.

Make them personal and write from the heart using your own words. Let your emotions and passion drive you. What do you desire? (Not your coach, teammates, parents or other people around you) What do you wish for or believe?

Make them specific and detail your goals. If you want to earn more money, rather than writing an affirmation like "I am earning lots of money", say how much you want to earn and how often. For example "I am earning $10,000 a month".

Use positive language only and state what you want rather than what you don't want. "I am…", "I do…", "I can…" and so on.

Once you've written them out, **stick them** on your walls, in your kitchen, on your fridge, mirror, computer, car steering wheel, at your desk, on the back of your toilet door – **anywhere and everywhere that you will see them constantly throughout the day.**

Say them out loud several times a day. Be proud of what you want to achieve. Speak slowly, positively and repeat them as often as you can. Even if it feels awkward at first, it will soon start to feel really natural to say and fully believe these phrases. Emphasise different words as you read them to give different meaning to the phrase. Repetition ensures they will form part of your subconscious.

Close your eyes and use visualisation to actually see yourself with the affirmation having come true. Truly believe it has already happened to you. Feel the emotion that it will evoke when it comes true.

I BELIEVE

Here are the affirmations I used in the lead up to the 2000 Olympic Games:

- I am a Sydney 2000 Gold Medallist.
- I am the best server in the world.
- My serving is accurate and has so much pace it will knock people over.
- My serving will win games – win the Olympic Gold Medal and prove that I am one of the best players of the decade.
- I stay behind the ball and see the block, hit past it and beat the defender.
- I am happy and compassionate.
- I am the best passer in the world.
- I am the best setter in the world.
- I am the best spiker in the world.
- I can play any shot I wish at any time.
- I give my partner strength and confidence.
- My body language on court is always positive.

- My knees are great and will never problem me.
- I am light, jump high and dominate the sand.
- I am the best and I LOVE TO SHOW IT.
- I am going to enjoy the crowd, laugh and smile.
- WE ARE AWESOME.
- I AM AWESOME.
- I LOVE LIFE!!
- WE WILL WIN THIS EVENT.
- WE WILL WIN GOLD.

This process is an extremely powerful way to imprint your goals, and the intention you have for your life, on to your subconscious mind.

As you start to use this technique, you'll be pleasantly surprised when you begin to attract the people or resources to yourself, that will help make the affirmations come true.

You'll be able to draw on your knowledge and experience under pressure.

And you will be able to solve problems and face challenges with greater calm and confidence.

KEY POINTS

Create affirmations that are specific and written from the heart.

Practise affirmations at least daily, to imprint them on your subconscious mind.

The scoreboard in our room during the Sydney Olympics. The way we saw it, we won every day even before we hit the sand!

CHAPTER 33
SEEING IS BELIEVING - VISUALISATION

> *When you imagine and visualise, expect and plan for it, when you work and commit and persist, passionately facing every challenge, it is not merely possible. It is certain to happen.*
>
> **Ralph Marston,** creator of 'The Daily Motivator' - www.greatday.com

Visualisation is simply the process of imagining yourself performing skills with *perfect* execution.

There is no *wrong* way to visualise. You may want to do it in a quiet room or use music. You can visualise for a few minutes or an hour. You can stand, sit or lie down. Whatever is most comfortable and works best for you.

Studies have shown that visualisation (sometimes called mental rehearsal) can help athletes of all levels improve their skill, confidence and relaxed state during competition. It's also been linked to increasing work ethic, motivation and the desire to improve.

There is no exact evidence that proves visualisation alone can improve performance. But most athletes say they benefit from it. And to me, that means it's worth a try. Why not? Even if there's only a remote chance it will improve your performance – take that chance.

BULLSEYE!

When I was working on improving the accuracy of my jump serve I used visualisation a lot to help give me the confidence to serve tough in pressure situations.

I would see my arm swing before I did it.

It started when I was practising hitting small targets on the other side of the net. No opposition. Just me and about 50 balls. The targets were the size of a small dinner plate and almost 20 metres away from where I stood to start my serve.

As part of the service routine that I'd created, I would look at the target and actually 'see' my arm come from behind my head and follow

> through straight at the target. I would 'see' the ball pass over the net at a particular point that was in line with the target and I would 'see' it hit the target.
>
> Now initially, to build that picture, I would physically swing my arm (without the ball) in the direction it had to go. This gave me the 'picture' that I would then see in my mind.
>
> Eventually, I stopped having to do the practice swing as I could 'see' the arm swing in my mind.
>
> This 'picture' became part of my routine and improved my serving by 200% within a very short space of time!

How To Create The Perfect Visualisation

Make sure you have no distractions. You may have to put headphones on to drown out other noise, or remove yourself to a less distracting place.

First, close your eyes and begin to imagine what it would look like to be performing the skills of your sport perfectly. It may be that you see the ball early, if you play a ball sport. You may see your stride as you run down the track.

Even if you're not that good at a certain skill yet, see yourself doing it perfectly.

Never visualise a mistake or a loss to an opponent. If you do happen to see yourself doing something that is not good, rewind the action and make sure you correct it positively before you go on. Always see yourself doing the best action and being in a winning position.

Remember, seeing is believing.

Add in the surrounding noises. The crowd, your opponent, even music if that's being played while you compete.

Make sure you aren't just watching yourself on video, *be in the game*. Feel each stroke in the pool. Feel the water between your fingers as you watch the black line. Feel the bubbles as they exhale your breath.

Put as much detail into your mind as possible and enjoy the movie!

The Best Time To Visualise

Visualisation can be helpful during practice, just before you compete and while you're competing. When you use it just *before* competition it's a powerful tool that will help get you in your best emotional state.

It doesn't matter exactly how much time you devote to a visualisation. It's trial and error – it may be five minutes, fifteen minutes or an hour. Whatever works for you. Just make sure you see yourself *beating* your opponent!

Depending on your sport, you may also have time to visualise (like I did with my serve) during your competition. It could help you if you need to relax or even fire up, during a time out or a break in play.

And, if you have the misfortune of getting injured, visualisation can help you maintain your skills during the rehabilitation process and help you stay motivated while off the field. Some say it can even help the healing process.

I suggest that if you want to try it out, do it at least three or four times a week and see if you get the results you want. It's free, it doesn't take a lot of time and you can make whatever movie you want to see, in your own mind.

Bear in mind that it must be done well in order to reap the benefits. Use vivid images and engage as many senses as you can.

Finally, if you struggle to create that perfect picture in your mind, you can always try watching a video of another athlete in your sport who has the technique you covet.

KEY POINTS

Visualisation can help you improve your skill, confidence and state of mind.

Engage all your senses to create the most effective visualisation.

CHAPTER 34
HABITS AND CONSISTENCY

We are what we repeatedly do. Excellence, then, is not an act, but a habit.

Aristotle, Ancient Philosopher

I truly believe that the difference between 'failure' and 'success' depends on our habits. To me, habits are more powerful than desires.

In his bestseller: *The 7 Habits of Highly Effective People*, Stephen R. Covey says: "Habits can be learned and un-learned… but it isn't a quick fix. It involves a process and a tremendous commitment."

If you think about how a typical day looks, it goes something like this: You get out of bed and go to the bathroom. You eat, shower and get dressed. You leave the house at the same time most days and drive to training or work. You take the same roads each time. You train, work or study and then maybe get groceries on the way home to make dinner. You cook, eat and clean up. Do some homework, study and then brush your teeth and go to bed.

This is your routine. These are your habits and you perform them consistently, day in and day out, without much conscious thought.

Some of your habits may be good habits, but some may be bad, debilitating, and destructive. They all create the results you have in your life right now.

Therefore, what Aristotle said – "excellence is not an act, but a habit" – makes perfect sense.

If your habits don't create results that lead you to your dream, then change the habits or change your dream!

Understanding What Motivates Us

The two basic motivators of behaviour are 'pleasure' and 'pain'.

Each one of us interprets these two motivators differently. Some people find pleasure in football, and others find it in belly dancing. Some people have a high pain threshold; others fall to pieces easily.

There are five basic principles that we follow when dealing with pleasure and pain. Can you think of an occasion when you have experienced each one?

1. We are willing to face pain if we can see the pleasure at the end (for example, childbirth!)

2. We will avoid pain if we can't see pleasure arising from it.

3. We will face pain in order to avoid a greater pain (for example, we'll work in a job we dislike to avoid the greater pain of poverty)

4. Avoiding pain today is a more powerful motivator than a vague future pleasure (for example, postponing the diet or the exercise, when we want to lose weight or get fit)

5. We are willing to face massive pain, when we have a very clear and inspirational future pleasure (most Olympic athletes have endured tremendous amounts of pain throughout many years of training – including injury, because of the clear 'pleasure' at the end: competing at the Olympics Games.)

Think of what you regard as 'pleasure' now. Is it actually causing you 'pain'? Do you have a habit, like smoking, that may *feel* good now, but is harming you beyond compare?

Do you avoid the 'pain' of early morning training sometimes, to enjoy the 'pleasure' of another half hour in bed?

Think about what pleasure and pain means to you, and think of how many bad habits are affecting your chance of achieving the Ultimate Big Picture. Habits such as:

- Poor or incorrect skills
- Procrastination
- Avoiding responsibility for the results in our lives
- Impatience and losing our tempers
- Poor training methods
- Smoking, drinking and other poor dietary habits

Evaluate Your Habits

In your Winner's toolbox, start a new page:

1. Draw three columns down the page.
2. In the first column, write down all the positive habits you have that lead you closer to your goals.
3. In the middle column, write down all the negative habits you have that lead you away from your goals.
4. In the third column, write down the new habits that you will need to create to replace the negative ones – in order for you to reach your goals.

Now you know what to do to create positive change to your daily actions!

It's only when you've created the vision of your desired future, and firmly believe in it, that you'll have any hope of changing those bad habits.

You must clearly see that the pain you are in is *greater than* the pain of changing your behaviours. And, you must *believe* that changing the behaviours will reduce the pain!

> *Once success becomes a habit, it's not hard to do anymore; it just becomes something you do."*
>
> **Kurek Ashley**, Peak Performance Coach

How To Break The Bad Habits

Now that you've identified the habits you want to change, you need to commit to changing them.

Break an old habit immediately by following the next few steps. Don't wait another second!

If you put if off until tomorrow, or when you have the time, it will go on the back burner and slip away until you forget. This is how your dreams will slip away from you. Don't let that happen – take action *now*!

Step 1 Make it hurt not to change

Write out a list of all the things that have been negatively affected by you not changing this/these habits.

- What has it cost you in terms of selection or representation of your country in your sport?

- What has it cost you financially?

- How has if affected your previous results?

- What experiences have you missed out on?

- How has it affected your relationships?

- How has it affected the team around you?

Step 2 List all the pros

List the all benefits you will enjoy as a result of the change.

- How much money will you save or make?

- What results could you get?

- What teams or competitions will you qualify for?

- How will this impact life after sport?

- How will it improve your health?

- How proud of yourself will you feel?

- How proud will your family, friends and teammates feel?

Step 3 Create the new habit

Now, you need to create a positive empowering habit to replace the old negative disempowering habit. This way you won't have an empty space in your life where you used to do something. Make sure the habit your replace it with is a positive one.

It you want to develop a new sporting technique habit, try this:

- When you're out on the court, do the new, correct action 20 times with absolutely perfect technique. Give it your sole focus and concentration. Do it as slowly as you need to, to make sure the technique is perfect. Get your coach or someone with similar skills to watch if necessary and ensure it is correct.

- Then sit quietly for 20 minutes and visualise about what it felt like, how much better you would be if you did it like this all the time. Think about every positive thing about the new action. Focus and don't allow interruptions. Take yourself to a quiet place.

- Then go back and do the same action perfectly again 40 times.

- Go back to your quiet place and reflect on it again but just for five minutes.

- Try the action again. Doing this should hopefully develop the new habit quickly because you will have stronger connections in your brain between the stored memory and the neurones that tell you what to do.

- If you continue doing this for about three weeks, you should notice a massive change.

Step 4 Tell your support network

Tell supportive, positive people about your new habit, and what you want to achieve. Keep them updated on how you are going and ask them to check in with you, to follow your progress. This makes you accountable and is a key motivator to keep it up.

Step 5 Reward yourself

Finally, reward yourself once you've accomplished this new habit because it is now part of your life! It's great to celebrate your achievement. Allow yourself this indulgence and really enjoy it (but don't indulge yourself with the old bad habit!).

Research suggests it takes three to four weeks to form a habit, so allow this amount of time to change an old habit to a new one.

Every hour, every minute that goes by without you indulging your habit brings you closer to breaking that habit. Don't give up – see it through. In three to four weeks that bad habit will be a distant ugly memory!

> *Tip: Use your new tools to help*
> Using affirmations and visualisation can really help to break a habit. Simply affirm to yourself and 'see' yourself doing the new habit.

Consistency – Make or Break

Lack of consistency is the killer of dreams. It applies to the way you play your sport and the skills you use, and it definitely applies to your mindset and the positive changes that you've made to date as you've read through this book.

Most people expect instant results and when they don't get them, they often quit – sometimes just moments before success shows up.

It's easy to charge out of the gates full steam ahead when you embark on a new and exciting journey. The hardest part is (and why not everyone is living his or her dreams), staying on track and being consistent.

You need to continue to do the things you've learnt and that you've told yourself that you'll do, long after the initial excitement has left you.

Once you've begun to achieve success, it actually becomes easier to live your life like this. You get into a steady routine which becomes habit and it's easier to be consistent.

It's not how or when you start, it's how you continue. It's why the tortoise beats the hare every time. Slowly, steadily and consistently.

How To Maintain The Momentum

If you start to lose momentum or get out of routine, just take a moment to consider the consequences and the impact it will have on your journey. Don't lose the momentum. Stay focused and be consistent with everything you do.

Have friends, family, teammates and your mentor remind you of your goals and dreams. Have them help you keep track of your progress.

Keep your goals, your "I am..." affirmations and all the things that motivate you visible and look at them every day. Put them all around your home, your car and your office.

CHANGING FORTUNE

Kurek had Natalie and I write down our top five goals on a piece of paper the size of a business card. He then laminated them for us.

He asked us to put our cards in a place that we were sure to go, each and every day. Mine ended up in my wallet so every time I bought something, a drink or lunch, I would quietly stand there and read my goals to myself while I was waiting for my change!

KEY POINTS

Identify the bad habits, and commit to change.

It only takes three to four weeks to create a new habit, so persist until you've made it.

CHAPTER 35
CONSTANT DAILY IMPROVEMENT

> *Go for it now. The future is promised to no one.*
>
> **Wayne Dyer**, Self-Help and Motivational Author

ACTION HERO

When I first met our Success Coach, Kurek Ashley, I noticed all the different tattoos he had on his body. (He'd been an actor in action movies in Hollywood, so it figured!)

One particular tattoo that resonated with me was on his wrist – C.A.N.I.

This stood for Constant And Never-ending Improvement

I loved this tattoo as it exemplified every thing that he was teaching us. He told me it reminded him every day that this was an opportunity to be one step better at something that day.

There is a sign on the door of the United States Olympic Training Centre dining room. It's also on the gym doors and on the doors to other training venues within the Centre. It simply says: - **Not Every Four Years, Every Day!**

It was put up there to remind the athletes, the coaches and everyone involved in teams striving for the Olympics that it's about improving each and every day.

I personally live by the mantra – 'Have no regrets'. With that in mind, I give everything my best and I'm always trying to improve.

Imagine if you could do one thing better by 1% each day? Do you think you could improve by 1%? It's not much, is it?

Well, if you multiply that by 100, you'd be 100% better in just over 3 months! Who wouldn't want that?

Yes, it's easy to say. But even if you got to 50% better, wouldn't that have a massive impact on your career and your life?

Apart from the skills of your sport and the new techniques and strategies you've learnt in this book, what other things can you learn and improve on?

How about doing some study (part-time or online)? You could read more about building your champion mindset or attend seminars on wealth creation. What about learning something new as a hobby?

Reading books is probably the easiest form of learning and improving while you're competing full time. It fits well with the time you need to relax and recover from the rigorous exercise. One book per month is a great target to start with. Especially if you're travelling, as you'll spend so much waiting time in airports.

I firmly believe that while a formal education will make you a living, self-education will make you a fortune.

Learn from people who have achieved the success that you want. Someone out there is already living your dream.

And, always be prepared to invest in your education. The cost of a great book is negligible compared to the results it could yield.

Have no regrets – you only get one chance at this!

> *Believe while others are doubting.*
> *Plan while others are playing.*
> *Study while others are sleeping*
> *Decide while others are delaying.*
> *Prepare while others are daydreaming.*
> *Begin while others are procrastinating.*
> *Work while others are wishing.*
> *Save while others are wasting.*
> *Listen while others are talking.*
> *Smile while others are frowning.*
> *Commend while others are criticizing.*
> *Persist while others are quitting.*
>
> William Arthur Ward

KEY POINTS

Give it your all – 100%.

You can be better, you can always improve. Keep learning.

Doing a little more every single day made shots like this hit the sand during the Olympics

CHAPTER 36
BALANCE

I believe that being successful means having a balance of success stories across the many areas of your life. You can't truly be considered successful in your business life if your home life is in shambles.

Zig Ziglar, Motivational Author, Speaker

When sport is your career, it can be easy to allow it to take over your life. As you continually strive to be the best, your training, diet, rest and recovery become all consuming and before you know it, your every waking moment is spent thinking about your sport.

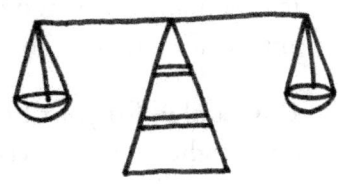

It's important that you schedule time out from sport to smell the roses and nourish the soul. Rather than pulling you away from your sporting success, time spent outside of your sport will actually have a positive impact.

It's all about balance. Balance is critical to preventing burn-out, and demotivation.

Without sufficient recovery time, you increase your risk of underperformance and injury. When we get out of balance, we risk collapsing and we definitely risk failure.

This can also be compounded if many of your friends outside of your professional career as an athlete use sport and exercise as their way to switch off from their day-job.

Firstly, they may all be exercising when you're ready to do something else. Secondly, they may also think your 'job' as an athlete is nothing like a real job anyway and that your main occupation involves taking time off and relaxing!

It can make you feel annoyed or even guilty to just switch off and socialise like everyone else.

How To Develop Balance

You may be an athlete but it doesn't define you or sustain you as a person. Try to develop balance:

- **Build breaks into your program** for rest and recovery.

- **Control demands** made by sponsors, media, school, parents and your social group of friends by planning your time so that you're not doing it all at once. Spread it out and add periods where you're not needed by anyone for anything and just have some 'me' time.

- **Have a plan for your future, *after* sport.** You don't have to be acting on it right now, but have an idea about what you'd like to do after sport. If it doesn't take away from your sporting career, start planning to spend time developing skills or learning something that you may want to do later.

- **Rest.** It's often the most overlooked activity of full-time athletes. Make sure it's planned into your schedule as clearly as each practice session.

- **Plan down time for fun activities with friends and family.** If you plan it in advance, you're so much more likely to do it. So often, you may have a day off and it ends up wasted, because you spend half the day trying to decide what to do and who to do it with.

- **Learn to say no, sometimes.** You can't do everything and you can't always help everyone. Many people have a hard time with this concept, but you must realise that in order to be fully loving and caring of anything or anyone else, you *must* fully love and care about yourself, which means putting yourself first. If you over-commit yourself to any one area of your life, it will be impossible to be present, in the moment, even though you might physically be there. Many times, people who over-commit will cancel plans or back out at the last second, leaving others feeling that you are unreliable. People will respect you so much more if you only commit to what you truly can balance into your time. Think of yourself first and then help others.

Balance Check-Up

Start a new page in your Winner's Toolbox. Write the six areas that we identified in Section One:

1. Health and Fitness

2. Family and Friends

3. Lifestyle

4. Wealth Creation

5. Personal Development

6. Athletic Career

...and add to this list any other specific area that you'd like to balance. For example, you may add:

7. Happiness

8. Your relationship with your partner

9. The time you spend with your partner

> 10. Practice
>
> 11. The relationship with your teammates
>
> Now, rate the balance in each area, giving 1/10 if it's extremely out of balance, through to 10/10 if it's perfect.
>
> Can you see a pattern? What do you need to do or overcome, in order to create more balance in the 'low-scoring' areas?

Sometimes it's important to work for that pot of gold. But other times it's essential to take time off and to make sure that your most important decision in the day simply consists of choosing which colour to slide down on the rainbow.

Douglas Pagels, Author

Let's work on developing some ideas for down-time.

Ideas List for Better Balance

While you have your toolbox out, make a list of all the ways you could take a break and enjoy yourself off the sports field.

Here are a few examples:

Take a holiday or even just a weekend break. Go somewhere you've never been before and have fun exploring.

Call up some friends you haven't seen for a while and go out.

Go hiking or camping with friends outside your sporting group.

Take an evening course or start a new hobby.

Arrange a lunch party or BBQ and invite all your family, especially those you haven't seen in a while. Get everyone to bring a plate of food to share.

> Go to see a concert, show or theatre.
>
> Schedule in some "me-time". Just you, on your own. Maybe do something you used to enjoy. Read a book or magazine in the park, go for a long walk, visit the day-spa, play a round of golf...
>
> Next time you're overseas and you know that directly after your competition you have some time off, use it to explore.

Some athletes 'work hard, play hard'. It might seem that they are living a glamorous lifestyle off the court or the field, but often, as revealed in the media at a later date, their lives are far from balanced.

OFF BALANCE, LOSING FOCUS

There were times when my life as an athlete was completely out of balance. My time was spent focusing on two things: my Volleyball and my relationship.

While it was OK some of the time, when my relationship wasn't going well, it pretty much destroyed my sport.

I remember one particular Beach Volleyball event, not long after a devastating breakup with my boyfriend, I was spending every waking moment thinking of him and only had him and my sport at the time (or so I thought!) I felt completely and utterly desolate.

It affected me so badly that while I was standing on the court that day, I could barely focus my eyes on the opponent just 10 metres away. I remember thinking that I needed glasses. I couldn't see the flight of the ball, I couldn't concentrate on any aspect of the game and we ended up losing to a much lower ranked team, quite badly. I was so sorry for Nat; there was nothing she could do. She also had no idea how bad I felt as I was trying to keep it a secret.

I learnt a really valuable lesson that day. I needed a more healthy balance in my life. It wasn't all about my relationship and my sport. I needed to spend time caring about other areas of my life, too. That

> way, if one part of my life wasn't going well, I would still have another area to fall back on to bring me happiness and success.

Stress and Panic

For fast-acting relief, try slowing down.

Lily Tomlin, Comedian

A by-product of being out of balance is stress. Stress can often lead to fearful, frantic thinking which zaps us of an enormous amount of energy. Stress can drain the creativity and joy out of your life. Practice saying: the more I relax, the more I get done.

If you have high, rigid and unrelenting standards, you may end up feeling like you'll never reach them. This can cause you to become preoccupied with detail and procrastinate. It can turn into a vicious cycle. I often fall in and out of this cycle and only really achieve when I sit back and 'let go' of little things.

Resist the state of desperation. Prepare yourself mentally in advance and know that you can live without this person, live without winning the trophy, live happily without a million dollars, or whatever.

Be happy. Find something important – other than your career, to care about.

KEY POINTS

Balance is critical to prevent burn-out, and to stay motivated.

Live life to the full. There is more to life than sport.

CHAPTER 37
HAVING AN ATTITUDE OF GRATITUDE

It's so easy to be thankful for all the great things in your life. It's character building to be thankful for the setbacks.

When you have an 'attitude of gratitude' you will easily be able to turn any negative into a positive.

And, you know the saying 'actions speak louder than words'. You can express gratitude by 'giving back'. No matter what stage of your career and no matter what your financial situation or profile, there is always an opportunity to give back.

As athletes we tend to become very selfish and self centred, because our lives revolve around ourselves and our results. You are truly blessed with many talents, some of which you may not even know you have yet. Have you ever been on the receiving end of someone else's generosity?

Just imagine how it would feel if you could enable others to achieve things just like you, if you could inspire others, encourage others…

You can truly make a difference and believe me, doing good really does feel good. You will also meet some amazing people along the way.

1. **Donate Time**

   Donating time costs you nothing and so many people could benefit from your time and your talents.

   You can give your time in any number of ways including:

   - Helping younger athletes get started, or improve their skills (at a local level or through your governing body).
   - Offering to help a charity that you feel passionate about.
   - Giving a talk, or teaching some sports skills at a local school.
   - Volunteering at a soup kitchen.
   - Spending time at an aged care facility.
   - Helping care for animals at an animal rescue shelter.
   - Visiting a children's ward at a local hospital.
   - Offering to shop for someone who finds it difficult to leave the house.

I suggest you work with a charity or organisation that's close to your heart – perhaps it's something that has affected you, your family or your community. This will really help you to feel committed and remain involved. You'll also feel like you are making a real difference to the lives of people close to you.

If you are not sure how to start, call them and discuss how you might be able to get involved. Be honest about your available time and your schedule. Only commit to something you know you can see through so you can block off that time in your schedule. You may not realise how much of a difference your assistance can make.

> *I try to spend as much time as I can at surf club "nipper" days. These kids are the future of my sport but also they are the kids that will grow up to patrol our beaches and keep them safe. Surf Life Saving is a fantastic organisation and the "nippers" are the future of this so I try to help improve their surf skills.*
>
> **Shannon Eckstein**, World Ironman Champion

2. **Donate Money**

    If you are in the fortunate position of being able to donate money, then choose carefully. Understand where your money is going and exactly how it will be used. Consider where your money will do the most good and make the most difference. Ask as many questions as you need to feel satisfied that you are making a good decision and that your money will be put to good use. Sometimes your dollars can make more of a difference in a smaller organisation than a large global one, but only if they are managed well.

> *In the quiet hours when we are alone and there is nobody to tell us what fine fellows we are, we come sometimes upon a moment in which we wonder, not how much money we are earning, nor how famous we have become, but what good we are doing.*
>
> **A.A. Milne**, Author

Remember To Be Thankful

Next time you have a whine about how bad your day's been, just think – your very worst day could be someone else's very best day. That person would give anything to have your kind of day. No matter how difficult you think your life is there are always others who have it far worse.

Anger and envy are very destructive emotions, and cannot co-exist with gratitude. When you learn to replace negative emotions with gratitude, you will soon find yourself in a positive and happy space.

- Be thankful for your challenges, because they help you learn, grow, build strength and character.

- Be thankful that you make mistakes, as they will teach you valuable lessons and prove that you *are* human!

- Be thankful when you're tired and sore, because it means you've completed a great day of training.

- Be thankful for the mess you're left to clean up after a party, because it means you've just been surrounded by friends.

- Be thankful for the tax you have to pay, because it means you're earning money!

- Be thankful when the alarm goes off at 6am for training, as it means that you're alive.

- Be thankful in advance of receiving your goals! That way it tells your brain that your goal is already coming and that creates the unwavering faith that keeps you on your path.

What Are You Grateful For Today?

I love doing this exercise at the end of each day. I do it with my child and it always brings a wonderful smile to our faces.

At the end of each day, make a habit of asking yourself these three questions:

1. What was the best thing about today?
2. What were you most grateful for today?
3. Who empowered you and made you feel great today?

> *Tip: End the day with gratitude*
> Pin these three questions up on your bedroom wall to read before you go to sleep. Or, tape them to the mirror in the bathroom to look at when you brush your teeth at night. Eventually, you'll get into the habit of reviewing in your mind, all the great things that happened that day. You'll then be able to drift off into a nice happy sleep.

And finally, never ever forget to *express* your appreciation and gratitude to others. Tell it to them often.

Let us be grateful to people who make us happy; they are the charming gardeners who make our souls blossom.

Marcel Proust, Author

HAVING AN ATTITUDE OF GRATITUDE

> **KEY POINTS**
>
> Be thankful for each and every day.
>
> There is always an opportunity to 'give back'.
>
> Express gratitude – often.

Giving back to school kids

CHAPTER 38
WHAT I'VE LEARNED – FINAL WORDS

To become successful, be prepared to make sacrifices.

No one achieves a long held dream without making some sort of sacrifice. Some pay out lots of their hard earned money; some leave behind family and friends. Some give up top paying jobs and consequently put themselves in a position of financial insecurity.

You have to be willing to sacrifice different things at different stages of your journey. Initially it may be time and other simple desires. Eventually, as you get close, the price will higher.

Are you willing to sacrifice? You have to give some things up in order to *go up*.

You've got to *want* to change and improve.

However, there is always a limit. Be careful not to compromise your values, sacrifice your beloved family or ruin your health. The end result will not be worth it.

Now that I have completed the journey of writing this book, having *lived* that journey and am *still* living that journey, I believe success comes down to just one thing – choice.

The choices you make every single day and every single moment lead you to the results that you have in your life. How you choose to think, feel and believe is your choice.

Sure, the circumstances that you're born into have a certain influence. Your education, parents, schools, coaches, peer groups and culture, have an effect on you. But, *you* control the way your life turns out because of the choices you make.

You can choose today to stop waiting for the perfect moment to start taking action, to stop wishing you had …., to start taking your journey towards your goals into your own hands. You can choose to take on those challenges and work your way through them. You can choose to rise above your worries and be positive. You can choose right now to design your own life.

I have given you many powerful techniques, strategies, exercises and tips to fill your Winner's Toolbox to the brim. It's now up to you to choose whether or not to make it happen.

If you are going to achieve goals you have never achieved before, you must be willing to do what you have never done before.

You need to be able to allow yourself to fail as a result of your choices and then learn from that to make better choices. If you want to succeed big, you sometimes have to fail big.

If you see that others around you are achieving greater success than you, the reason is simply that they have made different choices.

Different choices about how they approach their training and how they spend their time; different choices about how they deal with challenges and different choices about who they surround themselves with.

You have to consciously make these decisions so that you are in control of your own destiny.

Make the true choice today to be the best you can be and commit to it wholeheartedly. Then, you'll have no other option other than to take the actions necessary to achieve your dreams.

Being average has never been good enough for me. I've always wanted to be the best, which means: not being afraid of making mistakes or taking risks because of the choices I've made.

Have a goal, a vision, a dream and believe in it.

The greatest value of this book and your journey won't be what you get from it; it will be who you become by pursuing it.

With all the effort you've put into creating your Winner's Toolbox, make sure that you go through it *every* single day at least once.

You don't have to spend half an hour reading it, just flick through it and pick up on areas that may appeal to you at the time. Keep it by your bed and look at it when you wake up each day.

Look over past exercises and see if you're still on track. Re-do your goals if you need to. Explore your 'pick me up' pages and just have a smile. Remember, the quality of your actions will determine the quality of your results. Put the effort in and you'll most certainly be the best you can be.

The Future

Winning a Gold Medal hasn't just changed my life; it has *enhanced* it.

It has opened many doors of opportunity and these have provided some wonderful experiences and some financial gains, but unless you see those doors open and you're willing to do what it takes to go down the pathways, it may not add to your life at all.

It has allowed me to leave my mark in history within our own sport and within the sporting world of Australia.

It has brought me great respect as a motivational speaker and a Beach Volleyball coach. And, of course, it has provided me with an incredible tale to tell and wonderful experiences to inspire others!

But most importantly, it's given me the confidence and knowledge that *anything* in life is possible and that we can most certainly achieve almost anything we set out to do.

Anything is possible

CHAPTER 39

AFTERWORD – WHAT IT'S LIKE TO BECOME AN OLYMPIAN

It all starts with a dream. At some point in our sporting careers...a kind of 'light' comes on, a thought emerges and we realise that competing in an Olympic Games is possibly within our reach. This is the beginning of our dream. This is when the seed is sown and we begin the journey that will change our lives forever.

Now with that in mind, it doesn't just happen by itself. Over the next few years, or even a decade, we work hard for this dream and we embark on a journey, which includes many chapters. There are the hours of training, the competition, the wins, the losses, the sacrifices, the sleep deprivation, the sweat, the injuries, the challenges, the hurdles, and the limits that have to be overcome.

And then the moment of truth - the Qualification process. Will we make it or not? Will all that hard work pay off, or will we have to wait another 4 years?

For some this process may go on over many competitions and a period of up to two years in the lead up to the Games. For others, it may last a mere 10 seconds of sprinting over 100 metres on one day in just one race.

For each athlete that has made it to an Olympic Games, there are perhaps hundreds or thousands of other athletes that have made the same sacrifices, gone through the same preparation and dedicated the exact same amount of time and effort, and did not make it to the Games.

The moment of selection, the moment of elation, joy, reward upon hearing that you are now part of the team that will represent your country at an Olympic Games. Some feel relief; others feel joy or even sadness for their teammates that didn't make it. This is the first moment that you begin to feel special. You can now proudly say that you're going to the Olympics!

Soon it's time to receive your uniform. You grab your shopping trolley and hit the Olympic Uniform supermarket aisles.

There is more clothing than you think you could possibly wear in three weeks. The sizes are all right, bar a couple of small mistakes, because you were measured earlier in anticipation of this moment. You pack it all up in two massive suitcases, you say thank you to the awesome staff at the Olympic Uniform supermarket and off you go with your prized possessions. You won't find any of these items at Target!

It's time to check into the Olympic Village. Photos, passports, official forms, handprints and smiles all around. It's like being admitted into a maximum-security jail, except that once you're inside, you're free!

Walking around the village, exploring every corner, not wanting to miss out on anything. Checking out all the other athletes from all around the world. These people are all the best in the world at what they do. All of a sudden you realise that you are part of this group!

You enjoy a massive variety of food in the biggest food hall you'll ever eat in.

You're sitting next to athletes with the names of countries on their tracksuits that you've never even heard of. You feel humbled that you're just a small part of this huge world.

Here we all are, enjoying our meals in peace. No guns, no war, no religion, no politics, no fighting. Smiles all around.

Next, it's back to why you're there. Last minute training and preparation for your event. Seeing your venue for the first time and taking a moment to let it all soak in. You close your eyes and imagine the venue full with anywhere between 10,000 – 150,000 spectators. You try to imagine the rest of the world watching you on TV. The adrenalin is really starting to pump.

Your first match or your first race. If there were ever a crescendo of nerves, today is that day. The moment you step out in front of your crowd and the cheers reach your ears. That's the moment you've been waiting for. That's the moment when you sink or you swim.

And then, you make the semi-finals, the finals and then, the Gold!!! All hell breaks lose. For a split second you just can't believe it. The noise is deafening, has this really happened to me? You are instantly part of a new 'Club'. You even receive text messages, phone calls and emails from other Gold Medallists, welcoming you to the 'Club'.

Then, there it is. Your medal. It's coming towards you in a beautiful box. Being awarded by someone famous or important within your sport. You lean forward; they hang it around your neck and your first thought is how heavy it is! You straighten up, lift your hand to the sky and feel the most amazing sense of exhilaration you have ever felt in your entire life.

They play your National anthem and you proudly sing every word – because knowing every word was part of your preparation. You belt out that song like you're a rock star singing to your fans!! But, who cares, you've won the Olympic Gold. The most prized possession of any athlete in any sport... It only comes around once every four years.

Next there's the media merry go round. The cameras, reporters, news crews. Everyone wants a piece of your time. You speak to them about your amazing journey, thanking everyone who believed in you and helped you along the way. You are humble, yet proud of what you have achieved. You enjoy the attention.

The remainder of the time you have left until the curtain falls on this Olympics is spent celebrating, enjoying and being part of other athletes' successes. You go to every event that you can. You see more of your new Olympic friends win Gold and break World Records. You explore a little bit of the culture of the city that you're in and then celebrate with 10,000 other athletes at the Closing Ceremony.

Tears, joy, new friendships, great experiences, wins and losses – it all comes to an end right there in the middle of the Olympic stadium in front of the entire world.

As the buses leave the village to take you to the airport to go back to your home country you take in all the sights and imprint them into your mind, for never will you get to experience anything else like this again.

Will you be back in another four years? When do you start training for the next cycle? What do you aim for next? These are just a few of the questions you begin asking yourself as you leave behind an empty village full of the most amazing memories.

You are now a part of history – win, lose or draw. You're a role model for others, a teacher and if you decide to keep going, you're still a student. But, one thing will never change – You're an Olympian and no one will ever take that away from you.

In 1996 we were on the bottom rung, 3rd place after two Brazilian teams. This time, Sydney 2000, we were on top. The most amazing feeling in my entire sporting career!

KERRI'S ACHIEVEMENTS

Indoor and Beach Volleyball

Kerri represented Australia for 22 years (between 1982 and 2004) in Indoor and Beach Volleyball.

Indoor Volleyball:

National Indoor Volleyball team 1982 – 1992

National Indoor Volleyball team Captain 1992

National Champion under 17, under 18 and under 20 age groups from 1982 - 1984

National Champion Open Senior team 1982 - 1992.

Numerous MVP, Best Player, Best Spiker and Best Blocker awards at National Championships.

Beach Volleyball:

Kerri represented Australia in Beach Volleyball briefly in 1992 winning an Asian Circuit event in the Philippines. She then went on to represent Australia in Beach Volleyball from 1994 - 2004

Medal's won at International events:

Kerri played over 100 International Beach Volleyball events and won the following medals:-

Asian circuit Philippines	1992	Gold
Asian circuit Philippines	1994	Silver
Asian circuit Thailand	1994	Silver
Asian circuit India	1994	Bronze
Jose Cuervo Beach Tour California	1995	Silver
World Beach Volleyball Tour	1996 Japan	Gold
World Beach Volleyball Champs	1996	Bronze
Olympic Games Atlanta	**1996**	**Bronze**
END OF SEASON RANKING	**1996**	**3RD IN THE WORLD**
World Beach Volleyball Tour	1997 Korea	Silver
World Beach Volleyball Tour	1998 Brazil	Silver
World Beach Volleyball Tour	1998 China	Bronze
Goodwill Games	1998 USA	Silver
TEST SERIES VS. NZ	1998	1st
Brazil Nat. Tour	1998 Salvador	Bronze

Brazil Nat. Tour	1998 Goiania	Silver
World Beach Volleyball Tour	1999 Portugal	Silver
World Beach Volleyball Tour	1999 Mexico	Silver
World Beach V'ball Champs 4 on 4	1999 Brazil	Gold
World Beach Volleyball Tour	2000 Portugal	Bronze
World Beach Volleyball Tour	2000 Mexico	Bronze
World Beach Volleyball Tour	2000 Canada	Bronze
Olympic Games Sydney	**2000**	**Gold**
World Beach Volleyball Tour	2001 China	Gold
World Beach Volleyball Tour	2001 Italy	Silver
World Beach Volleyball Tour	2001 China	Bronze
World Beach Volleyball Tour	2002 Greece	Silver
World Beach Volleyball Tour	2002 Norway	Silver
World Beach Volleyball Tour	2002 Spain	Bronze
World Beach Volleyball Tour	2002 China	Bronze
World Beach Volleyball Tour	2002 France	Bronze
World Beach Volleyball Tour	2002 Switzerland	Bronze

(Kerri retired from International competition briefly between 2002 and 2003)

Olympic Games Athens	**2004**	**9th**

Individual awards - Indoor and Beach Volleyball:

Best Blocker Award	1983
Asian Junior champs	
FIVB International Team of the Decade	1990-2000
Part of Australia's No. 1 Beach Volleyball team for 9 years	1995 - 2003
Fastest female server in the world – 77km/ph 1996 Olympic Games	1996
Fastest female server in the world – 85km/ph 2000 Olympic Games	2000
Australian Sports Medal	2001
Order of Australia Medal (OAM)	2001
International Volleyball Hall of Fame Massachusetts	2007
(Only Australian inducted to date)	
S.A.S.I Best of the Best athletes over the past 25 years	2007

ADDITIONAL REFERENCES

Elite Athletes
Go Girl by Natalie Cook, Hardie Grant Books – www.nataliecook.com
Serious. John McEnroe, The Autobiography. Published by Penguin Putnam Inc. 2002.
Mark Skaife, Diary of a Champion. Published by Harper Collins Publishers 2002.
Andre Agassi, Open. An Autobiography. Published by Harper Collins Publishers 2009.
Muhammad Ali – The Greatest of All Time. By Robert Cassidy. Published by Publications International 1999.
John Eales, The Biography. By Peter FitzSimons. Published by ABC Books 2001.
Jonah – My Story. By Jonah Lomu. Published by Hodder Moa Beckett 2004.

Passion & Belief
The Winner's Bible, Rewire your brain for Permanent Change. By Dr. Kerry Spackman. Published in 2009 by THE WINNER'S INSTITUTE.
Success Beyond Sport, How to Retire from Sport and Keep Winning. By Annette Huygens-Tholen. Published in 2010 by Love Your Life Publishing Inc. www.successbeyondsport.com

Positive Thinking
'The Daily Motivator' www.greatday.com
Think and Grow Rich. By Napoleon Hill. Published by Wilshire Book Company
As a Man Thinketh. By James Allen (now available as a free e-book)
The Power of Positive Thinking. By Norman Vincent Peale. Published by Simon and Schuster
The Power of Focus. By Jack Canfield, Mark Victor Hansen and Les Hewitt. Published by Health Communications Inc 2000

Habits
Psycho-Cybernetics. By Dr Maxwell Maltz. Printed by Pocket Books 1969.

Public Speaking, Media, Social Media and Ettiquette
www.fripp.com/articleslist.html
Womensport and Recreation NSW, media conference: www.womensportnsw.com.au

Dale Beaumont's profile accelerator course - www.propelyourprofile.com/profileaccelerator
Social Media – www.socialrabbit.net
Business etiquette overseas - www.kwintessential.co.uk and www.cyborlink.com

Procrastination

The Procrastination Report by Jason Gracia www.motivation123.com/procrastination-report.html

Building the A-Team

Building your team - www.nswis.com.au and www.sportsmind.com.au

Nutrition, Hydration, Recovery

The Complete Guide to Sports Nutrition. By Anita Bean. Published 2004

Leaf A. Prevention of sudden cardiac death by n-3 polyunsaturated fatty acids. *J Cardiovasc Med.* (Hagerstown). 2007; 8 Suppl 1:S27-29

Source: http://sportsmedicine.about.com/od/sportsnutrition/a/EatForExercise.htm

http://www.womenfitness.net/sportsdrink.htm

The Survival Cookbook Series available from the AIS - www.ausport.gov.au/ais/nutrition

www.ausport.gov.au

http://www.drugs.com/cg/healthy-snacks-for-athletes.html

http://www.kidshealth.org/teen/food_fitness/sports/eatnrun.html

http://www.active.com/nutrition/Articles/Fluid_Facts_for_Athletes.htm?page=2

http://ezinearticles.com/?Recovery-from-Strenuous-Sports-Performance-Training&id=399334

http://EzineArticles.com/?expert=Dr_Wye_Mun_Low

http://sportsmedicine.about.com/od/sportsnutrition/a/EatForExercise.htm

http://www.kidney.org.au/KidneyDisease/Drinkwaterinstead/tabid/703/Default.aspx

http://www.pponline.co.uk/encyc/0824.htm

http://spartascience.blogspot.com/2010/02/better-athletes-sweat-more.html

http://www.active.com/nutrition/Articles/Fluid_Facts_for_Athletes.htm?page=2

http://www.pponline.co.uk/encyc/0824.htm

http://sportstrainingblog.com/sport-general/recovery-training-competition

www.sportsdietitians.com

www.remedialmassage.com.au

www.hammernutrition.com

SHARE YOUR OWN STORIES

I would love to hear your opinions of this book and how it has helped you on your journey to your goals.

I also invite you to send in your own personal story, particularly if this book has proven useful to you along the way. Any stories submitted may be used in subsequent publications of this book.

Please email your stories to info@thebusinessofbeinganathlete.com or mail them to:

Kerri Pottharst
PO Box 716
Manly NSW 1655
Australia

I hope this book proves useful to you and you enjoy reading it as much as I have enjoyed writing it for you.

This book may be purchased in bulk for educational, business, fund-raising or sales promotion use. For more information, please email info@thebusinessofbeinganathlete.com

BOOK KERRI FOR YOUR NEXT FUNCTION

Aside from writing books and winning gold medals, Kerri's vision is to continue to inspire and motivate through her warm and personal Keynote Presentations, Goal Setting Workshops and her fun, team-building Corporate Days on the beach. Further information on all Kerri's work can be found on her website - www.kerripottharst.com

"Yesterday I had the pleasure of listening to you at the PA Summit in Melbourne. I felt the need to contact you today to let you know you have changed my life....ok, for now you have changed my view on life, but I have already improved that 1% as you say on the way to changing the whole 100% of my life. Thank you so much.

I had what Oprah would call a «light bulb» moment whilst you were presenting, and believe me it has come at a time when I was really looking for something to motivate and inspire me. I didn>t realise it was going to come yesterday. It did.

I'm sure in your speaking you have had this effect on many people, you should be so proud.

You're a legend. Thanks"

— **Amanda - PA Summit**

"Great move having Kerri first up – fantastically inspirational. Awesome way to start the day!"

— ESSSuper

"Kerri Pottharst was BRILLIANT – what an inspirational speaker. She delivers a message that everyone can take on board. She is GOLD!"

- WHK Group

"Kerri, our team cannot thank you enough for your time and effortless energy you shared with us at our Goal Setting Workshop.

You engaged the group from the beginning, and even difficult to do (they are a rowdy bunch sometimes), you were able to hold their attention for the entire program. Your warm, friendly, uplifting nature made what could be a complex and extremely challenging program enjoyable and inspiring for all. You are 'real', honest and so supportive. The team opened up to you, and shared their personal experiences and plans for the future without hesitation. We all made a commitment and as promised, we'll follow it through. Your approach to goal setting and achievement is so simple, yet proven to be successful. You are proof of this. It's easy really and we now all understand, you can achieve anything if you break down the barriers of self doubt, make a commitment, formulate a plan and enjoy the journey!

Thank you for opening our eyes and hearts. Let the life changing goals unfold."

– Michelle, Step into Life

"Thank you Kerri for adding great value to our conference. Your obvious dedication and passion for your sport was an inspiration to our team and showed us that dreams can be a reality....It was a pleasure to see the transformation of a group of excited individuals into a proficient team by your simple but effective methods. To be able to accomplish this with a great sense of fun and humour is a credit to your skills. Well done"

- David, Metcash Trading Ltd Australasia

"We really needed to get our guys focused on team work and results – plus give them the chance to have some fun and learn some new skills. The session on the beach was ideal – entertaining, stimulating, insightful and fun. Just the right tonic to send the troops back refreshed and motivated."

- Martin, Palin Communications

Kerri is also available for Master of Ceremonies, School Presentations and is an Elite Level Beach Volleyball Coach. For more information or to book her for your next function please visit www.kerripottharst.com

FREE BONUS GIFTS

How to Claim your FREE bonus gifts...

As a special thank you for buying my book, I have put together some bonus items that I hope will help you on your journey to being a highly successful athlete. To claim your free gifts, go to www.thebusinessofbeinganathlete.com/bonus. Register, or log-in if you have registered before, to download each gift.

Good luck with your career and I really hope you will let me know how your journey progresses.

Best wishes,

Kerri Pottharst

Kerri Pottharst

info@thebusinessofbeinganathlete.com

FREE GIFT 1 – value $97.00

Winners Toolbox Templates and Worksheets

Completing these worksheets is a critical part of your journey to success. You can use your own notepad or folder, or you can download these templates to make things even easier to get started. Explanations on how to use these sheets are included within the relevant section of The Business of Being an Athlete.

- Passion - My Ultimate Big Picture

- Preparation (Time Management) - How Do I Spend My Time Each Week

- Preparation (Time Management) - Weekly Planner

- Preparation (Budgeting) - Income and Expenses

- Preparation (Keeping Records) - Tax Expense Record

FREE GIFT 2 – value $57.00

Two additional fantastic tools to help you with two key areas:

- **Sample Media Headlines** – sport specific media headline 'templates' that you can adapt to your own situation when writing media releases. Or just use them as inspiration to think up new ones of your own.

- **Structure for Preparing a Speech** – a hugely valuable step by step approach to preparing a speech. How to link the various aspects of your speech together professionally, ensure your key message is heard and leave your audience wanting more.

FREE GIFT 3 – value $27.00

You Are Your Brand

Winner of the NSW Telstra Micro Business Awards 2008 for her first start-up business Mocks (mobile phone socks), Australian entrepreneur Lara Solomon shares her in-depth knowledge of Social Media. She became so successful in this field that she started up another thriving business – Social Rabbit – www.socialrabbit.net which helps businesses use social media to engage with their customers to produce results. You Are Your Brand gives you her highly successful insight into how you can use Social Media to enhance your career as a professional athlete.

FREE GIFT 4 – value $29.95

How to Influence People

In this interview Michelle Bowden, Australia's presentation and influence expert shares some essential skills for better influencing the people around

you. Michelle is a Master Trainer and Corporate Mentor in Advanced Presentation and Influencing skills as well as a keynote speaker.
www.howtopresent.com.au

FREE GIFT 5 – value $27.00

5 Keys to Think Your Way to Sporting Success

Olympian Annette Huygens-Tholen takes you through her key steps on how to:

- Focus on what you want, not what you don't want

- Create clear goals

- Master your Emotions

- Ensure positive outcomes no matter what the result

- Take responsibility

Annette is a certified Master Results Coach and Trainer of NLP. She focuses on helping athletes develop the mindset of a champion to improve results both on and off the sports field.
www.annetteffect.com.au

FREE GIFT 6 – value $29.95

101 Lessons for Life

Dale Beaumont is the author of 16 best-selling books, 11 of which were published within a single year, earning him the title of 'Australia's Most Prolific Author'. He is now widely recognised as the expert for those that want to "build profile" fast and make more money. In this very personal MP3, Dale narrowed down his list to share his top 101 lessons for success in life. An absolute must for anyone wanting to reach the top of their game.
www.dalebeaumont.com

FREE GIFT 7 – value $37.00
21 Tips to Maximise Business Success
Having become a self-made millionaire at the tender age of 23, in this eBook Kirsty Dunphey shares 21 powerful tips to maximise your business success and create a happy life. Learn how to turn to obstacles into opportunities, how to find your life's purpose, how to become financial savvy, and how to create long lasting relationships.

FREE GIFT 8 – value $37.00
Great Public Speakers
In this fabulous question and answer chapter taken from Dale Beaumont's book "Great Public Speakers," Ron Tacci explains how anyone can overcome their fears and learn the skills to become a great public speaker. Ron has spoken at over 3,000 functions in front of over 1.5 million people and was the founder and managing director of Speakers Network International, which has grown to become one of Australia's leading full-service speaker's bureaus.